956.7044 Record, Jeffrey.
REC
      Hollow victory.

$22.00

HOLLOW VICTORY

Also by Jeffrey Record

Revising U.S. Military Strategy: Tailoring Means to Ends (1984)
Determining Future U.S. Tactical Airlift Requirements (1987)
Beyond Military Reform: American Defense Dilemmas (1988)

HOLLOW VICTORY

A CONTRARY VIEW OF THE GULF WAR

JEFFREY RECORD

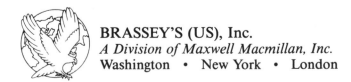

BRASSEY'S (US), Inc.
A Division of Maxwell Macmillan, Inc.
Washington • New York • London

To Carrie, Ian, and James

Brassey's (US), Inc.

Editorial Offices	*Order Department*
Brassey's (US), Inc.	Brassey's Book Orders
8000 Westpark Drive	c/o Macmillan Publishing Co.
First Floor	100 Front Street, Box 50
McLean, Virginia 22102	Riverside, New Jersey 08075

Brassey's (US), Inc., books are available at special discounts for bulk purchases for sales promotions, premiums, fund-raising, or educational use through the Special Sales Director, Macmillan Publishing Company, 866 Third Avenue, New York, New York 10022.

Library of Congress Cataloging-in-Publication Data

Record, Jeffrey.
   Hollow victory : a contrary view of the Gulf War / Jeffrey Record.
     p.   cm.
   Includes bibliographical references and index.
   ISBN 0-02-881046-5
   1. Persian Gulf War, 1991.   I. Title.
DS79.72.R43 1993
956.704'42—dc20   92-26885
                                         CIP

10 9 8 7 6 5 4 3 2

Printed in the United States of America

CONTENTS

Contents

1

Looking Back

THERE HAVE BEEN MANY books published on the 1991 Persian Gulf War and U.S. involvement in that extraordinary conflict. It is thus important to define here what this book is not and why it is different. It is neither a history of the Gulf War nor a survey of the operational and technological lessons learned from that experience. It is not an extended account of the diplomatic relations between the United States and Iraq prior to the conflict, nor a detailed recitation of the Bush administration's decision-making during the crisis after the invasion of Kuwait on August 2, 1990. It is not solely focused on lessons learned; perhaps never in history have so many lessons been learned by so many so quickly.[1]

What follows here, rather, are commentaries on the broader political, military, and strategic questions raised by the war and its aftermath—questions old, new, and unresolved. In this book, I have sought to raise important issues and to provide insights off the beaten path of so-called conventional wisdom about the war. I have tried to live up to my reputation for asking hard questions of the U.S. military and of political leaders. This may be even more important in the glow of what may turn out to have been a "hollow victory." For the United States in the post–World War II era, the war in the Persian Gulf was unique. It was short, victorious, and cheap. It was waged against a patently monstrous tyrant on behalf of the United Nations and in concert with genuinely helpful allies. It occasioned but modest domestic political dissent; on the contrary, it prompted a popular (albeit short-lived) outpouring of affection and respect for the U.S. military unprecedented since V-E Day. It seemingly vindicated not only the enormous investment in U.S. defense modernization made in the 1980s but also America's new post–cold war status as the world's only remaining superpower. It was also the only foreign conflict in American history that did not catch U.S. military forces unprepared and in which U.S. war costs were financed largely by foreign contributions. It was, in short, a splendid affair.

The war, however, raised some troubling issues that have yet to be fully or satisfactorily explored. Was the conflict, for example, avoidable? Before August 2, 1990, U.S. policy toward Iraq rested on an assumption that Saddam Hussein and his Baathist regime, presumably preoccupied with reconstructing an Iraq battered by eight years of brutal combat with Iran, could be molded into a force for moderation in the Middle East via U.S.

encouragement, credits, and technology transfers. Might a nonappeasing, sterner policy have dissuaded Saddam from attacking Kuwait?

The avoidability of war was also the principal issue joined by the prewar public and congressional debate over the efficacy of economic sanctions. There is little doubt that U.N.-imposed and U.S. Navy–enforced sanctions had crippled Iraq's economy and damaged its military readiness well before the beginning of Operation Desert Storm on January 16, 1991, although we will never know for sure whether a continuation of sanctions alone would have compelled an Iraqi withdrawal from Kuwait. Saddam's survival of both sanctions and war underscores both the difficulty of translating economic pain into political leverage, and the innate resilience of totalitarian states to external attempts to impose internal change.

It is far from clear, however, whether the Bush administration would have been satisfied with a resolution of the Kuwait crisis short of war. A voluntary Iraqi withdrawal from Kuwait would have satisfied the major declared political objective of the U.S.-led coalition, though it would have left Iraqi military power intact and Saddam himself (presumably) still in control of Iraq's destiny. The White House clearly harbored intentions against Iraq—the dictator's removal and his country's disarmament—that not only exceeded any strict interpretation of the U.N. mandate, but also, given Saddam's seemingly mindless intransigence from August 2, 1990, to January 16, 1991, could be accomplished only by war. This disparity between more limited formal objectives and ambitious, undeclared aims continues to hamper attempts at judging the war's ultimate success or failure.

The Gulf War also raised important questions about America's ability to assess accurately the military prowess of non-Western adversaries, and about the Bush administration's decision-making process. The U.S. intelligence community and other expert opinion as a whole significantly overestimated Iraq's actual military capabilities. The reasons included a cultural predisposition to exalt the quantifiable indices of military power at the expense of more difficult and subjective inquiries into such unquantifiable factors as historical performance, morale, quality of organization and operational doctrine, and cultural receptivity to modern warfare's institutions and technologies. Indeed, throughout this century the United States has, with respect to non-Western opponents, consistently underestimated their fighting power (the Philippine *insurrectos,* the Chinese in Korea, and the North Vietnamese army and its Viet Cong auxiliaries in Indochina) or given them far too much credit (the Iraqi army).

As for the decision-making process, there is no question that the much-applauded Goldwater-Nichols Defense Reform Act of 1986 paid off handsomely at the operational and tactical levels of command in the Gulf War. Unlike the American military effort in Vietnam, in the Persian Gulf there was a single command authority that counted, and he was accorded the necessary latitude to fight a single, integrated, joint-service and combined-national military campaign. There was only one war, not a collection of individual service wars, and in the air there was only a single daily air tasking order, not a bundle of several separate air wars.

From another perspective, however, the Bush administration's approach during the crisis was unsettling. Key decisions were made by a tiny group of people (the President, Secretary of Defense Dick Cheney, and the Chairman of the Joint Chiefs of Staff, General Colin Powell) that included no "devil's advocate," with the possible exception early on of Secretary of State James Baker. The White House scorned any congressional role in the decision-making process until early January 1991, when war had become inevitable, making a congressional rejection of the administration's orchestrated U.N. ultimatum to Iraq to get out of Kuwait or face war tantamount to a betrayal of the flag. On the contrary, the White House sought to use the combination of the United Nations and its twelve resolutions against Iraq as both a functional substitute for a formal congressional declaration of war and a bludgeon to cow the Congress into supporting the decision for war. Moreover, though the Defense Reform Act rightly increased the power and authority of the Chairman of the Joint Chiefs of Staff and theater commanders at the expense of the individual, parochial service chiefs, it cannot compel the President to seek military advice from the Chairman, nor the Chairman to provide advice.

According to Bob Woodward's and similar accounts, which remain undisputed by any of the principal Bush administration players during the Gulf crisis, the President did not solicit General Powell's advice before declaring, a few days after Kuwait's fall, that Iraq's aggression "will not stand." This statement expanded previously declared U.S. aims from simply deterring an attack on Saudi Arabia to reversing, by force if necessary, Iraq's invasion of Kuwait. Conversely, Powell, who at the time had greater confidence than Bush in the efficacy of sanctions, and who was deeply troubled by prospects of a major war with Iraq, apparently could not bring himself to confront the President directly with his concerns. Thus at a critical juncture on a matter of war or peace there was an absence of essential communication between the country's political leader and his senior military adviser.

The conduct of the war itself has sparked much controversy, at least within the U.S. defense community. For example, some commentators believe that Operation Desert Storm is a prototype for future American military interventions in the Third World, whereas others point to the difficulty of replicating the political, logistical, and operational foundations of Desert Storm's success. Another controversy involves the role of air power. Predictably, the Air Force has been wont to claim that air power, most notably the strategic bombardment components of the air war, won the war virtually by itself, thereby vindicating long-standing theories of air power's decisiveness. Critics of this view concede air power's dominating role in Desert Storm, but contend that the nature of the enemy, terrain, and weather in the Kuwaiti Theater of Operations (KTO) was unusually favorable to the application of air power. They further point out that Iraqi forces in Kuwait crumbled only with the advance of Coalition ground forces. Some critics also believe that the Coalition's extension of the strategic bombardment campaign to attacks on Iraq's economic infrastructure was both unnecessary and politically counterproductive. Within the U.S. aviation community, a debate also rages between proponents of land-based air power (i.e., the Air Force) and supporters of sea-based air power (the Navy), with the former asserting, as they did even in the 1930s and 1940s, that land-based air power, especially long-range aviation, offers a cost-effective substitute for carrier aviation. The Navy, on the other hand, points to the carriers' independence of air bases ashore, political access to which is becoming an increasingly scarce commodity in the Third World.

Still other issues, at least for military professionals, include the utility of light versus heavy ground forces; the Navy's predilection for such Cold War missions as sea control at the expense of such "peripheral" tasks as sealift and counter–mine warfare (where it was embarrassed on both counts in the Persian Gulf); the future of amphibious assault (eschewed by General H. Norman Schwarzkopf over Marine Corps objections in Desert Storm); the proper strategic mobility mix of airlift, sealift, and prepositioning; ballistic missile defenses for U.S. forces operating overseas (Saddam's primitive Scud missiles were only a preview of things to come); voluntary versus involuntary means of recruiting military manpower; and the implications of casualty minimization as a governing principle of U.S. military operations.

This last issue is of supreme importance because the domestic political imperative of minimizing American (and wartime enemy civilian) casualties not only dominated U.S. planning for Desert Storm, but also continues to place significant constraints on future U.S. military flexibility, especially in situations in which national security interests and moral considerations might be less self-evident than they were in the Persian Gulf. In terms of the potential expenditure of American blood in the Arabian desert, the experience of the Vietnam War hung over the U.S. Central Command in Riyadh like a solar eclipse stopped in mid-movement; both the operational planning and tactical execution of Desert Storm had to pass the "scrub" of casualty minimization with respect to both American forces and enemy civilians, and stringent rules of engagement produced thousands of aborted air attack sorties because targets were not visible enough to risk unwanted collateral damage. U.S. aversion to even the appearance of indiscriminate slaughter of Iraqi noncombatants was heightened in the Gulf War by a new phenomenon: instantaneous commercial television coverage of the effects of military operations on enemy forces and civilian populations alike, which influenced U.S. political and military decision-making. Saddam Hussein clearly recognized America's Vietnam-induced hypersensitivity to body bags, and while he may not have believed he could defeat the Coalition, he seems to have convinced himself that Iraqi forces in Kuwait could inflict enough casualties on the Americans to provoke a domestic political crisis at home. Future U.S. adversaries in the Third World may be more successful in this regard, as were the Chinese in Korea and the Vietnamese in Indochina.

A few comments are in order on nomenclature. The author has chosen the commonly used term the "Gulf War" to encapsulate the Persian Gulf conflict of 1990–91, even though the same term has been used to denote the 1980–88 Iran-Iraq War. Some favor the term "War for Kuwait" on the grounds that it was Saddam Hussein's invasion of Kuwait that provoked the subsequent international crisis and war, and that Kuwait's liberation was the principal declared formal objective of U.N.-sanctioned Coalition forces arrayed on and around the Arabian peninsula. Clearly, however, the scope of both Iraq's and the United States' ultimate objectives in the conflict extended well beyond Kuwait's fate, as did the scope of both sides' military operations, which were directed at targets far outside the KTO. Equally clearly, neither the terms "Desert Shield" nor "Desert Storm" will do; they refer only to the two distinct phases of the U.S. military response, encompassing neither Iraq's invasion of Kuwait nor Iraq's subsequent preparations to defend that country against the Coalition.

The author also has chosen to treat the Gulf War as a continuum from August 2, 1990, when the first Iraqi tank crossed into Kuwait, until March 3, 1991, when General Schwarzkopf imposed cease-fire conditions upon surrendering Iraqi military authorities. The absence of combat from Kuwait's fall until the beginning of the Coalition's air campaign on January 16, 1991, was simply an anomaly occasioned by Saddam's suspension of aggressive military action and an initially defensive Coalition military response. Such intrawar pauses are not historically uncommon. From ancient times through the eighteenth century, multiyear warfare in Europe was punctuated by long intermissions because of material exhaustion and the difficulties of mounting military operations in wintertime. A more recent example occurred in 1939–40 when Britain and France, following Germany's conquest of Poland, engaged in an eight-month-long sitzkrieg, standing by passively on the French frontier while the enemy prepared a fatal blow. The Gulf War began on August 2, 1990, not January 16, 1991.

Which brings us to a far more difficult and controversial definitional issue: the very term "war" itself. No two armed conflicts are, of course, alike, but the Gulf War, at least that phase of it beginning with Desert Storm, was historically unprecedented in its one-sidedness. One side, the Coalition, did virtually all of the fighting; the other, Iraq, did almost all of the dying and surrendering. The Dervishes at Omdurman, the Zulus at Rorke's Drift, the French at Sedan, Custer at Little Big Horn, the Egyptians in the Sinai, and the Argentines in the Falklands—all put up a better fight than did the "world's fourth largest army" in the Kuwaiti Theater of Operations. Even by modern-day historical standards of Arab military performance against the West (the French-Algerian War being the one major

exception because the Algerians waged guerrilla warfare), the Iraqi performance against the Coalition was comatose. Ezio Bonsignore has observed:

> The uniqueness of the Gulf War lies in the fact that it was virtually a
> one-sided affair. As a general rule, wars—no matter their causes, the
> technical level of the forces battling with each other, and the aims and
> goals of the involved parties—are fought through a series of battles and
> encounters, whose intensity and durations depend on a number of
> circumstances and conditions, until one side gives up and offers to
> surrender (or, in some cases, until one side suffers complete military
> defeat and unconditional surrender). . . . But in the Gulf, we have
> witnessed a totally new phenomenon. One of the two contenders
> actually waged war, following a coherent battle plan and hitting its
> targets very hard. The other has done nothing more than absorb ever
> more violent and lethal blows, while maintaining a defiant attitude and
> spitting hate and rancor until the very end. The best that can be said of
> Iraq's war strategy is that Iraq "fought back" against the Alliance the
> same way a punching ball would fight back against Mr. Tyson.[1a]

Indeed, numerous anecdotal accounts by U.S. soldiers, marines, and
pilots likened the conflict to training exercises back home at the National
Military Training Center, Twenty-nine Palms, and Nellis Air Force Base;
some even said that "combat" in the Gulf was easier. Many U.S. troops
confided that they were more concerned about being hit by their own fire
than by the enemy's, a fear seemingly borne out by the fact that an
extraordinary twenty-three percent of the 148 Americans killed in action
were killed by friendly fire; and perhaps the most common characterization
by American pilots of both the air-to-air war and the air-to-ground war was
a "turkey shoot."

None of this is to suggest that death, fear, and anguish were absent
among Coalition ranks; all were present at the tactical levels of combat, and
the families and loved ones of those who were deprived of life or limb can
hardly be expected to consider the Gulf War a military farce. Some Iraqi
units did fight hard, and there were some tough if fleeting clashes of
armored forces in the desert. Nor is it to suggest that the Coalition's swift
and stunning victory over Iraq was ascribable entirely or even mainly to
Iraqi weaknesses and mistakes, legion though they were. By January 16,
1991, the day Desert Storm began, victory for the Coalition was hardly in
doubt. What was in doubt was the time it would take, and especially its
price in blood. The war did last forty-three days, longer than some expected,
because of the Iraqi military target array's sheer size, unexpectedly bad
weather, and the scope and elusiveness of Iraq's mobile ballistic missile
force. The great surprise, however, was victory's cheapness. Compared to
Iraq's loss of perhaps tens of thousands of troops, Coalition losses totaled
less than 1,000 dead and wounded out of a committed force of 745,000.
Comparative combat losses in tanks, planes, ships, and other military
hardware were no less lopsided.

Clearly, the vastly superior training, generalship, technology, mobility, and morale of Coalition forces overwhelmed Iraq. There was more at play, however. Saddam Hussein was seeking to refight *his* last war—a static, attritional affair à la the Somme and Passchendaele. In contrast, the United States, determined to avoid a repeat of *its* last war, Vietnam, served up a prototype of futuristic, twenty-first century warfare, in which the combination of electronic combat, computer chips, space-based surveillance and navigational systems, night-vision equipment, "brilliant" munitions, radar-eluding aircraft, and, above all, thoroughly trained and highly motivated professional soldiers never seemed at a loss in defeating a demoralized, ill-led force incapable of effectively absorbing military modernity. The Gulf War was essentially two separate wars: one sluggish, obtuse, and irrelevant; the other nimble, quick-witted, and decisive. It was a modern-day equivalent of a nineteenth-century colonial conflict between an organizationally and technologically superior industrial power and a premodern culture, despite Iraq's outward trappings of military modernity.

The abyss in military prowess separating the two sides makes it very difficult to draw meaningful lessons for the future. Was the Coalition really that good, or the Iraqi military so awful? What are the chances of ever again encountering so incompetent an opponent in the Third World? Was the war really a meaningful test of U.S. military effectiveness, given Iraqi weaknesses and stupidity, to say nothing of the unusually favorable political, operational, topographical, and climatological conditions both Desert Shield and Desert Storm enjoyed? Could a more worldly, intelligent, and enterprising Iraqi leadership have derailed Desert Storm, or at least raised its cost in blood to politically unacceptable levels for the United States? Was it really a war, or little more than a live-fire exercise? Was it a harbinger of future U.S. military interventions, or a singular, aberrational event devoid of useful lessons for the future? And what lessons from the Gulf War are being drawn by other countries, especially other aspiring regional hegemons with ambitions at odds with U.S. security interests, including a now vengeful Saddam Hussein? What worked in the Persian Gulf that didn't in Korea and Indochina? What difference, for example, did the Cold War's demise make?

How replicable are the conditions over which U.S. forces had little or no control? Could Iraqi forces in Kuwait have been forcibly ejected without prior politically assured U.S. military access to Saudi Arabia's abundant ports and air bases? To what extent did flat terrain, a relative absence of natural and man-made cover, and mostly clear weather contribute to the Coalition's success? What if Saddam Hussein had chosen not to grant the Coalition 163 days of uninterrupted Iraqi passivity to amass overwhelming force on his very doorstep? Indeed, how different would the war's duration, price, and outcome have been with an Arab equivalent of Mao Zedong or Vo Nguyen Giap at the helm in Baghdad, instead of a rank military amateur? What if the United States had entered the war having learned nothing from its experience in Vietnam—a premier assumption of Saddam Hussein's?

The analytical difficulties in capturing the real meaning of the various facets of the Gulf War posed by that conflict's extreme one-sidedness are compounded by the yawning disparity between Desert Storm's unarguably impressive military accomplishments, especially at the operational and tactical levels of combat, and its increasingly apparent failure to have engendered desirable political change in the Persian Gulf region. Like the Israelis' stunning triple military victory over Egypt, Syria, and Jordan in the 1967 Six-Day War, Desert Storm seems to have put paid to few if any of the sources of political and military instability that gave rise to the Gulf crisis of 1990 in the first place.

To be sure, Desert Storm quickly accomplished its foremost declared political objective: Kuwait's liberation. However, in failing to topple Saddam Hussein and his Baathist gang of thugs in Baghdad, Desert Storm left intact the principal source of instability in the Gulf—and make no mistake about it, the underlying if implicit premise of the entire enterprise was that Saddam and his henchmen could not politically survive the kind of military punishment the Coalition planned to inflict on Iraq. Saddam did survive, as has much of his chemical, biological, and nascent nuclear weapons capability, the magnitude and quality of which were grossly underestimated by Coalition intelligence agencies before the war. And the world must now deal with a Saddam Hussein bent on revenge against those responsible for undertaking the very war that failed to bring him down. The dictator has returned to his stock-in-trade of butchering his own citizenry; he has amassed an impressive record of successfully defying U.N. sanctions and demands; his forces have repeatedly violated the U.N.-established demilitarized zone separating Iraq and Kuwait; and strong evidence suggests that Iraq is arming Kurdish rebel groups in Turkey as payback for Ankara's prominent if indirect support of Coalition military operations during the war. Baghdad's capacity to unleash weapons of mass destruction against its neighbors has been dealt a severe blow, but as the 1981 Israeli strike on Iraq's Osirik nuclear complex demonstrated, diminishing Iraq's capabilities addresses only the symptoms of the disease; the core of the threat lies not in weapons of mass destruction themselves, but rather in their dogged development and ultimate possession by a megalomaniacal regime willing to use them. Even Saddam's departure would offer no guarantee of a benign, compliant successor.

The author believes that Saddam's survival and postwar behavior—and U.S. and allied inability to compel his compliance with the U.N. cease-fire's provisions or to remove the dictator altogether—must be counted as a major American political defeat, given the enormity of the international diplomatic, political, and military effort marshaled against him during and after the Gulf War. Moreover, the United States, fearful of a "Lebanonized" Iraq—i.e., an Iraq based on effective self-determination for each of its disparate peoples—bears a significant measure of responsibility for Saddam Hussein's survival, in the form of a premature cease-fire, a hasty evacuation of occupied Iraqi territory, a hands-off attitude toward subsequent *White House-encouraged* Kurdish and Shia uprisings, and failure to meet Saddam's continuing defiance of the cease-fire's provisions with an adequate display of force. Even many Iraqis—Kurds and Shias, of course, but also many educated middle-class Sunnis—seem to have been deeply disappointed in America's failure to go the last mile in ridding their country of its tyrant. Especially embarrassing was the belated and grudging humanitarian assistance to beleaguered Kurdish forces trapped in the mountains of northern Iraq. There is scant evidence of the "new world order" in the Gulf today.

Less significant but in some respects more embarrassing has been the postwar behavior of Kuwait's ruling al-Sabah dynasty. Though the war was not fought to make Kuwait a democracy, the performance of the Sabahs, both during the war (which found most of the family safely ensconced in a luxury hotel in the Saudi resort city of Taif) and after Kuwait's liberation, outraged Kuwaitis and non-Kuwaitis alike. The exiled emir's principal concern throughout the crisis appeared to be avoidance of any interruption of his prodigious nightly pleasures of the flesh and maintenance of his opulent life-style; he delayed his return to his liberated though shattered country for the two weeks it took to have one of his seven palaces restored. And his returning government initially proved to be more of an obstacle to Kuwait's political and economic reconstruction than its agent. It initiated an ugly, indiscriminate pogrom against Kuwait's economically indispensable Palestinian community, most of whose members remained loyal to the country during the Iraqi occupation, and displayed a startling political obtuseness toward those reform-minded Kuwaitis unfortunate enough to have been trapped in the country by the Iraqi invaders.

Saudi Arabia, on whose behalf the Gulf War was really waged, also quickly reverted to its prewar theocratic regimentation, and resumed its traditional resistance to any highly visible military connection with the United States. The House of Saud, terrified at prospects of a Shia takeover in Baghdad, pressured the United States to go easy on Saddam Hussein, and has paid little more than lip service to renewed American efforts to craft an Arab-Israeli settlement. Saudi Arabia, moreover, has rejected U.S. requests to leave behind in Saudi Arabia a U.S. Army heavy division's worth of equipment and supplies, which would greatly facilitate another joint U.S.-Saudi defense of the kingdom against a militarily resurgent Iraq or Iran. Riyadh has instead pressed the United States for the wherewithal to create a smaller, Saudi version of the heavy U.S. Army's Seventh Corps that formed the backbone of Kuwait's swift liberation on the ground—even though this would entail a massive transfer of U.S. high-technology weapons and equipment to a small, inexperienced military establishment that with few notable exceptions has not demonstrated a convincing ability, any more so than Iraq, to absorb modern military technologies and forms of organization effectively. Saudi Arabia seems not to have grasped two of the war's major lessons: that the kingdom, with its vast empty spaces and open border, and relatively sparse and significantly alien population, cannot hope to defend itself against its far more populous and militarily powerful neighbors to the north and across the Persian Gulf; and that, as Iraq and so many other Third World countries have demonstrated, military modernity cannot be purchased by simply writing checks for large numbers of advanced foreign weapons.

Nor, despite some early hope, does the Gulf War as yet appear to have altered the Middle East's landscape so as to offer a real chance for an enduring Arab-Israeli settlement. The Bush administration's prodigious efforts in this regard have broken new ground; the international Middle East peace conference convened in Madrid in October 1991 and attended by the United States, Soviet Union, Israel, Arab states, and a Palestinian delegation represents a singular achievement—the result in part of U.S. pressure on Israel unprecedented since the Suez crisis of 1956. However, as long as Israel refuses to trade land for peace, as long as it continues to construct new settlements in the territories it occupied in the wake of the 1967 war, prospects for real peace remain dim, as they do for an end to Palestinian violence in those territories, against which Israel's conventional military prowess is all but irrelevant. Indeed, the Gulf War may serve to reinforce Israeli intransigence because it discredited the Palestine Liberation Organization's leadership, and eliminated, at least for the time being, Iraq as a major external threat to Israel's security. Many Israelis also seem to believe that they did the United States a favor, and that the United States therefore is in Israel's debt, by refraining from retaliating against Iraq in response to Saddam's Scud missile attacks of Israeli cities—when in fact retaliation would have been, from Israel's standpoint, both politically and strategically nonsensical.

The two Middle Eastern states that have profited most handsomely, and at virtually no cost, from the Gulf War are Syria and Iran, hardly a welcome development in the long run for the United States. Both countries are every bit as hostile to democratic institutions at home and U.S. security interests in the region as is Baathist Iraq, and both countries are still in the business of sponsoring terrorism at home and overseas. Iraq's military prostration, though hardly permanent, has increased the relative weight of Syria and Iran in regional affairs, and Syria's token participation in the Coalition's military operations against Iraq was purchased by America's tacit approval of Hafez al-Assad's establishment of a Pax Syriana over all of Lebanon north of the small Israeli security zone. In Damascus the United States is courting yet another, if cleverer, Baathist thug as a force for moderation and stability, just as it did Saddam Hussein before the Gulf War, and before Saddam, the arrogant, indecisive Shah of Iran. As for the Gulf itself, the war has left Iran not only more than 120 shiny new French- and Soviet-made aircraft, courtesy of defecting Iraqi pilots, but has also put that country in a position, as by far the largest of the Gulf states with the most military potential, to regain the hegemonial status it enjoyed under the Shah, though hardly, as with the Shah, as a surrogate for U.S. military power.

A most unwanted political legacy of the Gulf War is America's entanglement in Iraq's internal affairs, and prospective entanglement in a web of implied defense commitments and obligations that have been incurred on behalf of Iraq's Kurds, already twice betrayed by the United States. These new responsibilities could require a display of military power, especially on behalf of marooned Kurdish populations along the Iraqi-Turkish border. Moreover, as the chief enforcer of the continuing embargo of Iraq and of the U.N.'s cease-fire provisions—all of which compromise Iraq's sovereignty —against a defiant Saddam Hussein, the United States may be compelled once again to undertake military action inside Iraq, and indeed has already threatened to do so.

Since the war ended the United States also has sought more concrete military relationships with all of the Gulf monarchies, relationships which, while not involving formal, ironclad, NATO-like defense commitments, by their very nature convey heightened obligations where none before existed. The United States has already entered a new military relationship with Bahrain and Kuwait involving arms transfers, military access rights, prepositioning of key U.S. equipment, and joint training exercises; and the very fact of Desert Storm effectively commits the United States to Kuwait's and Saudi Arabia's defense in the event of future aggression from the north. However much the Saudis would like to believe that they can ultimately achieve defense self-sufficiency, the reality is greater defense dependency on the United States. This commitment by extension applies to the other Gulf monarchies when confronted by a clear and overwhelming outside threat, since Saudi Arabia's security is inextricably bound up with their own. A United States willing to overturn aggression against Kuwait, a country that before the war had been a major bankroller of the PLO and publicly anti-American and anti-Semitic, could hardly stand idly by while the Gulf's other small and defenseless states were gobbled up by a militarily resurgent Iraq or Iran.

The difficulty of translating Desert Storm's unarguable military success into political gains is but one of the many issues addressed in the commentaries that follow. Chapter 2 tackles the knotty issue of whether the Gulf War could have been avoided altogether: specifically, whether prewar Kuwaiti behavior and U.S. policy toward Iraq unwittingly encouraged an Iraqi move on Kuwait; whether different stances might have deterred Baghdad; and finally, whether, once confronted with Iraq's occupation of Kuwait, there were insufficiently pursued possibilities open to both the United States and Iraq that might have obviated the need for Desert Storm.

Chapter 3 deals with the related question of the U.N. economic sanctions' efficacy in compelling an Iraqi evacuation of Kuwait, recognizing the distinction between economic hardship imposed and its relation to desirable political decisions in Baghdad. Were sanctions never really given a chance to work, or were they an inherently faulty tool for influencing Saddam Hussein's behavior?

Chapter 4 examines prewar professional and other U.S. assessments of Iraq's fighting power, and why they so often overestimated Iraqi strengths and failed to grasp critical Iraqi weaknesses. Historical antecedents of U.S. misjudgments of other non-Western adversaries' military capabilities are also explored.

Chapter 5 scrutinizes the operational setting of Desert Shield and Desert Storm, particularly the elements of time, space, topography, and the military conventionality of both sides. The implications of all these factors are weighed in terms of their contribution to the war's duration and outcome. Comparisons are also made with previous wars.

Chapter 6 assesses Saddam Hussein's qualities as generalissimo of his country's military establishment, focusing on his key decisions during the crisis as well as on the impact of Iraq's political culture on Iraqi military effectiveness. The issue of whether a more worldly, imaginative, and resourceful Iraqi leadership could have derailed Desert Storm—and how— is also examined.

Chapter 7 investigates the relative contributions of air, ground, and naval power to the war's outcome. Particular attention is paid to claims of air power's decisiveness, and to the key distinction between the air campaign's strategic bombardment and other components. Also discussed is the replicability of those "objective" conditions that so favored the effective Coalition application of air power against Iraq.

Chapter 8 addresses, in the context of the Defense Reorganization Act of 1986, the relation of U.S. military advice and presidential decision-making at the strategic and operational levels, during both Desert Shield and Desert Storm. Particular attention is paid to the unusual phenomenon of unsolicited and unproffered military advice that characterized the initial phase of U.S. decision-making in the Kuwait crisis; to the White House's decision unilaterally to terminate hostilities; and to the conventional wisdom that U.S. military planning and operations were free of intrusion by civilian authorities.

Chapter 9 examines some of the political, strategic, operational, and technological lessons of the war that have already been drawn by other professional analysts and organizations, and postulates the author's own conclusions concerning what lessons can—and cannot—be safely drawn not only by the United States but also by potential future Third World adversaries.

The last chapter comments on certain features of the war's political aftermath, especially its failure to alter the seemingly intractable underlying sources of instability and violence in the Persian Gulf region.

A word on sources. The interpretive character of this work has permitted the author to rely entirely on abundant open primary and secondary sources. Few of the basic facts regarding events in the Persian Gulf (and Washington, D.C.) from the spring of 1990 through the immediate aftermath of the war for Kuwait are in dispute, although the reasoning behind much of Iraq's behavior and some of its actions (and inactions) must be inferred. Where there are disputes in the literature over matters of fact or interpretation, the author has duly noted them, as he has insufficiently supported claims and assertions, especially on the part of suspect sources.

The reader should also know that the author supported the use of force to eject Iraqi forces from Kuwait and to strip Iraq of its now-forbidden weapons, although he was and remains highly critical of prewar U.S. diplomacy toward Saddam Hussein, and of several aspects of the U.S. government's handling of the Gulf War and its aftermath in the Persian Gulf region.

2

Was War Avoidable?

THEORETICALLY, MOST WARS NEED never take place. If one side or the other in a war-threatening dispute is prepared to appease or surrender in advance—i.e., to satisfy the demands of the other, unilaterally eliminating issues in contention—then the reason for war presumably disappears. If in the 1850s, for example, the American South had abolished slavery, or at least desisted from demanding its extension to the western territories, and had renounced the right of secession and its supporting Calhounian doctrine of states' rights, there would have been little cause for civil war in the 1860s. Or, if in the 1930s, for another example, President Franklin D. Roosevelt had accepted Japanese imperial ambitions in East Asia, including access to Southeast Asia's oil and mineral resources, and had refrained from imposing punitive trade sanctions on Tokyo, then Pearl Harbor probably would not have been rudely awakened on the morning of December 7, 1941.

For better or for worse, however, nation-states acting in a near-anarchic international political environment often have conflicting interests, and few are prepared to compromise their own sovereignty willingly, and certainly not prospects for their very survival. Moreover, in war-threatening crises rationality and objectivity commonly give way to fear, confusion, and impulsiveness. States, like individuals, are prone to miscalculations about the strength and intentions of their neighbors, and in some cases must deal with adversaries who seek nothing less than their extinction, thereby creating a situation where no amount of appeasement short of willing suicide will propitiate the enemy. In the fateful summer of 1914, a terrified Serbian leadership capitulated to an Austrian ultimatum that would have stripped Serbia of most of its sovereignty, but Austria, determined to extinguish Serbia once and for all (and surprised by Serbia's acceptance of the ultimatum), rejected Serbian compliance and instead declared war. With respect to the Persian Gulf crisis of 1990–91, it can be convincingly argued, at least in retrospect, that nothing Kuwait could have said or done in the spring and summer of 1990 would have altered Iraq's march toward war—that Saddam Hussein was bent on gobbling up Kuwait regardless of the risks involved.

The issue of whether the Gulf War could have been avoided centers on two distinct phases of the crisis: whether an Iraqi invasion of Kuwait could have been forestalled by diplomatic and other means; and whether, once

Kuwait's conquest by Iraq was a *fait accompli,* the U.S.-led Coalition's resort to force to reverse Iraq's aggression could have been avoided. Implicit in the issue is an assumption that had the key players in the crisis—Kuwait, Iraq, and the United States—behaved differently before and after August 2, 1990, events would have taken a different, war-less course. But there is a large chasm between what those actors theoretically or objectively might have done and what they actually ended up doing. In each country there was, to varying degrees, a combination of misperceptions, miscalculations, and perceived interests and domestic political imperatives that governed national policy responses, and in some cases blocked alternative avenues of resolving the crisis short of war.

Could an Iraqi invasion of Kuwait in the summer of 1990 have been deterred? No one can say for sure. It is the author's contention, however, that an Iraqi armed assault of some kind on Kuwait was virtually inevitable, *given* (1) Iraq's economic desperation and the nature of its regime, (2) Kuwait's reckless prewar diplomacy and behavior toward Iraq, and (3) America's (and the West's) witless appeasement of Saddam Hussein beginning in the early 1980s, but especially during the period 1988–90. The author is also persuaded that the subsequent U.S. and allied military campaign to dislodge Iraqi forces from Kuwait could have been avoided through actions by either the United States or Iraq. However, chances of war avoidance were in reality rather slim, primarily because of stultifying Iraqi intransigence. This was encouraged in part by Saddam Hussein's conviction that the United States was less interested in a peaceful solution to the immediate issue at stake—Kuwait's fate—than in removing the dictator himself from power and at erasing a decade and a half's worth of mammoth Iraqi military investment.

The author believes that the moral and political blame for the tragic course of events in the Persian Gulf cannot be assigned entirely to Saddam Hussein. To be sure, Saddam was and is a dictator with a record of megalomania and brutality comparable to the likes of Idi Amin, Pol Pot, and Stalin,[2] and he did little to conceal his military and nuclear ambitions, or his belief that he was a modern-day Saladin anointed by history to create a single Arab nation-state—the one enduring theme of his opaque and opportunistic Baathist "ideology." Like his predecessors in Baghdad, he certainly made no bones about Kuwait's status as a "lost" province of Iraq, though he was happy, of course, to have the emirate's generous diplomatic and financial assistance during his misguided war with Iran. Without question, Saddam was the principal culprit responsible for the Gulf War, though his actions, while morally reprehensible, were politically explainable—a key distinction to keep in mind when assessing the behavior of all the major actors in the Gulf crisis.

But if Saddam was guilty of gross misperceptions and miscalculations, especially regarding America's predictability and resolve, so, too, were many others, including America's Arab friends like Egypt's Hosni Mubarak and Jordan's King Hussein, who were stunned by Iraq's invasion. Blame also may be generously assigned to France, Germany, and those other West European states who fell all over themselves in the 1970s and 1980s to arm Saddam to the teeth. As for Kuwait, its prewar demeanor toward Iraq could not have been more needlessly provocative, and seemingly rested on fatal illusions about Saddam's intentions as well as American attitudes.

Kuwait also ignored concrete signs of impending Iraqi military action, including an early-July warning from its military attaché in Baghdad that an invasion was planned for August 2.[3] "Clearly," write James Dunnigan and Austin Bay, "a major layer of blame for the disaster falls on Kuwait. Kuwait sat on its bankroll and ignored all of the war signals."[4] Kuwait's postinvasion image in the United States as a benign, innocent victim of Iraqi perfidy was largely manufactured after the fact with the assistance of New York's high-priced public relations firm Hill and Knowlton;[5] it bears little resemblance to the reality of Kuwait's prewar arrogance and dissembling.

As for the United States, it also completely misread the nature of the regime it was dealing with in Baghdad, in part because the White House and the Departments of State and Commerce wanted, despite mounting evidence to the contrary, to see in Iraq both a stabilizing force in the region and an ongoing lucrative market for U.S. agricultural and other products. At no time did the United States provide clear and consistent signals indicating what it would not tolerate in Baghdad's behavior toward its neighbors; indeed, the administration and its emissaries actively sought to deflect congressional and other criticism of Saddam's brutality, and ignored evidence of his preparations for empire. The contradictions in U.S. policy quickly became apparent shortly after the invasion, and the White House's embarrassment at having been so abruptly exposed as being so wrong about Saddam Hussein may have contributed to President Bush's personalization of the subsequent U.S. contest of wills with Iraq. Saddam Hussein, who had figured in preinvasion official and semi-official characterization as a "force for moderation" in the Gulf (Assistant Secretary of State John Kelly) and "the kind of leader the United States can easily be in a position to influence" (Senator Robert Dole),[6] suddenly became an Arab Adolf Hitler. An administration that on the very eve of the invasion had been lobbying Congress against passing trade sanctions against Iraq for its egregious human rights violations, including the gassing of Kurdish villages and the torture of children, suddenly determined that nothing short of a total economic embargo would suffice to deal with Saddam. And so it went.

What follows is a more detailed examination of the factors that prompted Saddam's invasion of Kuwait and his belief that he could get away with it. Again, the author's intention here is neither to justify nor to condemn what happened, but rather to explain how and why it happened, with an eye to judging whether the invasion could have been deterred.

IRAQI DESPERATENESS

Saddam Hussein had several motives for undertaking military action against Kuwait in the summer of 1990, all of them (at least in his own mind) legitimate, and some of them compelling. Moreover, he had little reason to believe that the United States and the rest of the world would react to his invasion of Kuwait the way they did. In tiny, defenseless, super-rich Kuwait, Saddam saw a host of opportunities: for economic salvation, for territorial expansion, for regional hegemony, for revenge, and for keeping his idle and discontented army busy.

Topping the list were economic and financial imperatives. Saddam's disastrous miscalculation of 1980, when he attempted to take military advantage of the Islamic revolution in Iran, had entangled an economically vibrant Iraq in a bloody conflict lasting eight years—the longest and one of the most destructive conventional wars of this century. That war arrested Iraq's promising economic development and gutted the Iraqi treasury. Because the war's costs greatly exceeded Iraq's ability to pay for them, Baghdad was forced to borrow huge sums, mostly from Saudi Arabia, Kuwait, and the other rich Gulf countries. When the Iran-Iraq War ended in the summer of 1988, following an isolated and even more exhausted Iran's acceptance of a U.N. cease-fire resolution, Iraq was bankrupt. It was saddled with $80 billion in foreign debt and an estimated reconstruction cost of $230 billion over a twenty-year period—against annual oil revenues at the time of only $13 billion.[7] Moreover, world oil prices, the barometer of the Iraqi economy, were declining, in part because Kuwait, the United Arab Emirates, and others were deliberately pumping oil far above the quotas assigned to them by the Organization of Petroleum Exporting Countries (OPEC); during the period from late February to early June of 1990 alone, the price dropped from $19.50 to $15.00 a barrel.[8] Iraq, which during the years 1975 to 1990 spent $65 billion on conventional armaments,[9] found itself unable to pay the interest on its debts, let alone the principal, and by the end of 1989 its credit had plummeted so low that France and other suppliers suspended arms shipments to Baghdad.[10]

Compounding Iraqi woes was rampant unemployment, which prohibited any significant demobilization of Saddam's million-man army. Hundreds of thousands of regulars and older recalled reservists, including the large ranks of infantry populated predominantly by Shia Muslims who had plenty of other reasons for discontent with Saddam's Sunni-dominated regime, were retained on active duty at a time when they had hoped to return home to their families and the prosperity of the kind that had prevailed in Iraq before the war.

The economic crisis directly threatened Saddam's regime, which had always managed to stay in power because Iraqis were prepared to tolerate its totalitarian brutality and political suffocation as long as the government could deliver rising living standards. Saddam, whose paranoia was hardly lessened by four reported coup and assassination attempts made against him from October 1988 to January 1990,[11] understood that economic collapse endangered his own survival by breaking his regime's implicit contract with those it ruled. By the spring of 1990, an "immediate economic breakthrough had thus become," write two critical biographers, "literally a matter of life and death."[12]

Closely related to Saddam's economic imperatives was a perceived necessity to rectify a major and long-standing geographical weakness permitting enemies past (Iran) and future (the Coalition) to strangle Iraqi commerce at will: lack of secure access to the Persian Gulf. Iraq's access to the Gulf is both narrow and dominated by others—in the east by the presence of Iran along the shared Shatt al-Arab waterway, and to the south by the Kuwaiti islands of Warbah and Bubiyan, past which Iraqi oil tankers and warships must sail to leave or enter Iraq's naval base and port facility of Umm Qasr. Every Iraqi government since independence in 1932 has always asserted that Kuwait was rightfully part of Iraq, by virtue of its past history as an administrative district in the Ottoman imperial province of Basra, and on at least four occasions—1961, 1963, 1973, and of course 1990—Iraq has either threatened to invade, or invaded, part or all of Kuwait.[13] At a minimum, Saddam and his predecessors believed, Iraq should be granted control, through sale or lease by Kuwait, of Warbah and Bubiyan, and Kuwait's refusal to consider transferring the islands ranked as one of the *casus belli* of the Gulf War.

Saddam, however, had other, more legitimate reasons to be angry at the tiny emirate along Iraq's southern border. As we shall see, Kuwait probably was, as Saddam charged, stealing Iraqi oil by horizontally drilling into the Iraqi side of the shared Rumaila oil field straddling the Iraq-Kuwait border; it was also pumping its own oil at more than twice its OPEC-assigned quota, thus contributing to the very oil price depression that was driving Iraq's economy down the drain.[14] Saddam considered Kuwait's oil activities tantamount to a declaration of war against his country, and he was not alone in believing in the desirability of military threats to compel Kuwait's compliance with its OPEC quota.

The wartime alliance between Kuwait and Saudi Arabia has obscured prewar Saudi attitudes toward the Kuwaitis, which bore a remarkable similarity to those of the Iraqis. The Saudis have long regarded the Kuwaitis as politically arrogant and morally lax, and for at least a year before the Gulf War complained of the emirate's deliberate overproduction of oil.[15] Indeed, the evidence suggests that the Saudis, who themselves were suffering from depressed oil prices, actively encouraged Baghdad's saber-rattling in the hope that it would frighten the emirate into complying with OPEC's pricing guidelines.[16]

No less irritating to Saddam Hussein was Kuwait's refusal to forgive its wartime loans to Iraq and to grant new sums to the dictator, who during the war had conducted what amounted to a protection racket among the rich

Gulf states—protection from Iran in exchange for cash. Other Gulf states that had loaned Iraq money during the war had informally written the loans off, perhaps in recognition of Iraq's insolvency and their own military weakness, and perhaps in grudging appreciation of the service that Saddam had performed, admittedly for his own selfish reasons, in preventing a forcible expansion of Iran's Islamic revolution into the politically vulnerable and militarily helpless southern side of the Persian Gulf. After all, the United States had courted Iraq in the 1980s for the same reason. By the spring of 1990, "the Saudis were no longer even bothering to keep a record of the loans to Iraq on their books," unlike the Kuwaitis, "who foolishly kept reminding the Iraqis of their debts and trying to use them as a bargaining chip."[17] Kuwait, which had been the most territorily exposed of the Gulf monarchies to Iranian military power, and which owed its survival to Iraq's tenacious defense of Basra and the Faw Peninsula, also refused Iraqi demands for new sums of cash—specifically, Saddam's "request" for an outright grant of $10 billion as an attempt to humiliate his country.[18]

A number of seasoned observers of Middle Eastern politics have argued that by 1990 Saddam Hussein had worked himself into a situation where he could ill afford *not* to invade Kuwait, or at least a situation where the perceived rewards of doing so seemed irresistible. For example, former Assistant Secretary of State Richard Murphy, a key architect of what in the 1980s became a virtual American alliance with Iraq against Iran, has said that "Saddam came to realize that he was being regarded as one of the world's worst credit risks and was facing bankruptcy," and reasoned, not illogically, that "to get out of bankruptcy, you rob a bank."[19] Once-prosperous Iraq seemed headed for the status of a permanently and hopelessly indebted Third World state, despite its vast oil reserves and usable military power.[20] There can thus be no gainsaying Kuwait's multifaceted attractiveness to Saddam. The emirate was filthy rich, militarily vulnerable, and virtually friendless; it conquest would, moreover, make Iraq military master of the Gulf and establish Iraq as the preeminent military power in the Arab world.

Moreover, as we shall later discuss in greater detail, Saddam had every reason to believe that action against Kuwait would not elicit a strong American reaction, in part because he failed to perceive how the Cold War's demise and the Soviet Union's growing economic desperation were laying the foundations of a tacit U.S.-Soviet *alliance* in the Persian Gulf. Unlike the more insightful Hafez al-Assad, who saw in the Cold War's end an imperative to improve Syria's relations with the United States, Saddam seemed not to have understood that the United States now had a relatively free diplomatic and military hand in the Gulf. On the contrary, he appears to have interpreted the collapse of Communism and the global recession of Soviet military power as liberating himself from long-detested Soviet attempts to curb his regional ambitions.

KUWAITI RECKLESSNESS

Historically, relatively small and defenseless states compelled to share borders with large, untrustworthy, and militarily powerful neighbors have commonly sought to preserve their security in one or more or a combination of three different ways. The first way, especially appealing to states with some measure of human resources and such natural barriers to invasion as mountainous or water-laced topography, is to create defenses which, while insufficient to stop a determined invasion, nonetheless offer the prospect of raising the price of invasion to militarily or politically unacceptable levels to the invader. Sweden, Finland, Switzerland, and what was formerly Yugoslavia, all of which have compulsory military service and excellent defensive terrain, are examples of small states that have chosen this route to security. Alternatively, the small state, particularly if it lacks manpower, geographic depth, and natural barriers to invasion (e.g., Denmark, Luxembourg), may pursue an alliance with a friendly major power able to counterbalance the enemy's military threat. This, in a very fundamental sense, was the essence of the North Atlantic Treaty Organization; the countries of Western Europe, which neither alone nor together could hope to balance the enormous military might of the Soviet Union, sought and received security compensation in the form of an alliance with the United States. A third route is appeasement. The small or militarily weak state makes the necessary territorial or political concessions to remove any reason for war with its threatening neighbor. This was the course followed by France and its continental allies vis-à-vis Germany during the 1930s, even though the disparity between French and German military power was far less profound than believed at the time.

A small state lacking defenses, allies, and a willingness to appease is an open invitation to aggression, especially if it is either rich in natural resources or strategically critical territory—and certainly if it pursues a foreign policy based on the illusion of its own inviolability. During the 1930s, for example, Poland, a relatively small, flat country lacking modern military forces and sandwiched in between two military behemoths that each had hostile designs on Polish territory, behaved as if it, too, were a major European power. Unlike Finland, which was in a similar predicament, Poland refused to accept the reality that its survival hinged on appeasement of, or outright military alliance with, either Nazi Germany or the Soviet Union; its militarily useless 1939 alliance with France and Britain amounted to too little, too late. The result was Poland's destruction by both German and Soviet forces.

Kuwait's position in 1990 was not dissimilar to Poland's in the 1930s, except that Kuwait seemed even more oblivious to the dangers it faced. Lacking all but token military forces, and as naturally defenseless as Denmark, Kuwait neither sought alliance with a compensating military power nor attempted to accommodate even Iraq's legitimate complaints, such as Kuwait's probable theft of Iraqi oil from the Rumaila oil field and its certain violation of OPEC production quotas. It pursued a policy of defiance that at the time was regarded as unnecessarily provocative by other Arab states, including Saudi Arabia, Egypt, and Jordan.[21] None of this, of course, excuses Iraq from responsibility for invading Kuwait, and for inflicting unspeakable atrocities upon its citizens; but neither does it absolve Kuwait's leadership of its irresponsibility. Just like the hot-rodder who likes to play "chicken" at the railroad crossing with oncoming trains, Kuwait went looking for trouble and found it.

Ironically, during the Iran-Iraq War Kuwait exhibited far more strategic common sense than it did after that conflict. Confronted by both Iranian-sponsored attempts to subvert its dynasty and a direct Iranian military threat to its territory, Kuwait, though at the time harboring suspicions of Saddam Hussein's ultimate intentions toward the emirate, nevertheless entered into a virtual alliance with Iraq. It bankrolled much of Iraq's war effort, turned its ports over to Iraqi commerce, and even permitted the stationing of Iraqi air force units on its territory.[22] By all accounts, however, Kuwait failed to recognize the implications for its own security of Iran's defeat, which left Iraq—a country that had long regarded Kuwaitis with contempt and their country as rightfully part of Iraq—as the militarily predominant power in the Persian Gulf. Alarm bells certainly should have clanged loudly by early 1990, when the combination of Iraq's refusal to demobilize its giant army and Saddam's increasingly hostile rhetoric toward Kuwait demolished any notion of a war-induced Iraqi foreign policy of restraint and reasonableness.

Even as Iraq began massing 100,000 troops along the Kuwaiti border in mid-July 1990, "the Kuwaitis failed to grasp the seriousness of the situation," remaining "amazingly complacent."[23] And reckless—as manifest in their behavior at the critical Jiddah (Saudi Arabia) conference, convened on August 1, the day before the invasion, at the request of Egyptian President Hosni Mubarak in a last-ditch attempt to forestall Iraqi military action—from which Saddam agreed to refrain pending the conference's outcome. Though both Saddam and the emir of Kuwait had agreed to attend the conference, the Jiddah effort was torpedoed by the emir's last-minute boycott of the meeting, which compelled an insulted Saddam to withdraw.[24] The resulting conference lasted only two hours and consisted mainly of an invective-hurling match between the Iraqi and Kuwaiti delegations.

Kuwait's diplomatic recklessness is now a matter of historical record. Unanswered is the question of motives. Some have suggested that the Sabahs' innate arrogance blinded them to the threat that was staring them in the face, while others claim that Kuwait's leaders simply could not bring themselves to believe that any Arab state, even Iraq, would dare invade another Arab state, which indeed had been an unwritten taboo in the Arab world since the withdrawal of the European colonial powers.[25]

More intriguing is speculation that the Kuwaiti leaders, perhaps with memories of American protection provided to Kuwaiti shipping during the Iran-Iraq War, had convinced themselves that the United States could and would quickly come to their country's defense if Iraq attacked. Though preinvasion U.S. policy toward Baghdad remained one of appeasement, and though U.S. spokesmen denied any such commitment to Kuwait, the Kuwaitis apparently believed that both the Americans and the British would rush to their defense. At the Jiddah conference, Kuwait's Crown Prince Saad al-Sabah reportedly advised the Iraqi delegation: "Don't make threats. Kuwait has powerful friends. We have allies as well. You will be forced to pay us the money you owe us."[26] Jordan's Crown Prince Hassan, in an attempt to account for defenseless Kuwait's defiance of Saddam, reportedly concluded that the emirate had America's tacit support, and even possibly was in cahoots with Washington "to set a trap for Saddam Hussein."[27]

The problem with such a conclusion is its utter inconsistency with every other aspect of prewar U.S. policy toward Iraq.

AMERICAN WITLESSNESS

Any assessment of prewar U.S. policy toward Iraq, especially to the extent that it focuses on the issue of whether American actions or inactions may have consciously or unknowingly encouraged Iraq to invade Kuwait, or at least to believe that it could invade without incurring unacceptable risks, must start with a major caveat: namely, that the situation objectively may have been one in which nothing the United States might have said or done otherwise would have dissuaded Saddam Hussein from grabbing the emirate. For Saddam, the conquest of Kuwait, as we have seen, was a political and economic imperative. Moreover, one of the most consistent features of the dictator's behavior throughout the crisis, during both its preinvasion phase and the period of America's subsequent massive military buildup in Saudi Arabia—which ought to have alerted Saddam to the seriousness of U.S. intent—was his apparent conviction that the United States would not, indeed could not for domestic political reasons, bring itself to employ force against Iraq. Even after the Coalition launched its devastating air campaign against Iraq, which by most accounts took the Iraqis completely by surprise, the evidence suggests that Saddam still believed the United States lacked the guts to tangle with Iraqi forces on the ground in Kuwait. Saddam's attitude undoubtedly derived in part from his own ignorance of, and illusions about, the United States, a paper tiger still traumatized by its experience in Vietnam—and about the Soviet Union, a has-been superpower incapable of wielding significant influence in world affairs. As is not uncommon among "personality cult" totalitarians, he surrounded himself with no one knowledgeable or courageous enough to believe or tell him otherwise; moreover, to assume the Americans would fight was to entertain unpleasant consequences for his personal and imperial ambitions.

In hindsight, it is difficult to imagine what the United States might have done before August 2 to deter a desperate and determined Iraq from marching into Kuwait—short of a clear ultimatum accompanied by the dispatch of powerful U.S. ground forces to Kuwait, possibilities certain to have been categorically rejected by a Kuwaiti leadership oblivious to its impending doom and by U.S. congressional and public opinion. As we shall see, even after news of the invasion reached the White House, President Bush hesitated before concluding that Iraq's aggression could not be permitted to stand, by which time Kuwait's defense had become a moot issue; and it was not until late October that the President authorized the deployment to Saudi Arabia of U.S. forces sufficient to recapture Kuwait.

At a minimum, however, the record reveals that the United States, in part because it misread Baghdad as much as Baghdad misread Washington, did little if anything to convey to Saddam the risks that invasion might entail. On the contrary, U.S. policy during the decade before the invasion not only encouraged Iraq's militarization and Saddam's sense of self-importance, but also promoted on Saddam's part a belief that he would have a free hand in dealing with Kuwait. To put it bluntly, the overall burden of U.S. behavior toward Iraq right up to the invasion, and especially during the period between the end of the Iran-Iraq War and August 2, 1990, was a combination of indifference and appeasement. The United States was preoccupied with events elsewhere in the world, particularly in Europe and the Soviet Union in the late 1980s, and entertained convenient illusions about Saddam and his ambitions—illusions promoted by powerful domestic U.S. political forces with a vested interest in policies that ignored the dictator's brutality and lust for regional hegemony. The combination of American signals not sent, and of Iraqi signals missed by U.S. policymakers, reinforced the web of misperceptions and miscalculations that led to war.

The American courtship of Iraq began in the early 1980s, and for reasons that at the time, and still in retrospect, appear rational and even compelling. In Iran, the fall of the Shah in 1979 and his replacement by a radical, virulently anti-Western Islamic regime abruptly removed a major pillar of stability and surrogate for U.S. military power in the Persian Gulf. The Ayatollah Khomeini's seizure of American hostages in Teheran and his expansionist theocratic ambitions appeared to threaten not only the survival of the Sunni-dominated regimes in Iraq and the Arabian peninsular Gulf states, but also the U.S. position in the Middle East itself. A wave of Iranian-inspired terrorism swept the region: deadly bombings in Kuwait and an assassination attempt against the emir; an attempted Shia coup in Bahrain in 1981; the bloody assault on Mecca's Grand Mosque in 1979, during the annual pilgrimage; and Anwar Sadat's assassination in 1981. These acts were supplemented by direct attacks against Americans and American interests in the region, including numerous airliner hijackings, and the Hezbollah attacks of 1983 on the U.S. embassy in Lebanon and on the U.S. Marine Corps garrison in Beirut. The Ayatollah also targeted Iraq, calling for the overthrow of its Baathist regime, and actively fomented rebellion among the large populations of his Shia coreligionists in the strategically critical southern regions of that country. The Iranian challenge to Saddam's minority Sunni-run regime in Baghdad was a significant factor in the Iraqi dictator's ill-considered decision to invade Iran in September 1980, and though the subsequent eight-year war between the two countries absorbed most of Iran's military energies, not until the war's last year did Iraq finally gain the upper hand.

However, Iraq's ability to survive its contest with its far larger and more highly motivated Persian neighbor, to say nothing of ultimately prevailing over Iran, hinged from the outset upon access to vast amounts of foreign cash, credits, military assistance, and armaments, all of which were only too happily supplied by other Arab states terrified of an Iranian victory, by Western defense contractors hungry for new military orders, and by a United States that had a clear strategic stake in containing the spread of radical Islam in the Gulf and in preventing the emergence of a hostile Iran as the region's unchallengeable military hegemon.

Though U.S. policy toward Iraq during the war with Iran was guilty of much shortsightedness, many excesses, and a lot of wishful thinking, its strategic premise was both sound and long-standing: to prevent the Gulf's domination by any single hostile power, be it the Soviet Union (the focus of U.S. policy in the Gulf during the Cold War) or Iran (in the 1980s), or Iraq (in the 1990s). Allegiance to this premise, however, did not dictate what became a virtual wartime alliance with Iraq. Nor did it demand the sharing of sensitive intelligence information and advanced technologies that could later be turned against the West. It certainly mandated neither an apparent failure to recognize that the marriage of U.S. and Iraqi interests during the war was purely one of convenience, nor a postwar official blindness to the emergence of a threatening Iraq as the Persian Gulf's aspiring successor superpower.

To be sure, the United States was not, especially when it came to transferring arms to Iraq, the only or the most egregious offender. The Soviet Union supplied, in terms of dollar amounts, the largest single share of Iraq's imported military arsenal, mostly fighter aircraft and weapons and equipment for Iraq's huge army. Iraq in the 1970s and 1980s was, after all, a Soviet client state, and to its credit, Moscow consistently sought to discipline Saddam's regional ambitions by denying Iraq access to certain weapons and technologies, and by creating significant Iraqi logistical and production dependencies on the Soviet Union. Saddam's Soviet patrons denied their client information related to maintenance of Soviet equipment, refused to permit Iraq to manufacture Soviet weapons under license, and on more than one occasion used the "stick" of actual or threatened suspension of arms deliveries as political leverage against Baghdad. Indeed, it was a combination of abiding Soviet distrust of Saddam and the dictator's own belief that Moscow wanted to reduce Iraq to a vassal state that propelled Saddam to enter the Western arms bazaar in search of military independence.

These and other details of the Soviet-Iraqi military relationship are comprehensively chronicled in Kenneth R. Timmerman's *The Death Lobby: How the West Armed Iraq,* the definitive if sordid account of how the West's arms industry, with the connivance of Western governments, knowingly created in Saddam Hussein the military and nascent nuclear monster that was finally called to a reckoning in the Gulf War.[28] It is a depressing tale of "the greed of Western businesses, misguided analyses by the foreign policy establishment, and the incompetence of regulatory officials."[29]

Perhaps topping the list of irresponsibility and dishonesty were France and Germany. France, which sold Iraq a staggering $20 billion in arms and military production facilities from 1970 to 1990,[30] saw in Iraq a model of progressive, secular economic development in the Third World, as well as an opportunity to make money and to open a wedge of French influence in a region long dominated by the Anglo-Americans. To Iraq the French sold their best weapons and technologies, and unlike the Soviets, exhibited few reservations about assisting the Iraqis in establishing a viable indigenous arms industry. The Germans concentrated on helping Iraq build an independent capacity to produce biological, chemical, and nuclear weapons, thus creating the foundation of Iraq's rise as a genuine international threat. Without the assistance of German companies acting with the connivance of the Bonn government, Saddam could not possibly have made the progress he did in almost becoming a nuclear power, and many of those same German firms continued to do business with Iraq after that country was embargoed by the United Nations.[31]

Direct American complicity in arming Iraq was less notable, in part because of relatively strict arms export laws and enforcement procedures, and latent congressional aversion that surfaced strongly in the late 1980s. The Defense Department also staunchly opposed, though not always successfully, many technology transfer programs being promoted by the departments of State and Commerce, and by the U.S.-Iraqi Business Forum, a powerful, homegrown American lobbying organization of agribusinesses and defense industries that served as a de facto shill and apologist for Iraqi interests. However, through the Department of Agriculture's Commodity Credit Corporation the United States from 1982 to 1990 advanced billions of dollars' worth of credit to Iraq for the purchase of American foodstuffs, which permitted Saddam to reallocate to the acquisition of arms resources that would otherwise have been devoted to feeding his people. Moreover, during neither the Iran-Iraq War nor its aftermath did the United States exhibit any significant concern over what its Western allies were doing in the way of creating a future military challenge to Western interests in the Persian Gulf. On the contrary, U.S. behavior toward Iraq beginning in the early 1980s reflected a mounting desire to assist Iraq in its struggle with Iran, and later, confidence that Iraqi ambitions could be tempered via a mix of dependence on U.S. imports and repeated professions of desire for friendship.

What amounted by the end of 1987 to virtual U.S. cobelligerency with

Iraq against Iran began in the early 1980s in fear of the consequences of an Iranian victory. Moreover, Iraq was as eager to engage the United States against Iran as Washington was to help Baghdad. Indeed, Iraqi policy sought, with ultimate success via the so-called tanker-war, to provoke Iran into provoking the United States into entering the war's periphery on the Iraqi side.

The first two years of the war were disastrous for Baghdad. By the spring of 1982 Iraqi forces, poorly handled by a Saddam Hussein who micromanaged them from one setback to another, had been ejected from much of their initial gains inside Iran and were fighting desperately to prevent numerically superior Iranian forces from overrunning key Iraqi defensive positions along the Shatt al-Arab and the Faw Peninsula. Iranian victories were sparking Shia riots in Basra and elsewhere in southern Iraq, and Saddam, sensitive to the questionable loyalty of his own Shia-dominated infantry, was reluctant to commit them to battles that promised high casualties. In early April Iraqi fortunes were dealt yet another blow when Syria, tacitly allied with Iran, closed down the Iraq-Mediterranean oil pipeline and seized all Iraqi oil in storage, thus foreclosing to Iraq a major source of desperately needed foreign exchange. On June 9 and 10, in an attempt to entice Iran into a cease-fire and settlement based on the status quo ante, Saddam ordered all Iraqi forces to withdraw from Iranian territory and to observe a unilateral cease-fire—an early bid for peace that ran aground on Iranian insistence on the removal of Saddam Hussein and his Baathist regime as a precondition for any negotiations.

By early 1983 Iraq had apparently concluded that it could not hope to prevail over Iran, a country with great strategic depth and three times Iraq's population, without mobilizing world opinion against the Iranian threat and by broadening the war. This made imperative a widening of the war in a manner that would bring at least the United States into the Gulf, thereby provoking a violent Iranian countermove. Baghdad embarked upon this venture with ultimate success.[32] Even before 1983 Iraq had on at least one occasion attempted to broaden the war, in this case by diverting Iranian attentions toward Israel. In the hope of luring Iran into a temporary cessation of hostilities in favor of united action against Israel, which, ironically, was secretly supplying weapons to Iran on the principle that "the enemy of my enemy is my friend," Iraq directed its terrorist agents to assassinate Schlomo Argov, Israel's ambassador to Great Britain, on June 3, 1982,[33] which contributed to Israel's decision to invade Lebanon three days later.

It was in this context of events that the State Department, following two meetings in Paris between Secretary of State George Shultz and Iraqi Foreign Minister Tariq Aziz in October 1982 and May 1983, struck Iraq from the list of states sponsoring terrorism, thereby opening renewed trade with the United States. In June 1983 the Reagan administration authorized the sale to Iraq of sixty helicopters for "agricultural use" and granted Iraq a $400 million credit to purchase 147,000 tons of American rice.[34] Also in

1983, the United States launched Operation Staunch, a campaign to dissuade U.S. allies from supplying arms to Iran. It began supplying Iraq, via Saudi Arabian intermediaries, information on Iranian forces and their movements obtained from U.S. reconnaissance satellites and AWACS surveillance aircraft, which had been operating from Saudi bases since September 1980. A year later the United States resumed diplomatic relations with Iraq, which had been severed since the 1967 Arab-Israeli War.

Thus began America's long courtship of one of the world's most brutal and ambitious dictators, and its slide into cobelligerency against Iran. The critical turning point came in 1987, when the Reagan administration agreed to place Kuwait's eleven oil tankers under the U.S. flag and the U.S. Navy's protection. This decision effectively allied the United States to a major ally of Iraq, Kuwait, which was not only bankrolling much of Iraq's war effort but also permitting Iraq access to Kuwaiti territory for the purpose of conducting military operations against Iran. It also placed U.S. warships in the Gulf on a mission virtually certain to attract violent Iranian responses, which indeed were not long in coming. The Reagan administration, fearful of Soviet naval intrusion in the Gulf (Kuwait had cleverly made a similar reflagging request to the Kremlin), wishing to offset the damage to U.S. prestige in the region inflicted by revelations in 1986 of its attempted arms-for-hostages swap with Iran, and concerned that an Iran now armed with Chinese-supplied antiship Silkworm missiles was preparing attacks on major-power shipping in the Gulf, unfortunately ignored Iraq's obvious interest in using the reflagging as a means of inciting a U.S.-Iranian clash. Indeed, the reflagging decision, which was further encouraged by the May 17, 1987, "accidental" Iraqi Exocet missile attack on the USS *Stark* that killed thirty-seven American sailors—an incident interpreted by President Reagan as somehow Iran's fault—[35] represented an Iraqi strategic triumph of the first order. Iraq finally succeeded, using its ally Kuwait, in bringing into the conflict against Iran a superpower already favorably disposed to teach Teheran a lesson.

Hostilities came quickly. On July 24, 1987, three days after U.S. naval escorting operations began (Operation Earnest Will), the tanker *Bridgeton* struck an Iranian mine. A month later U.S. helicopters attacked and destroyed the *Iran Ajr,* an Iranian mine-laying vessel, and for the remainder of the war U.S. forces ran into other mines, engaged Iranian oil platforms, and sank Iranian warships. On July 3, 1988, less than three weeks before an Iran exhausted by disastrous defeats on the ground, Iraqi Scud missile attacks on Iranian cities, and the impossibility of dealing with the demands imposed by the American "second front" at sea, announced its willingness to accept a U.N.-sponsored cease-fire, the USS *Vincennes* mistakenly shot down an Iranian commercial airliner.

America's undeclared war on Iran, and its deliveries of foodstuffs, technology, and intelligence information to Iraq, contributed significantly to Baghdad's victory over the country it had so ill-advisedly invaded in 1980. In so doing, the United States, aided and abetted by its European allies and rich Arab friends in the Gulf, managed to contain within Iran itself the threat of the radical Islamic revolution spawned by the Ayatollah Khomeini, and to prevent the establishment of Iranian military hegemony in the Persian Gulf. In the process of containing one hegemon, however, the anti-Iran coalition laid the foundations for the rise of another. Yet American policymakers failed to grasp the implications of Iran's defeat and to understand the true economic plight and postwar ambitions of Saddam Hussein's Iraq. The American foreign policy establishment assumed, not illogically, that postwar Iraq would be too preoccupied with domestic social and economic reconstruction to engage in yet more military adventures beyond its borders.[36] A 1990 Army War College study, sympathetic to Iraq and highly dismissive of Saddam's American critics, concluded, for example, that "for the foreseeable future, debt repayment will fully occupy the regime; it will have neither the will not the resources to go to war."[37] It was further assumed that whatever latent malignant ambitions Baghdad might have could be assuaged by a continuation of business as usual. As Assistant Secretary of State for Near Eastern and South Asian Affairs John Kelly summed up the Reagan and Bush administrations' approach to Iraq during the two years separating the end of the Iran-Iraq War and Iraq's invasion of Kuwait, "Our policy towards Iraq has been to attempt to develop gradually a mutually beneficial relationship with Iraq in order to strengthen positive trends in Iraq's foreign and domestic policies."[38]

At a time when a fundamental reassessment of the wisdom of continuing the 1983–88 marriage of convenience with Iraq ought to have been conducted, the United States embarked instead on an even greater effort to romance Saddam Hussein into international respectability. Commerce was expanded, agricultural credits doubled, more technologies transferred, and politically soothing messages delivered—all amidst mounting evidence of Baathist terrorism run amok at home and of military preparations for more adventures abroad. Saddam's poison gas attacks on his own Kurdish citizens at the conclusion of the Iran-Iraq War were followed by expanded Commodity Credit Corporation guarantees to Baghdad. On the very day before Saddam invaded Kuwait, the Bush administration approved the sale of advanced data transmission equipment worth $695,000 to Iraq, bringing total U.S. technology sales to Iraq during the period 1985–90 to 771, including advanced computers, sophisticated machine tools, radio equipment, VIP helicopters, imaging devices for reading satellite photos, and computer mapping systems.[39]

Even after it became clear, by late 1989 or early 1990, that Saddam Hussein had no intention of pursuing a benign foreign policy in favor of internal reconstruction, the administration continued to appease the dictator. Congressman Stephen J. Solarz, a prominent Democratic supporter of the administration's postinvasion toughness toward Iraq, including the decision for war to liberate Kuwait, criticized the administration's preinvasion lack of backbone:

> There was no excuse for putting our policy toward Iraq on automatic pilot for two years after its war with Iran ended—which is exactly what the administration did, when it opposed congressional efforts to impose trade sanctions on Iraq, on the naive assumption that by kowtowing to Saddam we would be in a better position to influence his behavior. By declaring that we had no obligation to come to the defense of Kuwait, and by taking no position on Iraq's border dispute with Kuwait, administration spokesmen clearly contributed to a perception on Saddam's part that we would not resist his use of force in the Gulf.[40]

The most perfidious aspect of U.S. policy, certainly in hindsight, was the stream of political signals sent to Baghdad that quite understandably were interpreted by Saddam as a combination of American fear of Iraq and a willingness to appease his appetite for some or even all of Kuwait. For example, the Bush administration consistently and until the very end staunchly opposed congressional attempts to impose trade sanctions on Iraq for its heinous human rights abuses and manifest efforts to build a nuclear bomb, trotting out all the old worm-eaten arguments about how sanctions would hurt American business and eliminate any remaining U.S. leverage over Iraqi behavior. Opposition to sanctions, long favored by such congressional odd couples as Senators Claiborne Pell and Jesse Helms, continued through the spring and early summer of 1990 as Saddam publicly threatened to incinerate half of Israel, executed British journalist Farzad Bazoft, and made increasingly bellicose pronouncements against the United States itself. On April 26, 1990, Assistant Secretary of State Kelly, who on February 12 had journeyed to Baghdad to tell Saddam Hussein that he was a "force for moderation" and that the "United States wishes to broaden relations with Iraq,"[41] testified before a House subcommittee that sanctions would "hurt U.S. exporters and worsen our trade deficit," adding, "I do not see how sanctions would improve our ability to exercise a restraining influence on Iraqi actions."[42] The administration's dogged opposition to sanctions continued down to the invasion itself, prompting at least one Republican senator, William Cohen of Maine, to accuse the administration of appeasement worthy of the British at Munich:

> [L]et me say that at one point in our history we heard the tap tap tap of Neville Chamberlain's umbrella on the cobblestones of Munich. Now we . . . hear the rumble of the [American] farm tractor on the bricks of Baghdad. Make no mistake about it, we are following a policy of appeasement and we are never going to lead in the fight against terrorism. We are never going to lead in the fight against the spread of chemical weapons, or that of high military technology, because of the argument that our allies are unwilling to follow our example. Therefore, we are left with the argument that we must follow the herd, follow it

right down the path of feeding Saddam Hussein while he continues to terrorize, attack, gas, or simply threaten to do so. This is a policy of appeasement. . . . [43]

If Saddam was grateful to the White House for blocking congressional sanctions against him, he must have been positively ecstatic about the things the White House and its emissaries were saying. On April 12, 1990, a delegation of U.S. senators consisting of Minority Leader Robert Dole, Alan Simpson, James McClure, Frank Murkowski, and Howard Metzenbaum, most of them Republicans from farm states with a vested interest in maximizing agricultural exports to Iraq, were granted an audience with Saddam in Baghdad. Among other things, Senator Dole, later a leading warhawk, reassured the dictator of President Bush's continued opposition to sanctions and desire for better relations with Iraq. Senator Simpson, a man known for ill-considered remarks later recanted, averred that Saddam's problems with the United States "lay with the Western media and not with the U.S. government," and went on to denounce a "haughty and pampered" American press. Senator Metzenbaum, the only Democrat and liberal in the delegation, allowed as how he had "been sitting here and listening to you for about an hour, and I am now aware that you are a strong and intelligent man and that you want peace."[44]

Then came, on July 25, 1990, a week before the invasion, but one day after the first Iraqi armored divisions began deploying along the Kuwaiti border, the infamous performance of the U.S. ambassador to Iraq, April Glaspie, in another audience with Saddam. Glaspie, a fervent promoter of U.S.-Iraqi trade, made a gushing display of sympathy with virtually every utterance of Saddam's during the dictator's long monologue on Iraq's tribulations. After declaring that she had "a direct instruction from the President to seek better relations with Iraq," Glaspie sympathized with Iraq's unfair treatment at the hands of the British Colonial Office: "We studied history in school. They taught us to say freedom or death. . . . we as a people have our own experience with the colonialists." She sympathized with Iraq's desire for higher oil prices: "We have many Americans who would like to see the price go above twenty-five dollars because they come from oil-producing states." She sympathized with the dictator's dismay over a critical American television program: "I [also] saw the Diane Sawyer program on ABC. And what happened in that program was cheap and unjust. And this is a real picture of what happens in the American media. . . . I am pleased that you add your voice to the diplomats who stand up to the media. . . . If the American President had control of the media, his job would be much easier." She sympathized with Saddam's indispensability to Iraq's future well-being, and seemingly, with Iraq's anger at Kuwait: "I admire your extraordinary efforts to rebuild your country. I know you need funds. We understand that and our opinion is that you should have the opportunity to rebuild your country. But we have no opinion on Arab-Arab conflicts, like your border dispute with Kuwait."[45]

The one aspect of the dictator's remarks to which she did not respond except with silence was his thinly veiled threat to unleash terrorism against the United States if it tried to stand in his way.[46]

Ambassador Glaspie's obsequiousness could hardly have alerted Saddam to the possibility that his impending move against Kuwait might elicit any response from Washington other than more appeasement. Indeed, Glaspie herself had anticipated the likelihood of some kind of limited Iraqi aggression against Kuwait, as she later confided to Elaine Sciolino;[47] she and others in the State Department apparently believed that an Iraqi-imposed revision of the Kuwait border was a tolerable price to pay to keep Saddam happy.[48]

In fact, veteran Middle East correspondent John Cooley has reported a U.S. willingness to appease Saddam's territorial ambitions even *after* the invasion was launched. This came in the form of a U.S. proposal drafted on August 2 by the American ambassador to the United Nations, Thomas Pickering, subsequently approved by Secretary of State James Baker, and then transmitted to the Jordanian U.N. delegation in hopes of its delivery to Baghdad. The proposal, which for unexplained reasons never reached Iraq, reportedly called for Iraq's withdrawal from Kuwait and the emir's restoration, but it also conveyed American flexibility over the Iraq-Kuwait border dispute, acknowledged Iraq's need for better access to the sea, and suggested that Iraq call for a U.N.-sponsored plebiscite in Kuwait to permit its people to decide their future.[49]

Ambassador Glaspie's "green light" was the penultimate signal. The final one was delivered by the ubiquitous Kelly on July 31, 1990, when he repeatedly emphasized before a House subcommittee that "we have no defense treaty relationships with any other [Gulf] countries," and "We have historically avoided taking a position on border disputes or on internal OPEC deliberations. . . . "[50]

Clearly, the invasion, and certainly its scope, caught the White House by complete surprise, despite mounting intelligence reports of Iraqi forces along the Kuwait border and the failure of the Jiddah conference. The possibility of a limited Iraqi move into the disputed border areas and Warbah and Bubiyan islands was entertained, but the country's complete conquest was not. Presidential national security adviser Brent Scowcroft reportedly was "stunned,"[51] as were Egyptian president Hosni Mubarak and Jordan's King Hussein, both of whom had tried to broker a nonviolent resolution of the dispute. Certainly the Kuwaitis were completely taken aback; many senior officers were on leave, and virtually no military precautions had been taken. And President Bush characteristically chose to place greater confidence in the judgment of his good friends President Mubarak and King Hussein than in intelligence information that could not answer the question of whether Iraqi military activity was the beginning of the real McCoy or simply a bluff aimed at intimidating the Kuwaitis. As Salinger and Laurent have noted:

The President had believed, right until the last moment, that Iraq would not invade, simply because two leaders he had trusted, King Hussein of Jordan and President Hosni Mubarak of Egypt, had constantly assured him of this. Bush had considered them more reliable sources of information than all the secret reports and satellite photos that arrived hourly on his desk.[52]

The surprise was in large measure strategic. The administration, as we have seen, had always believed that Saddam could be "managed" with proper incentives. Indeed, President Bush

> had personally invested in the idea that Saddam's behavior could be moderated. It was *assumed* all along that Iraq's saber-rattling should be seen as using threats to force concessions from Kuwait, a case of coercive diplomacy rather than the unfolding of a trajectory leading to war. This assessment led to a second key mistake: the failure to signal U.S. intentions.[53]

Furthermore, the administration in 1989 and 1990 was understandably preoccupied with earthshaking events in Europe and the Soviet Union, including the collapse of Communist political authority in Eastern Europe, the demise of the Warsaw Pact, unilateral Soviet troop withdrawals from Eastern Europe (and Afghanistan), the destruction of the Berlin Wall and other events signaling Germany's reunification with NATO, and clear signs of the Soviet Union's own impending disintegration. The invasion caught Secretary of State Baker in the Soviet Union on a visit with Foreign Minister Edward Shevardnadze, Secretary of Defense Dick Cheney fishing in Colorado, and President Bush vacationing in Maine.

It is moreover far from clear what the administration could have done militarily to deter Saddam even had it been so predisposed. Until the invasion, none of America's Arab friends, including Kuwait, Saudi Arabia, Egypt, and Jordan, were prepared to encourage, much less host, potential U.S. military initiatives such as, for example, the dispatch of U.S. air or ground forces to Kuwait. They wanted an Arab solution to the crisis, not visible U.S. military action that seemingly would confirm Saddam's claim that the rich Gulf states were little more than surrogates for American interests. Even had he wished to, President Bush could not appear to be seen as getting out in front of the Arabs militarily on a matter that appeared to be, after all, a long-standing Arab boundary dispute involving no important U.S. interest.

In sum, the evidence argues strongly for the conclusion that Iraqi military action against Kuwait in the summer of 1990 was highly probable, even inevitable. The combination of Iraq's economic desperation and Saddam's long-standing territorial ambitions; Kuwait's reckless provocations of Baghdad and apparent failure to recognize either its own helplessness or Saddam's seriousness; and America's unwitting encouragement of the dictator—all joined to produce Iraq's invasion of Kuwait. Nor was there, in the eleventh hour, much that the United States, having appeased Baghdad for almost a decade, could have credibly done to deter the invasion. Certainly, Saddam Hussein had little reason to anticipate the United States' subsequent response to his aggression. After all, the United States had backed Baghdad in its war on Iran; provided critical intelligence and foodstuffs; placed American lives in jeopardy in the Gulf to ensure the flow of Iraqi arms imports via Kuwait; made no fuss over the attack on the *Stark;* turned a blind eye to Baathist atrocities inside Iraq; and dismissed the border dispute with Kuwait as a purely Arab affair.

WAS DESERT STORM INEVITABLE?

If, however, Iraq's invasion of Kuwait was probably inevitable, can the same be said of Operation Desert Storm? Both President Bush and Saddam Hussein could have "canceled" Desert Storm—Bush by simply abjuring a decision to retake Kuwait by force, Saddam by removing the reason for Desert Storm. In the case of Saddam Hussein, throughout the 163-day period separating the invasion of Kuwait and the initiation of Desert Storm, it was within his power to avoid Desert Storm by simply ordering his forces to withdraw from Kuwait voluntarily. That he did not do so saddles him with the primary responsibility for the fate that finally befell his forces in Kuwait, if not the enormous damage inflicted on Iraq's economic infrastructure by the Coalition's air campaign. However unwittingly encouraged by others, Saddam was the transgressor, the agent that ignited the Gulf Crisis of 1990–91. His refusal to evacuate Kuwait before January 15, 1991, despite many opportunities to do so, was a product of mindless stubbornness, or so it appears in hindsight.

But was it? Given the outcome of the war for Kuwait, Saddam's unwillingness even to order a partial withdrawal from the emirate, back to, say, the disputed border areas, as the United States and its Coalition partners amassed overwhelming force against him in Saudi Arabia seems irrational, even idiotic. But, in fact, there were understandable, even compelling reasons for the dictator's inflexibility—reasons that at the time may not have been apparent or fully grasped by the United States and its allies. The first and perhaps the most important was a combination of personal pride and political desperation. Saddam saw in Kuwait's conquest the only answer to the Iraqi economic crisis that in his own mind was endangering his regime's political future. Kuwait's acquisition also would bolster his image as a strong leader capable of inspiring Arabs everywhere—a new Nasser prepared to stand up to the United States, Israel, and the effete Arabian oil principalities. The importance to Saddam of holding on to Kuwait was dramatically underscored on August 15, 1990, by his stunning acceptance of Iranian terms for a formal peace settlement of the Iran-Iraq War (though the fighting had ended in August 1988, no peace treaty had been concluded). With understandable alacrity, the surprised

Iranians accepted Saddam's offer to return Iranian territory still occupied by Iraqi forces, recognize Iranian control of the eastern half of the Shatt al-Arab waterway, and begin a prisoner exchange. Saddam's initiative freed hundreds of thousands of Iraqi troops along the Iranian border for redeployment to Kuwait, by in effect canceling the whole *raison d'être* for the Iran-Iraq War, and in so doing, underscored the lengths to which Iraq was prepared to go to preserve the fruits of its aggression against Kuwait. Iraq's enormous sacrifices in its war with Iran were in effect declared null and void in order to strengthen Baghdad's ability to hold on to Kuwait. The capitulation to Iran also hardened Saddam's resistance to any voluntary evacuation of Kuwait. As noted by Roland Dannreuther, the "concessions to Iran could only be ultimately justified if Saddam was to gain substantial rewards from his adventure in Kuwait. . . . the agreement with Iran made it far more difficult . . . to consider withdrawing without . . . probably fatal loss of face."[54]

The arrival and buildup of U.S. forces in Saudi Arabia made a voluntary evacuation of Kuwait even more difficult, since any withdrawal would appear to be flinching under pressure; on August 8, the day U.S. troop deployments were formally announced, Baghdad announced the formal annexation of Kuwait. Saddam Hussein was not, and could not be seen to be, frightened by the prospect of a Western military response to his conquest of a country that he and most Iraqis had always regarded as rightfully part of Iraq, but for the turn-of-the-century machinations of the British Colonial Office. Saddam could no more leave Kuwait without some kind of fight, if not the "mother of all battles," than could the Argentine junta in 1982, having grabbed the Falkland Islands in part to divert popular attention away from their failed policies at home, have countenanced a peaceful withdrawal from the islands before the arrival of British expeditionary forces. To have cut and run would have jeopardized Saddam's political future and even personal survival. Saddam's attempt to expand the political agenda of the crisis, from simply a determination of Kuwait's fate to a redistribution of wealth away from the rich Gulf states toward the larger and poorer Arab world, and most notably, his suggestion that Iraq would evacuate Kuwait if Israel abandoned occupied Palestinian lands and Syria withdrew from Lebanon, must be seen in this light. To leave Kuwait under U.S. pressure for any less a reward would be construed as a defeat. As Saddam told PLO leader Yasser Arafat on August 26, 1990, "If I tell the Iraqis I'll withdraw from Kuwait because I solved something like the Palestinian problem, they'll understand. But if I pull out only for the islands [Bubiyan and Warbah] and the [Rumaila] oil fields, the people will never accept it. It will be bigger than losing the war."[55]

There is, too, the matter of Saddam's interpretation of U.S. intentions. Until at least November 8, when President Bush announced a doubling of U.S. troop deployments to Saudi Arabia "to insure that the coalition has an adequate offensive military option should that be necessary to achieve our common goals,"[56] Saddam had little reason to believe that U.S. intentions included the forcible ejection of Iraqi forces from Kuwait. Consider the following: Until late November at the very earliest, U.S. ground forces in Saudi Arabia, composed mainly of early-arriving, strategically mobile light formations like Marine ExpeditionaryBrigades and the Army's 82nd Airborne and 101 Air Assault divisions, lacked the firepower and tactical mobility to take on Saddam's heavier and far more numerous forces in what later became known as the Kuwaiti Theater of Operations[57]—or at least take them on with any confidence in a relatively swift and easy victory. Indeed, it was this deficiency that President Bush's announcement of November 8 sought to remedy—by calling up from U.S. deployments in Germany and the United States an entire heavy U.S. Army corps.

Moreover, until November U.S. deployments to Saudi Arabia were publicly advertised by administration spokesmen as solely defensive in nature, aimed at protecting Saudi Arabia from possible Iraqi aggression. On the day of the invasion, President Bush, when queried by reporters, declared that "we're not discussing intervention. . . . I'm not contemplating any such action."[58] At his press conference on August 8, after Saudi Arabia had requested the dispatch of U.S. troops, Bush said nothing about Kuwait's liberation, focusing instead on the defense of Saudi Arabia, "which is of vital interest to the United States." Iraq, he said, "may not stop using force to advance its ambitions. Iraq has amassed an enormous war machine on the Saudi border capable of initiating hostilities with little or no additional preparations," and "to assume that Iraq will not attack . . . would be unwise and unrealistic."[59] The President then stated categorically that the "mission of our troops is wholly defensive. Hopefully, they'll not be needed long. They will not initiate hostilities but they will defend themselves, the Kingdom of Saudi Arabia and other friends in the Persian Gulf."[60] He added, in response to a direct question, that "to drive the Iraqis out of Kuwait . . . is not the mission."[61] Three weeks later, on August 29, Secretary of Defense Cheney told ABC Television News correspondent Sam Donaldson that "our [military] dispositions in the [Persian Gulf] region are defensive. We're there to deter and to defend. . . . we're not there in an offensive capacity, we're not threatening Iraq."[62] To be sure, President Bush had earlier declared that Iraq's aggression against Kuwait would not stand, but until November the nature of the U.S. military response remained palpably defensive, and the administration's emphasis on sanctions to force Saddam Hussein out of Kuwait was offered as an alternative to war, not its precursor.

Even after it became clear that the United States and its Coalition partners were assembling air and ground forces in the Arabian desert far in excess of that needed for the defense of Saudi Arabia—even after November 29, when the U.N. Security Council passed Resolution 678 authorizing Coalition forces to use all necessary means to expel Iraq from Kuwait if Iraq did not withdraw by January 15, 1991—Saddam apparently could not bring himself to believe that the United States would actually go to war to do so. As we shall examine in greater detail in a later chapter, Saddam regarded the United States as an effete society still traumatized by its experience in Vietnam, and therefore incapable of sustaining the kind of casualties he believed his forces in the KTO could inflict. During his July 25 interview with April Glaspie, the dictator, reminiscing on the sacrifices his troops had made to defeat Iran, lectured the U.S. ambassador on the subject:

> I assure you, had the Iranians overrun the region, the American troops could not have stopped them, except by the use of nuclear weapons. I do not belittle you. But I hold this view by looking at the geography and nature of American society into account. Yours is a society which cannot accept 10,000 dead in one battle.[63]

In his own mind, Saddam could point not only to the effects of the Vietnam experience, from which he apparently concluded the Americans had learned nothing, but also to the botched Iranian hostage rescue mission of 1980, and to the disastrous U.S. intervention in Lebanon in 1982–84, in which the action of a lone terrorist armed with a truckload of explosives, in killing 241 American marines, had prompted a humiliating U.S. withdrawal. A country prepared to cut and run after losing several hundred marines hardly had the stomach for a "real" war. Saddam also may have taken note of the American domestic political controversies occasioned even by the quick and cheap U.S. military interventions in Grenada and Panama.

Moreover, the Iraqi dictator, who displayed no real knowledge of the world outside Iraq, and who was, one can surmise, ignorant of the vast improvements in U.S. military effectiveness since Vietnam and of the entirely different kind of war he faced in switching enemies from Iran to the United States, believed that he could inflict a politically unacceptable level of casualties upon American forces. This conviction undoubtedly was reinforced by postulations of casualties, some of them bordering on hysteria, that were being bandied about in the American public and congressional debate over the Gulf crisis. On August 21, 1991, Iraqi Foreign Minister Aziz warned that "if the American leader thinks that this is a vacation like they had in Panama or Grenada, they are mistaken. . . . It will be a bloody conflict, and America will lose and . . . be humiliated."[64] And, in fact, Saddam's strategy for Kuwait's defense rested almost entirely on an assumption that he could dish out to the Americans on the battlefield at least some of the pain and suffering that his forces had inflicted on the Iranians.

Saddam also recognized the Coalition for what it was: a fragile marriage of convenience among disparate states, many of whom had had their allegiance to the Coalition purchased with Saudi and Kuwaiti money, other financial incentives, such as U.S. forgiveness of over $7 billion in Egyptian debts, and political rewards, such as tacit U.S. approval for Hafez al-Assad's establishment of a Pax Syriana in Lebanon. Characterized by one Arab observer as a "cash-register coalition" and a "posse of desperados and bounty hunters,"[65] it was in fact a coalition that in the event came very close to being shattered by the prospect of Israeli entry into the war following Saddam's technically inaccurate but politically well-aimed Scud missile attacks on Israeli cities. The enormous energy and resources that President Bush devoted to building and maintaining the Coalition testify to what both Washington and Baghdad correctly perceived as the Achilles' heel of the anti-Iraq international array.

Finally, Saddam, like so many totalitarian enemies of America before him, misread vigorous prehostilities domestic political debate in the United States as a wartime asset, failing to understand the high probability of strong public and congressional support for the administration that President Bush would, and did, receive once the shooting started. President Bush himself warned Saddam against making just such a mistake, though to no avail. In a letter to the dictator that Tariq Aziz refused to accept from Secretary of State Baker at their Geneva meeting on January 9, 1991, Bush cautioned: "You may be tempted to find solace in the diversity of opinion that is American democracy. You should resist any such temptation. Diversity ought not be confused with division. Nor should you underestimate, as others have before you, America's will."[66]

In sum, though Saddam could have ordered his forces out of Kuwait before the expiration of the U.N. deadline on January 15, 1991, he chose for quite understandable reasons to stay put. As compelling as the arguments were for getting out, the reasons for staying were even more so. Leaving without a fight was more politically dangerous to Saddam than fighting and losing. An honorable military defeat was preferable to a humiliating political capitulation without firing a shot, and the fact that Saddam and his regime not only survived Desert Storm but also consolidated their grip on Iraq, just as Gamel Abdel Nasser had managed in the Suez crisis of 1956 to convert military defeat into political victory, testifies to the correctness of Saddam's choice. For Saddam, the fate of his military forces in Kuwait was a consideration always secondary to his own political survival, and when confronted by the choice of losing his forces there or placing himself in jeopardy, his decision was never in doubt. A fight for Kuwait would advance the image of an Iraq unwilling to cower before American imperialism and would spare Saddam the humiliation of conceding defeat.

It is worthwhile to recall that the United States also could have withdrawn its forces from Vietnam any time before the Tet Offensive, which fatally undermined public support for the war. Like Saddam in Kuwait, however, the United States by 1968 had invested enormous prestige in Vietnam, and believed that it could ultimately prevail, or if not, that it had to endure whatever was in store in order to uphold its honor and reputation for at least a willingness to fight for perceived vital interests. Saddam's refusal to quit Kuwait except under fire is in hindsight no more or less objectively nonsensical than America's refusal to abandon Indochina even after all hope for a militarily decisive solution was lost.

The question remains whether the United States, given Saddam's intractability, could somehow have "managed" the Iraqis out of Kuwait by means short of war. The answer is probably "yes," had the primary U.S. objective in the crisis remained confined to Kuwait's liberation. An Iraqi withdrawal orchestrated in a manner that avoided the appearance of a retreat under American guns—for example, a removal of Iraqi forces from Kuwait in exchange for a withdrawal of U.S. forces from Saudi Arabia, and coupled with U.N.-sponsored negotiations to resolve Iraqi-Kuwaiti oil and territorial disputes—might well have been acceptable to Saddam, especially if accompanied by U.S.-sponsored Arab-Israeli talks. However, by the time Desert Storm was launched, U.S. objectives in the crisis had expanded from, initially, a defense of Saudi Arabia, to Kuwait's liberation by force, and finally to Iraq's effective disarmament and, by repeated presidential suggestion, Saddam's removal from power. These latter objectives, under the circumstances, could be achieved *only* by war. Pre–Desert Storm French, Soviet, and Arab initiatives to broker a peaceful settlement of the crisis ran afoul of Saddam's insistence on attaching a host of conditions to any Iraqi withdrawal from Kuwait. But they also ran aground on U.S. insistence on Iraq's unconditional withdrawal as a precondition for discussion of any other crisis-related issues. The administration's rigidity on this matter was consistent with the admirable principle of refusing to reward aggression in any way, but by making hostilities virtually inevitable it afforded an opportunity to do more than just liberate Kuwait. The emirate's liberation was, after all, one of four initially declared U.S. objectives in the crisis—the others being the emir's restoration to power, protection of American lives in the region, and the catchall goal of "establishing security and stability of the Persian Gulf."

Moreover, the course of events from early November 1990 to January 15, 1991, to say nothing of the scope and character of the strategic bombardment campaign subsequently launched against targets in Iraq outside the KTO, strongly suggests that well before the expiration of the U.N. deadline on January 15 the Bush administration had decided on war. War, with or without Kuwait's liberation, was the only means available to destroy Iraq's offensive military capabilities, especially its disturbing weapons of mass destruction, and to provoke Saddam's internal removal from power—i.e., to ensure the security and stability of the Persian Gulf. Early loss of White House confidence in the efficacy of sanctions; the doubling of U.S. troop deployments to gain an offensive option; mounting official expressions of concern over Iraq's nuclear, biological, and chemical weapons programs; administration reliance on the United Nations rather than the less malleable Congress to legitimize U.S. actions; and the President's own appeals to the Iraqi people to rid themselves of Saddam—all suggest the rather early formulation of an agenda in which Kuwait's liberation was in a sense incidental, and which could be fulfilled only by hostilities.

Elizabeth Drew, in numerous pre–Desert Storm off-the-record discussions with key administration officials, has concluded that it "was clear from very early on that some officials saw sanctions and diplomacy as the necessary political precursors of war in that each would be, as one official put it, 'a box to check.' "[67] She also noted correctly that Bush's eleventh-hour willingness to seek formal congressional approval of his march toward war, which he had earlier dismissed as unnecessary, entailed none of the political risks it might have in October or November, because "the President had got himself, and the country's prestige, so committed to the deadline set by the United Nations (at our behest) that by the time the [congressional] debate began, on Thursday, January 10, there was no question as to the outcome of the vote."[68] Indeed, the U.S.-sponsored U.N. Resolution setting a deadline for Saddam's departure from Kuwait was designed in part to compel congressional support after the fact. As Secretary of State Baker conceded after the war, the resolution authorizing the use of force against Iraq "would put us, frankly, in the position of being able to say, to congressmen who would not vote for this: 'You mean you're not willing to support the President, but the prime minister of Ethiopia will support the President?' "[69] The Bush administration moreover formally acknowledged that Iraq's disarmament beyond the elimination of Iraqi forces in Kuwait was a major war aim. In his speech to the nation announcing the launching of Desert Storm, the President declared: "We are determined to knock out Saddam Hussein's nuclear bomb potential. We will also destroy his chemical weapons facilities."[70]

None of this is to condemn the administration. War against Saddam Hussein's Iraq after January 15, 1991, was morally justified, and failure to take advantage of a war waged ostensibly on Kuwait's behalf to erase as much as possible of Saddam's wherewithal to commit future aggression would have been irresponsible. As we shall see later, postwar information gathered by U.N. and other teams inspecting suspect sites and activities in Iraq conclusively revealed that the scope and intensity of Iraq's nuclear, biological, and chemical weapons programs vastly exceeded prewar coalition estimates, and more ominously, that Iraq was but two to eighteen months away from building a usable atomic bomb—not the five to fifteen years that figured in so many prewar estimates.[71]

The point is that probably by mid-November 1990, and certainly by January 1991, war was inevitable, given Saddam's understandable intractability and *the presence of U.S. objectives that could not be satisfied by means short of war.* Indeed, in the fall of 1990 it was an open secret in Washington that the Bush administration's worst nightmare was a voluntary Iraqi withdrawal from most or all of Kuwait, which would have effectively eliminated war as an administration option. In late December 1990, House Armed Services Committee Chairman Les Aspin, among the most thoughtful and prescient observers of the Gulf crisis, addressed this issue in a speech:

> If Saddam Hussein [orders a partial withdrawal from Kuwait], we are left with the question of what the United States and the Allies would do next. This is clearly not an outcome that can be accepted. But in terms of

American public opinion, it will be difficult to see how the American people would believe that war was still necessary. This has not been called the "nightmare scenario" for nothing.[72]

A week later, Aspin warned:

The "nightmare scenario" in which Iraq partially withdraws from Kuwait . . . remains a strong possibility. This is clearly not a solution the United States could accept. It would, however, end the risk of war—neither the United States nor its Arab partners would be likely to attack if Iraq held on to the Bubiyan and Warbah islands and the sliver of Kuwait that contained the Rumaila oil field.[73]

The dilemma for the administration was that military action restricted solely to ejecting Iraqi forces from Kuwait would leave much of Iraq's army and virtually all of its nuclear, biological, and chemical weapons capabilities intact. Consequently, a peaceful Iraqi withdrawal from Kuwait became an outcome almost as dangerous as war. Liberating Kuwait by force would allow the United States to attack targets in Iraq whose destruction might prevent Baghdad from ever again threatening the Gulf's security and stability—and might even bring down Saddam himself. President Bush admitted as much to Hugh Sidey in an interview on the eve of Desert Storm's first anniversary. Referring to the prospect of a pre-Desert Storm Iraqi withdrawal from Kuwait, the President said, "I mean this was worrying me. What happens if [Saddam] does just haul all this armor back along the border, unpunished, unrepentant . . . ?"[74]

The November-announced decision to double U.S. deployments also contributed significantly to reducing prospects for war's avoidance, since it placed in Saudi Arabia a U.S. force too large to permit routine rotation of units to and from the United States. By calling forward so many additional units from the United States and Europe, which raised the U.S. troop level in Saudi Arabia from approximately 200,000 to ultimately 540,000,[75] the administration stripped U.S. deployments elsewhere of sufficient forces to form a rotation base. The pre-November deployment in Saudi Arabia could have been maintained indefinitely via unit rotation. In contrast, the larger deployment was in effect a "use it or lose it" force; the only alternative to using it would have been to have cut it back down to its pre-November level, which could have been interpreted as backing down to Saddam, and which in any event would have deprived the force of a capacity to retake Kuwait as quickly and as easily as the larger force subsequently did.

To sum up, it is difficult to see how Iraq's invasion of Kuwait and the international military response of Desert Storm could have been avoided, given Saddam's economic desperation, imperial ambitions, pride, internal political imperatives, and strategic incompetence; Kuwait's wealth, helplessness, and stupidity; and American and Saudi misjudgments of Saddam and fright over the possible consequences for Saudi Arabia of unchecked

Iraqi military power. Avoidance of war would have required not just a different decision here and another there, but rather fundamental alterations in the character of the key decision-makers—for example, a democratic and friendly Iraq, an alert and defensible Kuwait, an isolationist United States, or a Saudi Arabia either oilless or unwilling to countenance the presence of Western military forces on its territory.

3

Sanctions, Force, and
War Aims

ONE OF THE MOST vexing issues embedded in the pre–Desert Storm
debate on the efficacy of sanctions against Iraq—and one seemingly not
fully grasped by ardent sanctions supporters—was not their economic but
their political impact. The difficulty lay not in inflicting economic pain and
hardship on Iraq—that was easy; rather, it resided in translating that pain
and hardship into a *political* decision in Baghdad to quit Kuwait and
comply with the United Nations' other resolutions, and to do so *within a
politically and militarily acceptable amount of time.*

BAGHDAD'S ECONOMIC VULNERABILITIES

If ever there was a national economy subject to swift and severe damage
via a termination of its commercial intercourse with the outside world, it
was Iraq's in 1990. Politics and geography combined to make the shut-down
of that intercourse a relatively quick and easy enterprise, affording sanctions a degree of severity unprecedented in the modern history of attempted
embargoes for political purposes. In 1990 Iraq's economy, though weakened by debt, war damage, and low world oil prices, was in many respects a
modern, highly specialized, urban-industrial economy heavily dependent
on foreign trade. Unlike peasant economies characteristic of many Third
World countries, Iraq's was relatively mechanized, urbanized, and diversi-
fied, and contained a human and physical infrastructure that was in many
respects more modern, sophisticated, and socially progressive than those of
the rich Gulf states to the south or the oil-poor Arab states to the west and
southwest. City dwellers constituted over 70 percent of Iraq's total population,[76] and the country boasted the largest and best-educated middle-class
anywhere in the Arab Middle East—in part because the regime's strong
commitment to secularity encouraged the mass entry of women into the
professions;[77] even before the Iran-Iraq War, for example, women accounted for 46 percent of pharmacists.[78] Moreover, Iraq's Baathist regime,
whatever may be said of its political brutality, had vastly improved popular
living standards via mechanization and irrigation of agriculture, electrifica-
tion of almost every village in the country, development of modern

transportation networks, and provision of free education and health care to everyone.[79]

The richness and diversity of the country's military-industrial and civilian economic infrastructure was evident in the size of the U.S. Air Force's strategic target list for the air campaign against Iraq. Compared to the list of ninety-four strategic targets in Vietnam deemed worthy of attack by U.S. air war planners in the Vietnam War, Desert Storm planners began the air campaign with about four hundred, a number that by the campaign's end had mushroomed to over seven hundred.[80] These targets were stationary—government ministries, air bases, bridges, oil refineries, electrical power generation plants, military command centers, telephone exchanges, etc.; they did not include Iraqi field forces in Kuwait or mobile Iraqi Scud ballistic missile launchers.

The vulnerability of Iraq's economy to outside interference was underscored by its dependence on oil for 95 percent of its export earnings, and its dependence on imports for about 70 percent of its total consumption of food, including such staples as rice and wheat.[81] Additionally, 90 percent of Iraq's oil exports were carried through pipelines across Saudi Arabia (to the Red Sea port of Yanbu) and Turkey (to the Mediterranean port of Yurmutalik),[82] both of which were shut down as part of Saudi Arabia's and Turkey's participation in the mandatory U.N. economic embargo of Iraq proclaimed on August 6, 1990, in Resolution 661.

The *economic* consequences of the U.N. embargo were never in doubt, given Turkey, Syria, Saudi Arabia, and Iran all but completely sealing off land avenues of commerce, and the U.S. Navy shutting down seaborne trade. Within a few months, the civilian sector of Iraq's economy was grinding to a standstill, and military industries and operating forces, especially those dependent on advanced technologies and spare parts, were beginning to suffer. At the beginning of the crisis even the Bush administration voiced confidence in sanctions. On August 8, 1990, the President, in response to a question, declared:

> Economic sanctions in this instance, if fully enforced, can be very, very effective. [Iraq] is a rich country in terms of oil resources. They're a poor country, in a sense, because [Saddam Hussein] has squandered much of the resources on military might, and there are some indications that he's already beginning to feel the pinch. And nobody can stand up forever to total economic deprivation.[83]

In a late-October interview with the *Atlanta Journal* and *Constitution,* Coalition commander General Schwarzkopf, apparently bristling at reported pressure to speed up his own timetable for possible military action, countered by saying that "we are now starting to see evidence that sanctions are pinching. So why should we say, 'Okay, gave 'em two months, didn't work. Let's get on with it and kill a whole bunch of people?' That's crazy. That's crazy."[84]

In late November, former Secretary of Defense James R. Schlesinger told the Senate Armed Services Committee:

> The embargo, backed up by a naval blockade, is the most successful ever achieved aside from time of war. Early on it was officially estimated that it would require a year for the embargo to work. It now appears to be working more rapidly than anticipated . . . In time, the original objectives of the United Nations will be achieved.[85]

Schlesinger, also a former CIA director, added that the "world is now able to do without Iraqi and Kuwaiti oil. Thus, to sustain the embargo, no further price must be paid. In effect, we can leave Iraq in isolation until it comes to its senses."[86]

Former Chairman of the Joint Chiefs of Staff Admiral William J. Crowe, Jr., also voiced confidence in sanctions:

> The embargo is biting heavily. Given the standard of living Iraq is used to and the increasing sophistication of Iraqi society, it is dead wrong to say that Baghdad is not being hurt. That goes for the Iraqi military as well, which depends on outside support. . . . Iraq's civilian production has declined to 40 percent, export earnings have sharply dropped, and economic flexibility is rapidly decreasing. Military industry will likewise be hit. It is the most effective peacetime blockade ever levied.[87]
>
> Granted that the embargo is not working as rapidly as many would prefer; but if we wanted results in two or three months, clearly a quarantine was the wrong way to go about it. Most experts believe that it will work with time. Estimates range in the neighborhood of twelve to eighteen months. In other words, the issue is not whether an embargo will work, but whether we have the patience for it to take effect.[88]

Crowe concluded that "we should give sanctions a fair chance before we discard them. I personally believe they will bring [Saddam Hussein] to his knees."[89]

Testifying at the same set of hearings, William E. Odom, former director of the National Security Agency, claimed that the "industrial and military embargo combined with denying the sale of Iraqi oil is bound to cause severe damage to the military and economic infrastructure of the country. If it is continued for a year or two, the damage will be large." Odom added that whether the embargo "will cause Iraq to withdraw from Kuwait may be doubted, but we cannot know until it has been maintained for at least a year or so."[90]

The issue was again addressed in early December by CIA director William Webster. Appearing before the House Armed Services Committee, Webster asserted that sanctions had "all but shut off Iraq's exports and reduced imports to less than 10 percent of their preinvasion levels," thereby "eliminating any hope Baghdad had of cashing in on higher oil prices or its seizure of Kuwaiti oil fields." Webster went on to detail the impact of sanctions on Iraqi industry but noted that "they are affecting Iraq's military only at the margins," which could "probably maintain near current levels of readiness for as long as nine months" absent combat.[91]

SADDAM'S STAMINA AND TIME'S PERVERSITY

The problem with confident claims on behalf of sanctions was their failure to take into full account the political stamina of a police state, especially one as brutal and ruthlessly efficient as Saddam Hussein's Iraq, in insulating its survival and preferred policies from the economic effects of externally imposed deprivation. Proponents of sanctions also did not seem to understand that the Coalition did not have, from either a political or military standpoint, unlimited time to see how the sanctions might play out. Their human consequences fell first and foremost, of course, on an already brutalized Kuwait, the very country the Coalition sought to liberate. They fell next on those segments of Iraq's population—its politically atomized civilians, including women, children, the elderly, and the sick—least able to offer any real challenge to Saddam's authority and policies. As long as Saddam's three sources of power—Baathist officialdom, the Republican Guards, and the goon herds of the dreaded Mukhabarat (secret police)— remained well-fed, well-paid, and well-supplied with their customary perquisites and privileges (and every effort was made to assure their comfort), there remained little in the way of institutional threats to Saddam's continued control of Iraq.

The solidarity of this brotherhood of thugs was moreover reinforced by the fact that all three institutions were dominated by Sunnis, a minority in their own country that had every reason to stick together, as they did in the aftermath of the Gulf War, against potential challenges from Iraq's discontented Kurdish and Shia populations, and especially by the even smaller band of Tikritis, Saddam's fellow clansmen and villagers from his place of birth. The fact that Saddam and his regime survived not only six months of sanctions *but also* a forty-three-day drubbing by Coalition air and ground forces that wrecked his army in Kuwait and his economic infrastructure back home, *and then* a postwar continuation of the same prewar economic embargo, is testimony to the difficulty of trying to bring down a police state or alter its objectionable policies via economic pressure. Saddam Hussein's durability should have come as no surprise. Saddam, after all, had survived over two decades' worth of the most murderous national political "system" in the Arab world, rising to the top, as did Stalin in the Soviet Union, literally on the corpses of his political challengers and often their families. Saddam was no tin-pot dictator, but rather a well-entrenched totalitarian who brooked no internal or external challenges to his authority. Not even eight years of exposure to the full political and military wrath of the Ayatollah Khomeini had brought him down. Indeed, those who favored sanctions over war might have paid more attention to the enormous suffering and hardship Iraq had endured in its long war against Iran. In November 1990 former Assistant Secretary of Defense Richard Perle had warned the Senate Armed Services Committee that "the sanctions cannot possibly equal the pain and suffering of the eight years of war with Iran: 300,000 dead, 700,000 maimed, the economy wrecked. The privations of the embargo pale by comparison.[92]

Of course, no one can say for sure whether sanctions, given enough time, even several years, might have convinced Saddam to abandon Kuwait. The historical record is not encouraging. On the two previous occasions where the United Nations had imposed mandatory sanctions against a country, on Rhodesia in 1967 and on South Africa in 1977, it took thirteen and fourteen years respectively before the U.N. Security Council concluded that the sanctions had achieved their desired political effects. Even the combination of embargo and war has often required years before achieving success. Medieval sieges of towns and cities, far less economically viable entities than large, modern countries, often lasted years, and in some cases were abandoned. In the American Civil War, the Confederacy, though effectively embargoed by the Union Navy by the summer of 1863, continued to fight tenaciously until the spring of 1865.

More important was the seeming blindness of sanctions advocates to the limited time available to the Coalition for experimentation. The imposition of sanctions against Iraq in August 1990 took place in a specific political, diplomatic, and military environment that encouraged a resolution of the Gulf crisis sooner rather than later. There was, first, a limit on Saudi Arabia's tolerance of an indefinite continuation of the huge Western force presence on its territory, a presence that had been vehemently opposed by the Kingdom's own Crown Prince himself,[93] and that was exciting the suspicions and mounting hostility of the country's clerical authorities and *matawan* religious police—two key pillars of the House of Saud's political legitimacy as the protector of Islam's holiest shrines. Saudi nervousness over the political and social implications for their own conservative society was undoubtedly heightened by Saddam Hussein's attempt to exploit the issue during the crisis. This most secular of Arab dictators suddenly began speaking as a defender of traditional Islamic religious and social values now threatened by "infidel invaders . . . drunken, pork-eating whoremongers infected with AIDS."[94] Former Secretary of State Henry A. Kissinger feared that a prolonged Western troop presence would undermine the House of Saud:

> The issue in Arabia is not American staying power but the host country's domestic stability. Conditions in the Gulf are not even remotely comparable to Europe and Northeast Asia. There, American forces contributed to domestic stability; in Saudi Arabia they would threaten it. A substantial American ground establishment would soon become the target of radical and nationalist agitation.[95]

Certainly a delay in a resolution of the crisis that risked a major war during the annual *hajj* (pilgrimage) to Mecca in the spring of 1991 would be most unwelcome.

A second political consideration was deteriorating conditions inside Kuwait. The longer the Coalition waited to eject Iraqi forces from the emirate, the longer would be the nightmare for Kuwaitis of Iraq's occupation. As detailed in a mid-November report by the Middle East Watch, a human rights organization, Kuwait was being systematically looted, its citizens brutalized, its government's vital records destroyed or carted away to Baghdad, and its food supplies and medical services compromised.[96] Moreover, as noted, the embargo paradoxically fell first and most harshly on Kuwait. Kuwaitis were hardly at the top of Baghdad's list for priority distribution of ever-scarcer commodities.

A major factor arguing strongly against delay was the fragility of the Coalition itself. Such an unlikely grouping of politically and culturally diverse allies—the United States, Soviet Union, Great Britain, France, Syria, Iran, Saudi Arabia, Egypt, Turkey, and Israel (a silent partner insofar as it shared the common objective of preventing Iraqi military hegemony in the Persian Gulf)—was inherently vulnerable to disintegration. The fact that so many of its members' allegiance and enthusiasm had to be crudely purchased by cash, credit, debt forgiveness, and political rewards and promises testified to the Coalition's artificiality. Saddam Hussein clearly believed the Coalition's political cohesion was shatterable, and he had some limited success in his often clumsy attempts to break it up. He managed to marshal the forces of Islamic fundamentalism against the Coalition's policies in such countries as Morocco, Algeria, Tunisia, Jordan, Sudan, and Israel's occupied territories; and, had it not been for the Bush administration's strong condemnation of Israel's police excesses (notably the killing and wounding of 170 Palestinian demonstrators in Jerusalem on October 8, 1990),[97] and subsequent extreme pressure on Israel not to retaliate in response to Iraqi Scud attacks, the Coalition might well have fallen apart before the Gulf crisis ended.

Also undermining Coalition solidarity was the uncertainty of continued Soviet political cooperation, which was vital to American diplomatic and military flexibility in the Persian Gulf throughout the crisis. The Gulf crisis had caught the Soviet Union in the early stages of its later disintegration, and the possibility of a reactionary coup in Moscow—of the kind actually attempted just six months after the Gulf War ended—remained ever present. There was, too, the potential for serious domestic unrest in such key Coalition members as Turkey and Egypt, whose participation in the Coalition imposed heavy and mounting economic burdens due to loss of trade, oil pipeline revenues, and remittances from their nationals overseas.

The situation was hardly one that promoted a relaxed approach to the Gulf Crisis' resolution.

There was also the simple matter of weather. To have delayed military action beyond the spring of 1991 would have forced the Coalition to fight in the Gulf's searing summer heat and humidity, or to have waited until the winter of 1991–92—which would have kept U.S. troops in Saudi Arabia separated from their families and jobs back home for far too long to be acceptable in terms of the maintenance of both their morale and the President's standing in the popularity polls.

For the Bush administration, domestic political considerations were also paramount in arguing for a speedy resolution of the drama begun by Saddam Hussein's invasion of Kuwait. This was especially the case after November 29, 1990, the day the U.N. Security Council passed the White House–backed Resolution 678, essentially an ultimatum to Saddam to get out of Kuwait by January 15, 1991, or face ejection by force. Always sensitive to the "wimp factor," and having personalized the contest with the Iraqi dictator to a degree regarded by many critics as imprudent and even reckless, as well as having committed American prestige to a clear, favorable, and early resolution of the Gulf crisis, the White House simply could not afford to be seen as hesitant or procrastinating. Certainly, to have waited more than a few days beyond the January 15 deadline to strike would have encouraged suspicions of faintheartedness or a conclusion that U.S. policy all along had been one gigantic bluff. It would also have dismayed Bush's less than overwhelming support in the Congress, especially among such key Democratic supporters as Les Aspin and Stephen Solarz, who had stuck their political necks out to back the administration's hard line against Saddam Hussein. (On the eve of Desert Storm the Senate voted by a narrow 52–47 margin to authorize "all means necessary" to expel Iraq from Kuwait.)

To be sure, the President made no mention of domestic political considerations when he announced the reasons for going to war on January 16:

> Some may ask, why act now? Why not wait? The answer is clear. The world could wait no longer. Sanctions, though having some effect, showed no signs of accomplishing their objective. Sanctions were tried for well over five months, and we and our allies concluded that sanctions alone would not force Saddam from Kuwait. While the world waited, Saddam Hussein systematically raped, pillaged, and plundered a tiny nation. . . . While the world waited, Saddam sought to add to the chemical weapons arsenal he now possesses [and to build] an infinitely more dangerous weapon of mass destruction, a nuclear weapon. . . . Saddam clearly felt that by stalling and threatening and defying the United Nations, he could weaken the forces arrayed against him. . . . He remained intransigent, certain that time was on his side.[98]

Nor did President Bush mention that, as noted in the preceding chapter, his own key decision in late October 1990, announced publicly on November 8, a few days after the 1990 congressional elections, to double U.S. troop deployments to Saudi Arabia, had created a strong element of military inflexibility in U.S. policy in the Gulf that made a resort to war, assuming Saddam Hussein's continued intractability, virtually inevitable by the spring of 1991 at the very latest. James H. Webb, Jr., a novelist, highly decorated Vietnam War combat veteran, and former Secretary of the Navy, was one of many seasoned observers to grasp the profound implications of Bush's decision:

> [By] sending such a huge commitment of American ground forces, and at the same time escalating the rhetoric of the confrontation, the President has placed himself—and our troops—in a doubly unfortunate situation. First, the so-called logic of war and the danger of our country losing its credibility makes it difficult to reduce or adjust these ground forces, since we might be perceived as "backing down" without having forced the Iraqi army out of Kuwait. Second, since a majority of the U.S. Army is now overseas, and since two-thirds of the operational forces of our Marine Corps will soon be sitting in the desert, we cannot maintain the size of our commitment for much longer without running into problems of human endurance. Nor could we develop a rotational base for deployed units without decreasing the size of the commitment. In other words, the size and structure of our military commitment, rather than external events, risk becoming the dominant factors in whether force should be used.[99]

Other factors that may have contributed to a sense of urgency were possible pressure from Israel to "get the job over with," uneasiness at leaving Europe militarily destitute of the U.S. Army's Seventh Corps for too long, and the prospect of eventual significant leakage of trade to Iraq through the embargo. By January 15, moreover, Coalition air forces were ready to go—to launch a planned thirty-day air campaign preliminary to a final ground offensive.

COMPETING AMERICAN OBJECTIVES

It is important to recognize that the debate over the efficacy of sanctions was as much an argument about the desirability of going to war with Iraq, an issue that in turn hinged on differing opinions on the matter of what U.S. objectives in the crisis ought to be. Generally speaking, those who affirmed a belief in sanctions and counseled patience in permitting the embargo time enough to take full effect also regarded war as undesirable and believed that U.S. aims in the crisis should be limited to a restoration of the status quo ante—i.e., removal of Iraqi forces from Kuwait. Proponents of this view, the so-called doves, included James Schlesinger, William Crowe, James Webb, William Odom, Edward N. Luttwak, conservative columnist Patrick J. Buchanan, Joint Chiefs of Staff Chairman Colin Powell,[100] and the powerful and influential Senate Armed Services Committee chairman Sam Nunn. All were in varying degrees taken aback by the Bush administration's decision to double U.S. troop deployments in Saudi Arabia for the declared purpose of creating an offensive military option, which they regarded as an abrupt and unwise escalation of U.S. objectives in the crisis that made war increasingly probable. The doves were also wont to dismiss Kuwait's strategic importance, condemn the emirate's political system and prewar diplomacy, and ridicule Saudi Arabia's lack of democracy and religious freedom. Many also harbored great skepticism over claims that a military victory over Iraq could be gained swiftly and at relatively little cost in American blood and treasure. Luttwak, for example, appeared not to believe Saudi Arabia worthy of defense, much less Kuwait of forcible liberation, and noted the irony of the United States, a bastion of religious toleration, coming to the defense of a country characterized by

> the arrogant denial of religious freedom, by the corporal punishment of beer drinkers on behalf of whiskey-drinking princes, and by the intrusions of Saudi Arabia's "religious police," whose members now reportedly break into houses of Westerners suspected of hosting parties in which drinks are served and women are allowed to chat with men not their fathers and husbands.[101]

Buchanan said that the impending military confrontation with Iraq had "quagmire written all over it," and claimed that to "dig armored Iraqi troops out of Kuwait could require twelve to eighteen divisions, i.e., the entire U.S. Army," and that "America could find herself in a Korea-style meatgrinder."[102] Odom warned that "we could be surprised by the scale and intensity" of a war with Iraq, and though he had "no doubt that we could win it," he urged preparation "for a large, costly, and bloody campaign."[103]

The doves also expressed considerable dismay over the Bush administration's alignment with such unsavory "allies" as Syria, and over the prospect that the United States, once again, was being asked to assume the primary military burden for an enterprise from which others benefited far more and contributed far less. Among congressional opponents of war there was, too, anger at the administration's casual dismissal of Congress's war-making prerogatives.

In contrast, those who pooh-poohed sanctions and wanted a speedier resolution of the crisis were generally far more willing to resort to force, and believed that U.S. aims should not be restricted to Kuwait's liberation. This hawkish group included the President and his chief national security advisor, Brent Scowcroft, along with Henry Kissinger, Richard Perle, Stephen Solarz, Les Aspin, editorialist Charles Krauthammer, columnist William Safire, and some members of Congress, such as Senators Alan Simpson and Phil Gramm, who were probably embarrassed by their own association with the administration's prewar appeasement of Iraq. Most hawks regarded Kuwait's liberation as incidental to a larger and more ambitious agenda. They believed that Iraq's invasion of Kuwait and the international community's sharp reaction to it afforded the United States a unique opportunity to eliminate Iraqi military hegemony in the Gulf, especially the long-term threat to regional stability posed by Iraq's growing ballistic missile arsenal and chemical, biological, and nascent nuclear weapons capabilities. The hawks' worst fear was perhaps that sanctions would actually succeed in compelling Iraq's withdrawal from Kuwait, which would leave Saddam's military power intact. In late November 1990, Kissinger defined the issue this wary:

> American objectives have included fulfillment of stated U.N. goals of restoration of the status quo ante in Kuwait as well as the unconditional release of all hostages. But to contribute to President Bush's objective of stability in the Gulf, any solution to the crisis must also provide for a reduction of Iraq's offensive capability which now overshadows its neighbors. Without addressing this fundamental imbalance, a solution will only postpone, and probably exacerbate, an eventual resolution of Gulf instability.
>
> Were Saddam suddenly to accept the U.N. terms, he would in fact preserve the essence of his power, although it would represent a huge loss of prestige for him. Iraq would still retain its chemical and nuclear capabilities. Its large standing army would still preserve the capacity to overwhelm the area. Many nations might adjust to the perception that the mobilization of forces from all over the world cannot be repeated every few years.[104]

Perle was even more emphatic. Having fielded sufficient forces to ensure Saudi Arabia's defense, the United States, he argued, "should now make the transition from buying time to using it for the broader purpose of mobilizing for the destruction of Saddam Hussein's military machine."[105] Perle further contended that with "each passing day the risk increases that the coalition to which the President has made himself hostage will lose its sense of purpose and confidence. Saddam Hussein has kept it together by a foolish intractability that could, at any moment, give way to blandishments that could stay our hand."[106] As for sanctions, he argued, "even if they succeed, [they] aim too low. Iraq's withdrawal from Kuwait is a beginning; it must not become the end of American policy in the Gulf."[107]

Ironically, many of those who loudly applauded the Bush administration's inexorable march toward a military confrontation with Saddam Hussein later roundly condemned the White House for what they regarded as a premature cease-fire, and for Bush's failure to support post–cease-fire Kurdish and Shia uprisings against Baghdad and to use force again to compel Saddam's compliance with cease-fire terms. As *New York Times* editor A. M. Rosenthal put it, the United States, "having defeated Iraq militarily, fled victory."[108]

Perhaps the event most unsettling to doves and encouraging to hawks, other than the launching of Desert Storm itself, was the President's November 8, 1990, announcement that U.S. troop levels in Saudi Arabia were being doubled to provide an adequate offensive military option. It was certainly this event that cast suspicions in the minds of many that the White House had all along been dissembling in its public pronouncements on ultimate American political aims in the Gulf crisis, and that prompted

Senator Sam Nunn to hold a series of hearings highly critical of the administration's policy. In his opening statement at the November 27–30 hearings, Nunn, who questioned whether U.S. military action to liberate Kuwait "is wise at this time and in our own national interest,"[109] declared that with the decision to increase troop strength, "our overall strategy and the military mission of the U.S. forces in the Persian Gulf region changed abruptly."[110] Nunn went on to assert:

> The President's announcement was a fundamental shift in the mission of our military forces. After just three months, the Administration has gone from the original military mission of deterring further Iraqi aggression, defending Saudi Arabia, and enforcing the embargo to a military mission of liberating Kuwait.[111]

Nunn claimed that the President's decision raised a series of profound questions, including the possibility of a " 'use it or lose it' situation with the deployment of such a large U.S. force to the Persian Gulf." More important, he said, was the issue of political aims:

> . . . what should our ultimate military objectives in the region be? Should our military objectives extend beyond the restoration of Kuwait's sovereignty to the elimination of key aspects of Iraq's offensive military capability, particularly their ongoing nuclear efforts? What is the best estimate we have of Iraq's capability to build and use nuclear weapons?

Indeed, was it in "our vital interest to liberate Kuwait through military action . . . that could cost thousands of American casualties?"[112]

James Schlesinger also was disturbed by the administration's escalation of political objectives implicit in the troop increase, which he believed would encourage greater intractability on Saddam's part:

> . . . if the United States conveys the impression that it has moved beyond the original international objectives to the sterner objectives that Saddam must go, that Iraq's military establishment and the threat to the region must be dismantled or eliminated, etc., then whatever incentive Saddam Hussein may presently have to acquiesce in the international community's present demands and to leave Kuwait will shrink to zero. This may please those who have decided that the war option is the preferable one, but it makes it increasingly hard to hold together the international coalition initially put together to bless our actions in the Gulf.[113]

David C. Jones, former Chairman of the Joint Chiefs of Staff, worried that the military inflexibility of the new troop deployments "might cause us to fight—perhaps prematurely and perhaps unnecessarily," and warned against inflating U.S. objectives in the crisis beyond Kuwait's liberation and the emir's restoration:

> If U.S. policy attempts to expand these minimum objectives or to interpret them more broadly (for example, to include reparations, tribunals, dismantling of chemical and nuclear production facilities, etc.), we run the very real risk of exceeding the tolerance of some members of the coalition. A corollary risk is that we solidify Saddam Hussein's intransigence and foreclose a nonmilitary solution.[114]

In retrospect, of course, many of the doves' fears regarding the possible consequences of inflating both U.S. military power in Saudi Arabia and U.S. political aims in the crisis proved unfounded. As we shall see in a later chapter, whether Desert Storm made any enduring contribution to peace and stability in the Persian Gulf region remains an open question. However, the Coalition did not crumble, and military action against Iraq proved surprisingly swift and even more surprisingly cheap in terms of American lives lost. Moreover, the Gulf crisis was hardly a unique instance of expanded political objectives. A strong tendency to inflate victory's definition is inherent in war and in prewar military confrontations, which are commonly characterized by the placement in harm's way of ever-increasing amounts of national honor, prestige, and military power. This is essentially, though not always, the case in situations where victory turns out to be significantly more costly than first anticipated, thus mandating victory's redemption via expanded political rewards (thus the draconian peace terms imposed on Germany by the near-prostrate "victors" of World War I), and in situations where unanticipated military opportunities of strategic consequence present themselves.

An excellent example of the latter was the Korean War. The initial United Nations objective, following North Korea's invasion of the South, was simply a restoration of South Korea's territorial integrity, which, given the war's dismal first few months, culminating in the bottling up of U.S. and allied forces in the Pusan perimeter, seemed almost beyond reach. However, with MacArthur's surprise amphibious landing at Inchon and subsequent apparent disintegration of Communist forces throughout Korea, the United Nations abruptly escalated its war aims to include the reunification of the entire peninsula under Western political auspices. Then, of course, came massive Chinese intervention against U.N. forces overstretched along the Yalu, and the longest retreat in American military history, ending in stabilization of the front roughly along the prewar boundary at the 38th parallel. As a reflection of this new military stalemate, which lasted until the war's end, the United Nations reduced its political objectives to its original aim of a return to the status quo ante.

Whatever the wisdom and practical case for expanding U.S. objectives in the Persian Gulf crisis beyond Saudi Arabia's defense and then beyond Kuwait's liberation—i.e., to Iraq's disarmament and hopefully Saddam

Hussein's departure from power, it is certainly understandable that at some point in the crisis, probably fairly early on, the administration saw the opportunity not just to free Kuwait, but also to eliminate or at least severely damage Iraq's capacity to commit future aggression. If there was to be war, then it was to be a war that struck at both the symptom—Iraqi forces in Kuwait—and the cause—Iraq itself—of aggression.

Where the Bush administration may be fairly faulted was in its failure to make it clear from the beginning of the crisis, and certainly after early November, to both the Congress and the American people that war was a probability unless Saddam retreated from Kuwait voluntarily, and that if war came, the United States would not restrict its military operations simply to Kuwait's liberation. More candor in this regard might well have unsettled some reluctant Coalition allies, and probably would have done little to persuade Saddam to give up Kuwait; but it also might have muted congressional suspicions of a White House "hidden agenda" and irritation over the administration's refusal to consult key members of Congress even in private.

Moreover, by expanding the definition of success the Bush administration provided powerful ammunition to those who after the war understandably saw in Saddam's continuance in power, and the survival of much of Iraq's chemical and nuclear weapons potential, something considerably less than an unqualified American victory. The administration was in fact embarrassed by Saddam's continued defiance of the cease-fire's provisions and by postwar revelations of how much of Iraq's Republican Guard forces, ballistic missile arsenal, and nuclear programs escaped an air campaign the administration touted as the most successful in history.[115] Had the administration confined its definition of success solely to Kuwait's liberation, it could have rightfully claimed a complete victory in the Gulf War.

In hindsight, sanctions alone, while economically painful to Iraq, were probably never an efficacious means of removing Iraq from Kuwait or Saddam Hussein from Iraq, even had they been applied indefinitely. It took a war to achieve the former, though war failed to obtain the latter. Proponents of sanctions may have been plagued by cultural bias; in focusing on the sanctions' obvious and easily understood economic consequences, they seem to have ignored the far less familiar political nature of Iraq's regime, and the capacity of the Iraqi people to tolerate hardship and deprivation of a magnitude the American people would never accept. Similarly, many of those who pressed for war, though their confidence in the U.S. military's ability to beat Iraq at a politically acceptable cost in American lives was vindicated, also underestimated Saddam's tenacity and political durability as well as his Baathist regime's resilience in maintaining control over the country. Among many hawks there was an unspoken assumption that Saddam and his henchmen could not survive combat with a United States whose war aims encompassed the elimination of the Iraq that Saddam for twenty years had sought to create: military master of the Gulf and a source of awe, fear, and respect in both the Arab world and the world at large. It is no coincidence that many doves and hawks alike were disappointed with the outcome of the Gulf crisis—the doves, because it ended in war, and the hawks because the war was not carried far enough. Moreover, both doves and hawks, although to varying degrees, gave Iraq's military machine far more credit than it deserved, a subject to which we now turn.

4

Gauging the Enemy

ONE OF THE MORE remarkable aspects of the Persian Gulf crisis of 1990–91 was a near universal pre–Desert Storm overestimation of Iraq's conventional military capabilities by American official and other expert opinion. Almost without exception, those who sought to gauge Iraq's ability to fight credited "the world's fourth largest army" (a common characterization of the Iraqi military establishment throughout the crisis) with far more power than it deserved. Estimates of the Iraqi military's size and weapons inventories were reasonably accurate, notable exceptions being its ballistic missile arsenal and the scope of its nuclear programs. However, faulty judgments were the rule with respect to the more elusive matter of "fighting power," defined by military historian Martin van Creveld as "the moral, intellectual, and organizational" dimensions of military power as manifested in such things as "discipline and cohesion, morale and initiative, courage and toughness, the willingness to fight and the readiness, if necessary, to die."[116]

One need look no further than to the stunning swiftness of Desert Storm and to the even more breathtaking brevity of Coalition casualty lists to conclude that the Iraqi military, though certainly competitive against the armies of its neighbors, had little if any fighting power against the kind of foe it faced on January 16, 1991. Coalition air and ground forces pounced upon neither a skillful nor a tenacious enemy, but rather a military Potemkin village compared to the best Western armed forces. Coalition forces exposed the Iraqi army for what it really was: a mediocre mass formed in the delusion that genuine military modernity could be had by simply purchasing its outward trappings.

PREWAR ASSESSMENTS

Quite a different picture of the Iraqi threat prevailed, however, in the United States before Desert Storm. For example, two widely cited reports issued by the Army War College's Strategic Studies Institute, one of them an assessment of Iraq's performance in its eight-year-long war with Iran, credited the Iraqi army with excellent defensive capabilities, a high level of tactical innovativeness, and considerable skill at combined operations.[117] The first study, *Lessons Learned: The Iran-Iraq War,* traced the growth and apparently ever-improving performance of the Iraqi army from 1980 to

1988. It declared that "Iraq is superb on defense. Its army is well-equipped and trained to carry out mobile defensive operations."[118] The study further concluded that:

> Iraq's military leaders will fight for the regime, as long as it respects their dignity. Correspondingly, if they perceive that a military challenge from the United States threatens Iraq's vital interests, they will not hesitate to fight with great tenacity. Understanding this lesson from the Iran-Iraq War, it seems sensible to carefully weigh our future course of action in respect to Iraq. If we fight Iraq, we should be prepared to defeat it as quickly as possible, since the Iraqi military has shown that it fights well on the defensive. If the Iraqis do not capitulate in the first days of the conflict, we can expect them to "hedgehog." They will wrap themselves around Kuwait and force us to pry them loose—a hideously expensive prospect, in lives as well as resources.[119]

The second study, *Iraqi Power and U.S. Security in the Middle East,* asserted that Iran's defeat in 1988 represented "an authentic victory" for Iraq because the "Iraqis planned and successfully executed complicated, large-scale military operations and shrewdly managed their resources."[120] The study cautioned that it "does not seem sensible . . . to antagonize what is now the strongest power in so vital an area of the world,"[121] and urged the development of "good working relations" with Iraq.[122]

Other pre–Desert Storm assessments, some of which were published during Desert Storm, also overestimated Iraq's fighting power, particularly in defensive operations. Iraq's air defenses, for example, were widely heralded as among the world's finest. Consider U.S. Air Force Chief of Staff Merrill A. McPeak's characterization of them *after* they had already been rapidly overwhelmed by Coalition air power:

> . . . an [Iraqi] setup that can be described, I think, as state of the art. Perhaps as many as 17,000 surface-to-air missiles, on the order of 9,000 to 10,000 antiaircraft artillery pieces, very modern radars all lashed together with high tech equipment. Lots of principal control nodes hardened, buried under concrete bunkers and so forth. This is a first-class air defense—not a featherweight opponent that we had to operate against in the opening hours of the war.[123]

Prewar estimates of U.S. casualties, most of them well in excess of the actual number of Americans killed (148) and wounded (467) in combat in the war for Kuwait,[124] also reflected an exaggerated view of Iraq's fighting power. General H. Norman Schwarzkopf reportedly supplied estimates of up to 20,000 casualties to congressional delegations visiting Saudi Arabia before Desert Storm, which undoubtedly fueled antiwar sentiment.[125] Steven Canby, a noted military reformer during the 1980s, asserted that "the ground war will be a disaster for us . . . which will produce very high U.S. casualties.[126] The Brookings Institution's Joshua Epstein estimated that a U.S. attack limited to Kuwait's liberation could result in up to 15,000

American casualties, including 2,000–3,000 killed.[127] The Center for Defense Information's David Isenberg believed that it would cost 10,000 dead and up to 40,000 wounded to topple Saddam Hussein via a drive on Baghdad,[128] and the Center for Strategic and International Studies' respected analyst, James Blackwell, who marveled at "the incredible military machine the Iraqis had perfected in defeating the Iranians,"[129] estimated that 30,000 Americans could be killed or wounded in a march on Baghdad.[130]

General Schwarzkopf himself also was guilty of overrating Iraq's powers of resistance. After the war he vehemently denied that the U.S. Central Command had misjudged the Iraqi military, claiming that the charge "that we . . . overestimated the Iraqi capability is blatantly false and very misleading,"[131] But in March 1991 he told *Newsweek* correspondent C. S. Manegold that shortly after Iraq's invasion of Kuwait, he had given President Bush "terrible advice" in estimating that a Coalition ground offensive would require "about five times more force than I ended up getting," and last "seven to eight months longer than it took to do the job."[132] At a Central Command briefing ten days into the Coalition air campaign, he confessed surprise that the Iraqi air force "hasn't chosen to fight and also how easy it was to completely take out his air defense system."[133] In February, General Schwarzkopf told another journalist that the "reality that has surprised us probably more than any other is that they are nowhere near as tough as we . . . gave them credit."[134] And at his Central Command briefing at the close of Desert Storm the general declared:

> if we thought it would be such an easy fight, we definitely would not have stocked sixty days' worth of supplies at these log[istics] bases. . . . When you're facing an enemy that is over 500,000 strong, has the reputation they've had of fighting for eight years, being combat-hardened veterans, has a number of tanks and the type of equipment they had, you don't assume away anything. So we certainly did not expect it to go this way.[135]

Why was so much expert opinion off the mark? Before attempting to answer this question, it is perhaps worth bearing in mind that since the emergence of imperial Japan as a military threat to the United States in the 1930s, American military encounters with non-Western opponents, including Iraq, have been habitually attended by significant prehostilities misestimation of the other side's fighting power. For example, the quality of Japan's military technology, especially its ships and aircraft, was grossly underestimated before Pearl Harbor. The same was true of the ingenuity and daring of Japanese operational planning and the tenacity of imperial field forces—despite ample evidence of Japanese military prowess provided by Japan's performance in the Russo-Japanese War of 1904–1905. In the early stages of the Korean War, U.S. military leaders, most notably General Douglas MacArthur, pooh-poohed the prospect of Beijing's intervention, largely because the People's Liberation Army, notwithstanding the toughness and audacity it displayed during China's civil war, was regarded as a technologically primitive force (it was) incapable of surviving any collision with superior American firepower (it did). Over a decade later, despite the Korean experience, and the defeat of French expeditionary forces in Indochina just a few years before, the Pentagon entered yet another war in Asia against what many believed was a "third-rate" army (which it was by American standards) composed largely of ill-equipped, pajama-clad peasant conscripts.

What was unusual about the Gulf War in this respect is that Iraq represented the first major Third World adversary of the United States whose fighting power was overvalued rather than underrated. A contributory factor may well have been a Cold War–induced innate military planning cautiousness and preoccupation with "worst case" scenarios—reinforced by memory of the unpleasant Korean and Vietnam surprises. Better to exaggerate the enemy's military capabilities, and therefore estimated military requirements for defeating him, than to risk embarrassment on the battlefield. An inflated threat also confers inflated military significance to victory, if and when it comes.

CULTURAL BIASES

But cultural factors were probably far more significant sources of pre–Desert Storm U.S. misjudgments of the Iraqi military threat than traditional military planning conservatism. Prewar assessments of the Iraqi military threat paid scant attention to cultural and other nonmilitary factors at play. These included Iraq's Arab character and the political megalomania of its regime. Moreover, while the Iran-Iraq War of 1980–88 was studied extensively for clues as to how Iraq could or would perform against the Coalition, the significance of the fact that Iran, like Iraq itself, was also a developing non-Western country escaped most analysis. Even more notable for its absence was any broader historical inquiry into the performance of Arab armies in general against *Western* military power.

Such an inquiry would have revealed that in the four major Arab-Israeli military encounters beginning with the Egyptian-Israeli conflict of 1956, Arab forces were without exception swiftly vanquished—just as Iraq's were in 1991. The Arabs' only great success against a Western military power occurred in the eight-year-long guerrilla war waged by the Algerian FLN against the French. Thus, for U.S. planning purposes, lessons drawn from the performance of Third World adversaries against American and other Western military establishments are more instructive than lessons drawn from their performance against each other. Thus, for planners of Desert Storm, the Arab-Israeli wars of 1956, 1967, 1973, and 1982 were more pertinent than the Iraq-Iran War, even though Iraq did not participate significantly in any war against Israel.[136] As Syrian President Hafez al-Assad remarked to Egyptian officials before Desert Storm, "[Saddam Hussein] is crazy. He thinks because he fought the Iranians he can threaten the Israelis and the Americans. He has never fought the Israelis. He doesn't know what real military power is."[137]

A number of explanations have been offered to account for consistent U.S. misjudgment of non-Western military prowess, the most prominent among them being faulty intelligence information. The problem with this explanation, however, is that intelligence-gathering on foreign militaries traditionally has focused on the visible attributes of military power—i.e., the number, type, and location of ground divisions, air wings, and naval units—and is ill-suited to fathom the "moral, intellectual, and organizational" dimensions of military power. War is ultimately a clash of nations and cultures, not just of armies alone, and the ability of a given nation and its culture to make war effectively lies beyond the purview of traditional intelligence-gathering agencies, even though the history of a given culture's war fighting can teach much. For whatever reason, Arab culture does not seem to promote military effectiveness in attempting to challenge Western military power on its own terms. In contrast, such East Asian cultures as the Chinese, Japanese, and Vietnamese have compiled a far more impressive record against the West—the Japanese against Russia and the United States, the Chinese against the United States in Korea, the Vietnamese against both France and the United States—perhaps because they sense the futility of trying to out-perform the West in its own style of warfare.

Indeed, American cultural factors, far more so than faulty intelligence, of which there was aplenty vis-à-vis Iraq, may have contributed to U.S. misjudgment of Third World adversaries. In the case of Japan in the 1940s, China in the 1950s, and Vietnam in the 1960s, a strong dose of racial, technological, and other cultural hubris influenced American perceptions. After all, the three countries were Asian, lacked America's industrial might, and, in the case of China and Vietnam, navies and air forces capable of challenging U.S. mastery of sea and sky. None could hope to match the quality of American arms, to say nothing of the volume of American firepower.

The price of this hubris was steep. The cost of defeating Japan was unexpectedly high in terms of casualties incurred and the conflict's duration. In Korea and Vietnam this hubris blinded us to both the possibility and the fact of effective Asian organizational and tactical responses to overwhelming U.S. material superiority. In the distinctive art of guerrilla warfare and elusive conventional military operations targeted at both domestic and foreign political audiences, China and North Vietnam had fashioned a strategy and set of tactics that trumped U.S. firepower by simply denying it critical military targets, while at the same time imposing a steady drain on American blood, treasure, and will. Such a strategy was hardly an Asian invention; George Washington pursued a similar strategy against the British in the War for Independence.

As noted, perhaps in part because of a desire to avoid getting "burned" again, professional U.S. assessments of Iraqi military strengths before the Gulf War erred heavily on the "worst-case scenario" side of caution.

Compared to the foot-mobile Communist peasant armies in Korea and Indochina, the Iraqi military that invaded Kuwait was a thoroughly conventional force organized and equipped along the familiar Soviet model, and therefore much more impressive. Though the Iraqi army was not, in fact, the world's fourth largest,[138] Iraqi forces were large enough, and contained what on paper at least appeared to be formidable firepower and mobility. Iraq's million-man military establishment boasted fifty-five divisions, five thousand five hundred tanks (including over five hundred highly touted Soviet T-72s), more than eight thousand other armored fighting vehicles, almost four thousand pieces of artillery, and seven hundred combat aircraft, many of them quite modern.[139]

Approaches to assessing Iraq's fighting power were remarkably free of racial, cultural, and even technological hubris. However, a profound cultural bias propelled professional military judgments of Iraq to focus excessively on the quantifiable aspects of Iraq's military power at the expense of such unquantifiable factors as the quality of Iraq's military leadership, command and control, soldiery, operational doctrine, and past performance against Kurdish rebel forces and Iran.

It was the abysmal quality of these features of Iraqi military "capabilities" in relation to those of the Coalition's Western members that provided the foundation for the most lopsided military victory in modern times. Yet, since the days when Secretary of Defense Robert McNamara brought computers and quantitative analysis to the Pentagon, threat assessment has been dominated by an infatuation with what can be counted—numbers of enemy missiles, tanks, divisions, planes, ships, etc. This infatuation tends to discount by default the ultimately decisive "moral, intellectual, and organizational" facets of military power. It assigns the same combat power to a given tank or fighter plane regardless of whether it is crewed or piloted by ill-trained and demoralized Iraqis or superbly trained and feisty Americans, Israelis, or Britons. It ignores the fact that, except in rare cases of crushing numerical advantage, military superiority is ultimately a function of social organization at home. It ignores the potentially fatal impact on operational flexibility and ingenuity of a supporting political culture, such as Iraq's, in which all power is concentrated in the hands of a single military amateur. In their comprehensive assessment of Iraq's performance in the Iran-Iraq War, Anthony Cordesman and Abraham Wagner attributed repeated Iraqi setbacks in the early years of the war to a "gross overcentralization of command, mixed with high levels of politicization and incompetence at all levels of command," and concluded that "the armed forces of autocratic states are ultimately no more effective than their autocrats."[140]

There should have been no reason, considering Iraq's political culture and lack of any real experience in dealing with modern Western military power, to believe that Saddam Hussein's army would perform any better during the Gulf War than did Egypt and Syria against Israel in 1956, 1967, 1973, and 1982. On the contrary, there was every reason to expect an Iraqi military performance inferior to Egypt's and Syria's, given the irrelevance of Iraq's positional defense experience against Iran to the entirely different military challenges posed by Coalition forces. The Coalition also enjoyed far greater military advantages over Iraq relative to those of Israel vis-à-vis its past Arab opponents; in 1967 and 1973, Israel lacked strategic depth and was compelled to wage war simultaneously on two or three fronts. As General Schwarzkopf commented after the Gulf War, the Iraqis "were very good indeed at World War I, less good at grasping that seventy years and countless generations of weapons and systems had gone by since then."[141] Conversely, the French experience in Indochina from 1946 to 1954 and our own experience in Korea in 1950–53 should have alerted U.S. political and military decision-makers in the early 1960s to expect a long and potentially indecisive war against a tenacious enemy in Vietnam.

In the end, as we shall see later, it made little difference how many tanks and planes the Iraqis had in the Kuwaiti Theater of Operations, or how good they were. The Iraqi army was big and brutal, but also, against the Western foes it faced in 1991, clumsy, dim-witted, and technologically blind. Unlike Chinese forces in Korea and Communist forces in Indochina, whose strategy and tactics reflected a systematic and effective attempt to confront Western military power via a different style of warfare, the Iraqis tried to beat the United States at its own game. The Iraqi army represented an attempt to "ape" the armies of advanced industrial countries—to buy into military modernity by acquiring its outward material and organizational trappings. Like many, though by no means all, aspiring Third World hegemons, Saddam Hussein seems to have believed that military effectiveness was little more than a function of front-line troop strength and aggregate firepower. Paradoxically, the Coalition seemed almost as mesmerized by Saddam's military "trappings" as the dictator himself. The Coalition mistakenly judged Iraq's military capability on the basis of quantity rather than quality.

Nowhere was the gap between appearance and reality greater than in the behavior of the Iraqi air force. Of all the categories of military power, air power is the most technologically intensive, and strategically and operationally flexible, requiring incomparable human skill and imagination for its effective employment. As such, it is the most expensive and the most difficult form of military power for non-Western cultures to master—and indeed none have, to the extent of the best Western air arms.

Saddam Hussein spent a great deal of money on air power in the 1980s, and entered the Gulf War with the world's sixth-largest air force, boasting almost seven hundred combat aircraft, including over sixty very modern French F-1 Mirages equipped with the renowned Exocet antiship missile—"a fairly strong opponent" with "a very good infrastructure," in the judgment of U.S. Air Force Chief of Staff McPeak.[142] Of course, the outcome of the air war was never in doubt; Coalition air forces enjoyed decisive numerical and qualitative superiority. However, it was reasonable to expect that the Iraqi air force would inflict some damage somewhere. During the Vietnam War, North Vietnam's tiny air force of thirty-odd

Soviet MiGs downed dozens of American warplanes and severely complicated U.S. air operations over the North. During the Falklands War, Argentina's small air force, which included many decrepit U.S. A-4 Skyhawks, put up a highly spirited fight that came close to fatally disrupting Britain's attempt to retake the disputed islands.

During the Gulf War, however, there was no known instance of a successful Iraqi air attack against any Coalition ground, naval, or air unit. In the early stages of the conflict a few Iraqi aircraft did rise against intruding U.S. and allied planes. Thirty-five were shot down without a single Coalition aircraft lost in air-to-air combat. The remainder of the Iraqi air force either stayed put on the ground inside individual aircraft shelters, 375 (of 594) of which were destroyed or damaged with an estimated loss of 141 more aircraft, or fled to Iran (122 aircraft). Another sixteen were captured or destroyed by Coalition ground forces.[143] For all intents and purposes, Iraq had no air force on the day Desert Storm was launched, though it did have a lot of expensive aircraft and state-of-the-art air bases and aircraft shelters.

The shock of its first confrontation with real air power undoubtedly accounted for the Iraqi air force's comatose behavior against what unquestionably was the world's finest air force. Cultural factors, however, also contributed to Iraq's dismal performance in the air. As was the case in the Iran-Iraq War, Iraq seemingly could never quite figure out what to do with its air power. Air power was apparently never regarded as potentially decisive, because of a premodern preoccupation with ground forces and taking territory as the be-all and end-all of any military enterprise. Air power was employed in fits and starts, absent any unifying concept, and largely as an adjunct of land operations. The heavy politicization of the Iraqi air force's officer corps certainly did not encourage air power effectiveness, nor did a received and deeply ingrained Bedouin preference for limited raids against peripheral targets over sustained attacks on strategically important ones.[144] (The Arab armies led by T. E. Lawrence in World War I served as adjuncts along the Turkish periphery in Arabia to the advance of General Allenby's British main force through Palestine to Damascus.)

MISSING THE WORST

Ironically, the military capabilities of Iraq that the Coalition failed most miserably to gauge were those very components deemed the most threatening to Coalition forces and to prospects for long-term regional stability in the Persian Gulf: Iraq's ballistic missiles, chemical weapons, and nascent nuclear weapons programs. Perhaps the most embarrassing aspect of the Coalition's strategic bombardment campaign was its failure to destroy more than a fraction of Iraq's ballistic missile inventory and vast military-industrial infrastructure dedicated to the development and manufacture of hyperlethal (i.e., chemical, biological, and nuclear) munitions.

Discussion of the Coalition's air war against Iraq is presented in a later chapter. Suffice it to say here that the air campaign was waged in ideal strategic conditions: a politically and militarily isolated enemy, an abundance of air power and supporting facilities within the theater of operations, relatively good weather and open terrain, and an enemy air force that chose not to fight. Moreover, the Coalition had over five months to collect and analyze, via satellite, manned reconnaissance flights, and other means, information on the identity, size, and location of suspect sites. Yet according to published reports based on information obtained by numerous United Nations and other international teams that inspected suspect sites and activities in Iraq after the Gulf War was over, Iraq emerged from the conflict with significant weapon inventories intact. They included, among other things, no fewer than 819 Scud missiles (Iraq launched only 86 during the war); 46,000 loaded chemical bombs, shells, and missiles; 79,000 unfilled chemical munitions, 600 tons of chemical warfare agents, and three uranium/hydrogen bomb component factories.[145]

Indeed, of an estimated thirty to thirty-five facilities related to Iraq's mammoth prewar nuclear weapons program, which in terms of the number of people employed and its inflation-adjusted cost approximated that of the U.S. Manhattan Project of World War II, only three were attacked by Coalition air forces, one of them ineffectually and very late in the war.[146] Moreover, and perhaps most ominous for the future, the program's work force, estimated to include seven thousand scientists and thirteen thousand technicians, survived the war with few losses.[147]

The air campaign's relative ineffectiveness against those very components of Iraq's arsenal, whose elimination was perhaps the overriding U.S. objective in the war, has sparked a major debate over ecstatic claims made on behalf of air power in the war's wake. However, such a debate must be conditioned by recognition of two pertinent factors over which Coalition air campaign planners had little control. The first was a colossal failure of prewar Coalition intelligence collection and analysis to gauge the scope and intensity of Iraq's effort to acquire ballistic missile and hyperlethal munitions capabilities. Entire programs and many large facilities remained hidden from the Coalition's eyes and ears. Iraqi concealment measures were extensive; Western intelligence organizations were preoccupied before the war with events in Eastern Europe and the Soviet Union; and before August 2, 1990, the United States was not predisposed to seek out and expose potentially dangerous Iraqi military-industrial activities. As a result, Coalition air war planners were blinded to the very existence of many critical targets.

Iraq was known to have indigenously modified, extended-range Scud missiles, but intelligence agencies woefully underestimated Iraq's total Scud inventory, especially the number of mobile Scud launchers. Moreover, though Saddam Hussein never concealed his ambitions to produce the first "Arab" atomic bomb, U.S. officials doubted Iraq's ability to build one within even a decade. (Postwar estimates based on U.N. inspections and

45,000 pages of seized Iraqi documents point strongly to the conclusion that Iraq was two to eighteen months from having a usable atomic weapon.)[148] Agencies were certainly unaware that Iraq was employing four separate technological approaches in an all-out effort to manufacture plutonium and enriched uranium, including the "obsolete" calutron approach,[149] and that Iraq also had a parallel program to develop a hydrogen bomb.[150]

The second factor, unknown to Coalition air war planners, was the great degree to which Iraq's key military assets had been hardened or concealed in the decade preceding the Gulf War. Saddam's first real taste of Western air power came not in January 1991 but in June 1981, when Israeli F-16s destroyed his Osirak nuclear reactor near Thuwaitha. This experience with Western air power prompted him to disperse, harden, and hide much of his military-industrial infrastructure and even some of his operating forces. In an ABC Television interview after the Israeli raid, he told Barbara Walters that the attack had "taught not only the Iraqis, but all Arabs, that they must shelter their vital projects from all attack, so that even an atomic bomb will not be able to knock them out."[151] Thus the Israeli attack, while it clearly postponed realization of Iraq's nuclear ambitions, made it all the more difficult for Coalition air forces to erase Iraq's nuclear weapons program a decade later.

Beginning in the early 1980s, Iraq began undertaking extraordinary measures to protect existing facilities by burying them, and dispersing new ones across the country.[152] Deep underground shelters for Saddam, government ministries, and key command and communications centers were constructed in Baghdad. Existing air bases were hardened, and new bases, including three buried completely underground,[153] were built, many of them in remote areas. Chemical and biological weapons activities were scattered and often concealed in the guise of fertilizer, food-processing, and petro-chemical facilities. The evidence also suggests that Saddam's effort to bury or otherwise hide his "forbidden" programs may have been aided inadvertently by the satellite and other intelligence information the United States supplied to him during the Iran-Iraq War.[154]

Of course, Saddam was hardly the first Third World leader who sought protection against the threat of superior Western air power via such passive measures. The North Koreans, after their experience with U.S. air power in the early 1950s, long ago hardened their military-industrial infrastructure and some of their operating forces; and the very fact that so much of Iraq's now-forbidden infrastructure survived what has been widely heralded as the most successful air campaign in history undoubtedly will not be lost on other aspiring regional hegemons with ambitions contrary to U.S. security interests.

Nor was Saddam the first Third World leader to see in ballistic missile technology a relatively cheap and easy means of partially offsetting Western air power and of achieving, especially when joined with hyperlethal munitions, regional superpower status. The inability of Coalition air forces to extirpate Iraqi Scuds during the Gulf War significantly delayed the timing of the ground offensive. It also advertised the operational and strategic attractiveness of ballistic missile technology to other countries unwilling or unable to challenge Western air power on its own terms. The Coalition's difficulties in suppressing the Scud threat were all the more remarkable, given the Scud's relative technological primitiveness and the Iraqis' lack of imagination in employing them. The missiles themselves were inaccurate, incapable of maneuvering in flight, lacked decoys, and carried small conventional warheads. Moreover, though eighty-six Scuds were launched against Israel and Saudi Arabia during the war,[155] all were fired singly or in twos or threes rather than in barrage, which would have greatly complicated U.S. Patriot missile defenses. Indeed, the day before the war ended, U.S. special operations forces reportedly discovered a launch site in Iraq with twenty-nine Scuds positioned for a barrage attack on Israel.[156] Saddam also failed to target locations in Israel and Turkey where no U.S. Patriot antiballistic missiles were deployed. Finally, while Scud attacks on Israel were strategically worrisome because they were aimed at shattering the Coalition's political cohesion by provoking Israel's entry into the war, they had no direct military impact on the war's outcome; Scuds killed only thirteen civilians—twelve Israelis (eleven from indirect causes such as heart attacks) and one Saudi—and twenty-eight (U.S.) military personnel.[157]

The Scud threat did, however, compel diversion of up to 4,000 of the Coalition's approximately 68,500 combat air sorties to the detection and destruction of Scud launchers, and though the "great Scud hunt" succeeded in reducing the rate of Scud launches, the threat was never fully suppressed.[158] According to U.S. Air Force Chief of Staff McPeak, the combination of sorties diverted to Scud suppression and unusually bad weather added nine days to a planned thirty-day, pre–ground offensive air campaign.[159] And it goes without saying that both the strategic significance of the Scuds and the difficulty and urgency of suppressing them would have been greatly magnified had Saddam possessed more modern missiles (such as the Soviet SS-21s that Saddam sought from Moscow but reportedly was denied),[160] and certainly if his missiles had carried hyperlethal warheads.

Saddam's example is likely to be repeated. The very elusivity and relatively cheap cost of ballistic missiles are making them weapons of choice in Third World countries, which simply cannot compete directly with the challenges posed by Western conventional air power. By demonstrating the great difficulty in creating traditional air arms truly competitive with the West's best, the Gulf War inflated the attractiveness of theater ballistic missiles as the weapon of choice. Michael Armitage contends that the Scud experience showed that "the cycle of detection, location, targeting, strike and battle damage assessment by the Coalition air forces [was] literally outmaneuvered by the Iraqis,"[161] perhaps the only use of intelligent maneuver by the Iraqis during the entire war. Brookings Middle East expert William Quandt believes that there will now be a race to acquire missile technology. The only thing that Saddam demonstrated was that missiles can penetrate enemy defenses and that they can cause damage—not all the time and not always significant damage, but some. There will be a temptation to think that the next generation of missiles may do what this one was unable to do.[162]

FUTURE IRAQS

To sum up, considerable misjudgments characterized prewar U.S. assessments of the Iraqi military threat. Iraq's conventional military fighting power was significantly overestimated, whereas much of its ballistic missile force and hyperlethal munitions effort remained undetected until after the Gulf War ended. Threat assessments focused excessively on what could be seen and counted, and not enough on the political, intellectual, moral, and organizational dimensions of Iraq's military power. In the end, of course, misestimation of Iraq's fighting power made little difference, since by the time Desert Storm was launched, Coalition forces had placed themselves in a strategically and operationally unassailable position to defeat Iraq.

It was, of course, better to have overestimated Iraq's military prowess than to have underestimated it. The danger now is that there may be a tendency in some quarters of the U.S. intelligence community to "correct" the embarrassing overestimation of Iraq's fighting power by discounting that of future Third World adversaries. This danger is probably minimal in East Asia, where two unpleasant experiences have bred a healthy respect for North Korean, Chinese, and Vietnamese capabilities, especially when exercised in their preferred styles of warfare. In the Islamic and especially the Arab worlds, however, some may be wont to see in every aspiring regional hegemon little more than another Iraq, as threats to be polished off with a good dose of American air power and perhaps some supporting U.S. ground forces.

This would be a grave mistake. Whatever the sources of Arab infirmities when confronting Western military power on its own terms, few countries in the Islamic world, which includes Iran and other large non-Arab states, exhibit the unique plethora of vulnerabilities to American military power that Iraq presented to the Coalition in 1990–91. Countries like Iran, Algeria, Indonesia, and Pakistan, for example, are far larger, more mountainous, and economically and militarily less well developed than Iraq in 1990; as such, they are less vulnerable to a quick "take-down" by a Desert Storm–like air campaign. Moreover, it would be most imprudent to assume that other Islamic armies will register the poor morale that contributed to the easy dissolution of Iraqi forces in Kuwait. It is also unlikely that future Iraqs will have a Saudi Arabia next door—i.e., a hostile and logistically robust neighbor willing to open its territory to American combat forces.

Presumably, aspiring regional hegemons also will have learned something from Iraq's mistakes: don't commit so naked and outrageous an aggression in an area so vital to Western interests as to provoke a military response by dozens of other countries; don't confront the West without any meaningful allies; don't give the Americans almost six months to amass overwhelming military power on your very doorstep; don't underestimate the resolve and capacity of an aroused and determined United States; and above all, don't try to beat Western military establishments at their own game.

There will be more Iraqs to come—bids by well-endowed Third World states for regional military supremacy at the expense of U.S. security interests—and the United States cannot count on having the marvelous strategic and operational setting it enjoyed in the Persian Gulf in 1990–91.

5

The Strategic and Operational Setting

RARELY IN THE HISTORY of war has one side enjoyed such overwhelming strategic and operational advantages over the other as did the Coalition over Iraq in 1991. The purpose of this chapter is to examine the strategic and operational setting of Desert Storm, which the author believes made a relatively quick and decisive Coalition victory certain, and to compare that setting, where pertinent, to those of past U.S. conflicts, beginning with World War II.

In retrospect, it is difficult to identify any significant advantage Iraq mustered over the Coalition by the time Desert Storm was launched. As we shall see in Chapter 6, during the six-month period preceding Desert Storm there were opportunities available to Iraq to derail the Coalition's buildup in Saudi Arabia and to raise the price of Desert Storm when it came, but Saddam Hussein chose not to exploit those opportunities. Saddam also could not or would not employ his chemical and biological weapons, which along with his Scud missiles constituted the very components of Iraq's military threat that the Coalition was least prepared to deal with effectively. He did, of course, set ablaze most of Kuwait's oil wells, and dumped a large quantity of oil into the Persian Gulf. However, these acts were militarily no more than nuisances, and could never have begun to offset the inevitable consequences of the Coalition's crushing strategic and operational advantages.

IRAQ'S ISOLATION

Primary among those advantages was Iraq's political and military isolation. Iraq, a relatively small state with virtually no allies, was besieged by a vast international coalition led by the world's premier military power. Iraq's invasion of Kuwait aroused the anger of practically the entire world community, including all five permanent members of the United Nations Security Council, among them the Soviet Union, Iraq's long-standing military patron. The scope of Iraq's isolation was evident in the willingness of thirty-six countries to contribute military forces of one kind or another to Coalition deployments on the Arabian peninsula, in Turkey, and at sea.[163]

Moreover, with the exception of Jordan, a small and penniless country economically dependent on Iraq, Saddam was completely surrounded by political enemies: to the north, Turkey, which permitted Coalition air forces to operate from its territory; to the east, his blood enemies, the Iranians: to the west, his old Baathist nemesis, Hafez al-Assad's Syria; and to the south, of course, Saudi Arabia and the bulk of the Coalition forces.

French and Soviet adherence to the Coalition's policies must have been especially painful; both countries had served as Iraq's principal sources of foreign arms and spare parts, and Saddam initially may have convinced himself that Moscow, or at least Paris, would remain neutral in any showdown with the American-led Coalition. On the other hand, Saddam seemed indifferent to actions that propelled France into the Coalition. France's decision to send sizable military forces to Saudi Arabia was clinched by Iraq's gratuitous violation on September 14, 1990, of the French ambassador's residence in Kuwait and seizure of the Belgian, Dutch, and Canadian embassies—actions that reportedly enraged French President Mitterrand.[164] The Iraqi dictator may not have fully grasped another important consequence of U.S.-Soviet cooperation and the Soviet Union's own preoccupation with multiple domestic crises: the release of sizable U.S. ground forces deployed in Europe for possible transfer to the Persian Gulf.

Thus Iraq entered combat with the Coalition like Poland in World War II—with few friends (Jordan, Libya, Yemen, and Cuba), none of which were in a position to help him militarily. Such a condition was unique in modern American military experience. In World War II the United States had allies, and Germany and Japan, though having few significant allies, had, unlike Iraq, access within their respective empires to vast human, industrial, and natural resources for the purposes of waging war. In the Korean and Vietnam wars the United States faced regional enemies that had direct access to Soviet and Chinese military resources—and in the case of the North Koreans, the direct assistance of the Chinese army itself. U.S. attempts in both Korea and Vietnam to interdict the transfer of Soviet and Chinese weaponry and supplies to the battlefield never succeeded to the point of seriously affecting the enemy's ability to fight, and indeed the futility of U.S. interdiction efforts prolonged both wars, increased American casualties, and contributed to the erosion of public support for U.S. war efforts.

In the Gulf War there was no equivalent of the Yalu River crossings, the Sino-Vietnamese border, the port of Haiphong, or the Ho Chi Minh Trail. By the time Desert Storm was unleashed, Iraq was about as militarily isolated as a country could be, notwithstanding some measure of smuggling across the Iraqi-Jordanian and Iraqi-Iranian borders. Even Kuwait's fabulous wealth counted for little, since the closure of Iraq's oil pipelines across Syria and Turkey, and the U.S. Navy–enforced embargo of Iraq's sea-borne oil exports, eliminated any prospect of converting Kuwaiti or Iraqi oil into the foreign exchange needed to solicit arms from abroad.

Iraq's military isolation meant that it could not replace wartime losses of critical components of its arsenal, and therefore that war with the Coalition was likely to be far shorter and more unpleasant, in terms of its outcome, than the preceding war with Iran. In contrast, Communist armies in Korea and Indochina, which were logistically much leaner than Saddam's forces, could fight on indefinitely as long as the United States could not find the means of completely isolating North Korea and North Vietnam from Soviet and Chinese military assistance.

The reverse side of the coin of Iraq's isolation was, of course, the plenitude of allies, many of them militarily helpful, the United States enjoyed. Like Great Britain before it, the United States has long specialized in coalition warfare and, almost without exception in this century, has managed to pick fighting allies (i.e., those participating significantly in military operations) superior to those available to its principal adversaries. In World War II, the United States fought alongside the British Empire and the Soviet Union, whereas the Germans were stuck with the likes of Italy and Romania. In Korea, the United States fought under United Nations auspices and alongside military contingents from Britain, France, Greece, Turkey, and other countries. Only in the Vietnam War were America's fighting allies few in number, politically weak, and militarily mediocre.

In the Persian Gulf the United States was awash in politically critical and militarily impressive allies—ranging from France, Britain, and (tacitly) the Soviet Union, to Egypt, Syria, and Morocco. Indeed, some countries wishing to contribute military forces to the Coalition (e.g., Bulgaria, Honduras) had to be turned away because they could not be logistically accommodated in Saudi Arabia;[165] and, of course, with Israel, the Middle East's most militarily powerful state, the United States was placed in the paradoxical position of harshly refusing Israel's wish to join in the war against Iraq because Israel had become a political liability.

It is testimony to Saddam's utter obnoxiousness that in the space of a few short months he managed to array virtually the entire world against him, very much as had Hitler in the 1940s. Saddam had no allies, and Hitler had only a few weak "friends," because both dictators had not only imperial ambitions that threatened all of their neighbors, but also reputations for deceit and brutality that made them manifestly untrustworthy partners.

SAUDI ARABIA'S LOGISTICAL CORNUCOPIA

Next to Iraq's isolation, perhaps the next most important feature of Desert Storm's strategic and operational setting was the availability to the United States and its Coalition partners of a vast, modern, ready-made logistical infrastructure in Saudi Arabia, a cornucopia of over thirty air bases; eight port facilities, some of them among the world's largest and most modern; abundant supplies of refined petroleum products; and plenty of empty desert to which to deploy and train. The size and quality of the Saudi infrastructure, much of which had been built in the 1980s with the assistance of the U.S. Army Corps of Engineers and largely to U.S. military specifications—in anticipation of precisely the kind of contingency that arose in the Gulf in 1990—were impressive by any standard. As the Pentagon's own interim report on the Gulf War declared, "The Saudi coastal and military infrastructure ranks among the finest in the world— better than most European and Asian facilities; well ahead of all other Gulf, Middle East, or African countries."[166]

The Gulf War was the first instance since World War I in which major U.S. forces deployed to fight overseas without having to build most of their supporting infrastructure on the spot. In World War II, U.S. expeditionary forces, save for those established in Great Britain, had to build their own ports, air bases, supply dumps, and roads either from scratch or from the all-too-often demolished facilities left behind by retreating enemies. The human and material resources consumed by these activities often surpassed those dedicated to the actual fighting, causing manpower shortages in the combat arms, especially the infantry. South Korea in 1950 was almost completely barren of militarily useful logistical facilities, and in South Vietnam in the early 1960s, facilities left over by the Japanese and the French were woefully inadequate to support the half million U.S. troops deployed there by 1968. In Indochina, over three years of hectic construction were needed to satisfy burgeoning U.S. logistical requirements.

The deployment of a U.S. expeditionary force of over 500,000 strong to Saudi Arabia, and its readiness to fight within six months, would have been impossible without the unexcelled scope and quality of the kingdom's militarily useful infrastructure. Saddam Hussein could not have threatened a neighbor better suited to accommodate a rapid and massive foreign military buildup on his very doorstep. Moreover, as an oil-rich country with extensive refining capacity, the kingdom was in a position to supply U.S. forces with much of their fuel requirements, and thereby reduce the burden on precious American shipping. In both Korea and Vietnam all fuel used by U.S. military forces had to be brought into the theater of operations from great distances overseas. Former Assistant Secretary of Defense William Perry has identified "the quality and quantity of Saudi air bases and the ready supply of fuel within the theater" as "foremost" among the "many significant factors favoring the Coalition forces."[167] Naval expert Vincent Thomas, looking back on Operation Desert Shield in the context of previous U.S. experience, has observed that the buildup

> took place amidst conditions unique in comparison with any previous prelude to U.S. military action in our nation's history. Never before had there been, and probably never again would there be, more than thirty modern air bases available, and in most instances ready, for use by both

combat and logistics aircraft. Never had there been eight relatively new ports capable of handling any and all U.S. cargo. Never had there been an unlimited supply of necessary petroleum products available in-theater free.[168]

The Saudi Arabian government reportedly supplied about half of Coalition food and fuel requirements.[169]

Additionally, the vast empty lands of much of Saudi Arabia's interior provided abundant space for realistic training exercises well away from population centers and potential political trouble. In Vietnam, the inter-mingling of U.S. military forces and dense Vietnamese populations encour-aged unwanted behavior on both sides that played to Communist propaganda appeals and undermined the South Vietnamese government's political legitimacy. In Saudi Arabia, any rash of incidents involving American soldiers and liquor or local Saudi women could have threatened the House of Saud's very legitimacy and given credence to Saddam Hussein's propaganda about the monarchy's willingness to consort with unholy infidels. The quality of the training in the desert was in fact superb, in part because there were few distractions, including those of alcohol and women. Moreover, U.S. troops were not rotated once they arrived in Saudi Arabia. This permitted them to concentrate intensively on training on the very terrain in which they would be called upon to fight. The contrast with the Vietnam War, with the Army's reliance on comparatively inexperienced draftees and on a pernicious one-year individual rotation system, could not have been greater.

Indeed, the Gulf War was the first conflict in American history that did not catch U.S. military forces unprepared. From the War of 1812 through the early years of Vietnam, the United States had entered combat with forces unready for the war to come—peacetime forces too small, ill-equipped, or poorly trained. The results were almost invariably unpleasant: frenetic economic and manpower mobilization, and initial military paraly-sis, defeats, and disasters—e.g., the destruction of U.S. naval power and sea-borne commerce in the Battle of Queenstown Heights (1812); the follies of First Manassas (1861); the "Keystone Cops" mobilization against Spain (1898); the more than yearlong hiatus between America's declaration of war against Germany in the spring of 1917 and readiness for actual combat of U.S. forces in France a year later (Battle of Cantigny); the lost battles at Pearl Harbor, Bataan, Buna, and Kasserine Pass (1941–43); the retreats to Pusan and from Chosin (1950); and the surprise of North Vietnamese boldness and tenacity in the Ia Drang Valley (1965).[170] In contrast, the all-volunteer force of 1990, though requiring significant reserve component mobilization for the Gulf War, was about as ready for combat as any peacetime force could be, and certainly far more so than its small pre–World War II professional predecessor of *From Here to Eternity* fame, or the hastily thrown-together gaggles of amateurs, volunteers, and sometime draftees that fought the first battles of 1812, 1848, 1898, 1917, 1941, 1950, and 1965. Never has the United States fielded a force more ready for initial combat as it did in the Persian Gulf in 1990–91.

SECURE LINES OF COMMUNICATION

The United States enjoyed another advantage in the Gulf crisis, one that it had come to take for granted since World War II: secure strategic and operational lines of communication. Iraq's lack of a navy worth the name, or of an air force willing to challenge U.S. air supremacy even over Iraqi territory, meant that Coalition forces did not have to worry much about Iraqi attacks in transit to the Gulf or in the theater's rear areas. The Coalition did worry about possible Libyan mining of forces on their way to the Gulf, and during the crisis Italian, Belgian, and other Coalition naval units kept watch in the Mediterranean and the Red Sea.[171]

In Korea and Vietnam the United States also enjoyed immunity from assaults on its strategic lines of communication, although its intratheater land lines were often attacked and on occasion severed (e.g., at Chosin and Khe Sanh) by enemy regular and guerrilla forces. World War II, of course, provided quite a different experience. In the Pacific and especially the North Atlantic, the United States faced enemies that had the means, mainly submarines and long-range aircraft, to inflict severe losses on U.S. shipping carrying munitions and supplies to American and allied forces overseas.

Iraq had no such abilities, though it did have one category of weapons for which the U.S. Navy was (and remains) congenitally unprepared: sea mines. In the only known instance of Iraqi offensive military action against U.S. forces operating along other secure intratheater lines of communication (except for a few random Scud attacks), Iraqi mines collided with two large warships, the cruiser *Princeton* and the amphibious ship *Tripoli,* and severely damaged them both. As one disgusted naval commentator has written, the "Gulf War demonstrated once again that low-cost sea mines threaten the U.S. Navy's ability to operate. After the [U.S. Navy's experience in] the 1980–88 Iran-Iraq War, the danger should have been obvious."[172]

SADDAM'S CONVENTIONALITY

Still another important if less obvious advantage for the United States was the thorough conventionality of Saddam's military forces. Unlike the hearty and elusive Communist peasant infantries the United States faced in the rugged mountains of Korea and the jungles of Indochina, Saddam's army was little more than a smaller, and in many respects, cheap copy of the very Soviet conventional forces against which American military planners had planned to fight for over forty years. U.S. force structures, weaponry, and war-fighting doctrines, which all too often proved ineffectual and even counterproductive against the unconventional forces and tactics of the North Koreans, Chinese, Viet Cong, and North Vietnamese army, could not have been more efficacious against Saddam Hussein's large, visible, and logistically ponderous "military machine." U.S. forces that were ill-suited to deal effectively with Communist challenges in East Asia were eminently fungible against Saddam's Soviet-model army—witness the transfer of the U.S. Army's Seventh Corps from Europe to Arabia and its subsequent performance against the Iraqi army.

The conventionality of the Iraqi army—and its consequent vulnerability to superior conventional foes—were among Saddam's great gifts to the Coalition. Unlike Mao Zedong and Lin Piao, Ho Chi Minh and Vo Nguyen Giap, Saddam chose to try to copy industrial models of military power rather than to devise force structures and tactics designed to sidestep Western strengths and exploit Western vulnerabilities. The Iraqi army's conventionality stood it in good stead against Iran, as it would have against Saudi Arabia and even Syria, but it was an invitation to disaster against the qualitatively superior forces of the world's only remaining superpower and its allies. Perhaps Saddam never imagined tangling with Western opponents, although he had to assume possible encounters with Israel. In the wake of the Gulf War, Ezio Bonsignore commented:

No Third World country should think that by buying arms, even in enormous quantities, it is also acquiring the capability to mount a meaningful military resistance against the industrialized West. A Third World country may, indeed, effectively resist even a superpower, and actually beat it or at least force it to let go: Vietnam and Afghanistan are quite convincing demonstrations. In order to do so, however, a country must adopt unconventional and guerrilla warfare strategies and tactics, aimed at carefully exploiting the industrialized nations' structural and moral weaknesses. If a Third World force aspires to defy us on our own ground, he is lost without hope. Modern warfare—with its tanks, its guns, its aircraft—is a Western invention.[173]

OPEN COUNTRY

The vulnerability of Iraqi forces was also fortuitously magnified by the topography and weather characteristic of the Kuwaiti Theater of Operations. While unusually bad weather initially plagued air operations during Desert Storm (about 40 percent of all planned attack sorties in the KTO during the war's first ten days were canceled because of poor visibility and low overcast conditions),[174] conditions were ideal compared to the skies over Nazi-occupied Europe, North Korea, and Indochina (especially during the monsoon season). Equally important was the relative dearth of natural cover in the KTO. The tortuous mountains of Korea and rain forests of Vietnam were not available to shield Iraqi forces from detection by Coalition air and ground forces, and the combination of good flying weather and flat, arid terrain played heavily in favor of air power—the Coalition's greatest comparative advantage over Iraq. Not even skilled Iraqi use of camouflage, decoys, and other deceptive measures could conceal its major field force units from Coalition observation. During the War, General Michael Dugan, Air Force Chief of Staff until September 1990, commented: "If there ever was a scenario where air power could be effective, this was it. In Iraq and Kuwait, there is no triple-canopied jungle, no Ardennes forest, and the weather is usually clear."[175] Dugan's view was shared by British air power expert Air Vice Marshal R. A. Mason. "The sparsely occupied desert terrain was ideally suited to air attack. Iraqi ground forces, most of which were located away from towns, would either be dug in and static, or mobile, visible, and vulnerable."[176] As for the Iraqi air force, General Charles Horner, Desert Storm's air commander, concluded that Saddam Hussein "had no idea what air power is. . . . He had no air experience. There was nobody to teach him." Horner went on to state: "Any of my captains could have run his air force and caused much more trouble than he did."[177]

MORE AND BETTER FORCES

The Coalition also enjoyed an advantage over Iraq that had always eluded NATO in Central Europe: numerical superiority. Contrary to initial officially sponsored impressions of Desert Storm, Coalition forces outnumbered Iraqi forces in the KTO by at least three to two and perhaps by as much as three to one even before Desert Storm began. Coalition forces on January 16, 1991, numbered 745,000 soldiers, sailors, airmen, and marines (of which 540,000 were American), versus an officially estimated maximum of 540,000 Iraqis in the KTO.[178] The figure for Iraq is highly suspect, however. It assumes that all Iraqi units in the KTO were deployed at full manpower and equipment strength, when in all probability they were manned and equipped at something on the order of 70–80 percent or less. Most Third World armies habitually and significantly underman their units, and even during the Iran-Iraq War, Iraq maintained a very liberal furlough policy for domestic political reasons. London's International Institute for Strategic Studies has concluded that it is "clear that most [Iraqi] divisions were . . . not deployed at full strength and estimates of the Iraqi force strength were considerably revised. Iraqi ground forces [in the KTO] may have numbered as few as 350,000 at the beginning of *Desert Storm* . . ."[179] Another postwar assessment put the number at 250,000, or less than one half the original official estimate.[180] Middle Eastern warfare expert Anthony Cordesman also believes that low manning levels and high desertion rates had seriously depleted advertised Iraqi strength before Desert Storm.[181] James Dunnigan and Austin Bay have concluded that as many as 150,000 Iraqi troops mobilized for duty in Kuwait either failed to report to their units or deserted in Kuwait before and during Desert Storm.[182] Certainly by the time the Coalition ground offensive was launched, Iraqi forces in the KTO were but shadows of their former selves, courtesy of the Coalition air campaign. Gregg Easterbrook, for example, believes that Coalition armies fell upon Iraqi forces probably numbering no more than about 280,000 (or about 70 percent of the 396,000 U.S. Army and Marine Corps personnel committed to Desert Storm), "considering surrenders, troops who refused to shoot, and units depleted by the air campaign."[183] The result was a Coalition ground offensive far shorter and less bloody than anticipated, since it engaged significantly smaller than estimated Iraqi forces in the KTO, as well as forces utterly demoralized by thirty-eight days of air attacks. In the air and at sea, of course, the Coalition mustered a crushing numerical superiority, and even though Iraq had a modest advantage in tanks, artillery, and some other categories of ground weapons, it was an advantage completely erased by the Coalition's air supremacy and the superiority of Coalition armor. In Europe, the U.S. Army had always planned to "fight outnumbered and win"; in the Persian Gulf Saddam Hussein fought outnumbered and lost.

Far more contributory than quantitative superiority to the certainty of the Coalition's victory was its across-the-board qualitative superiority in manpower, morale, leadership, doctrine, and weaponry. Nowhere was this more evident than in the American all-volunteer force. During the Vietnam War U.S. military manpower quality steadily declined, in part because of the Johnson administration's decision to rely on draftees and refusal to call up trained reservists. The average age of American GIs in Vietnam, who usually had no more than one or two years of military service to their credit, was nineteen; in contrast, the average age of U.S. troops in the Gulf War was twenty-seven, and they had an average of seven years of military service under their belts.[184] The troops of Desert Storm were mature, superbly trained, undistracted, and ready—even eager—to fight. The quality of Saddam Hussein's conscripts in the KTO ranged from fair, in some Republican Guard and regular army units, to poor, especially in front-line infantry units, which were heavily populated by demoralized reservists in active service. Over half of all the Iraqi army's officers and men were older, recalled reservists, or young conscripts whose service had been extended, in many cases by several years.[185] Many had been numbed by service in the eight-year-long war with Iran. They were war-weary, not war-ready, and few were prepared to sacrifice their lives on behalf of Saddam Hussein's vision of a greater Iraq.

Worse still, Iraqi forces, while adequately trained in the essentials of individual combat, were trained largely to fight a relatively static, attritional kind of warfare on behalf of a regime always suspicious of military subordinates that exhibited too much independence, initiative, and willingness to challenge established ways of doing business. The impact of Saddam Hussein's coup paranoia proved near-disastrous in the war with Iran, and could hardly have been remedied by the time the Gulf War began. The Iraqi army in Kuwait was a premodern army that was paid not to think, only to do what it was told. It was completely unprepared to confront Coalition air power or the kind of rapid, shocking, and opportunistic armored blitzkrieg served up by General Schwarzkopf.

In contrast was a U.S. military force that from enlisted troops to generals was thoroughly trained in an entirely different kind of warfare: mobile, flexible, and sensitive to the synergistic effects of properly integrated and orchestrated employment of the various combat arms and of ground, sea, and air (including space) elements of military power—for example, the U.S. Army and Air Force's development of their joint AirLand Battle doctrine and techniques. It was also, contrary to apparent Iraqi misimpressions, a military that had trained extensively in desert environments. For two decades California and Nevada deserts had provided U.S. military forces superb desert warfare training in such places as the Army's National Training Center at Fort Irwin, the Marine Corps' Air-Ground Combat Center at Twenty-Nine Palms, and the Air Force's Nellis base. For over a decade, selected U.S. forces had also conducted joint exercises in the Middle East with Egyptian and other Arab forces, and the U.S. Central Command had been collecting invaluable data on the political, operational, physical, and climatological environments of the Persian Gulf. Iraq's military attachés in Washington, as well as Tariq Aziz himself, seem to have been completely oblivious to the American military's qualitative post-Vietnam recovery and its impressive store of desert warfare knowledge. How else to explain, among other things, the Iraqi foreign minister's boast to Secretary of State James Baker at Geneva seven days before Desert Storm began that "your Arab allies will desert you. They will not kill other Arabs. Your advance will crumble and you will be left lost in the desert. You don't know the desert because you have never ridden a horse or a camel."[186]

Indeed, the Iraqi army, contrary to Tariq Aziz's boast, had practically no experience in desert combat and lacked even a fraction of the U.S. Army's desert training experience. The Iran-Iraq War was not fought in a desert environment; most of its combat was waged in the swamps and along the waterways of the Faw Peninsula and the Shatt al-Arab, or in the rugged mountains along the northern stretches of the Iran-Iraq border. Both areas contained major natural obstacles to the kind of armored blitzkrieg permitted to the Coalition by the vast expanses of open terrain in the KTO and southern Iraq.

Professional Coalition military forces were not only incomparably better trained than Iraq's conscripted army; they also exhibited a vastly superior morale over their sullen and demoralized Iraqi counterparts. By all accounts, American military morale in Saudi Arabia was superb; AWOLs, desertions, and nonjudicial punishments were virtually nonexistent, in sharp contrast to the very high rates of indiscipline and low morale that characterized U.S. forces in the latter years of the Vietnam War. The only apparent major source of discontent was frustration over the seemingly endless delays in launching Desert Storm. Iraqi forces, on the other hand, had for the most part little stomach for a real showdown with the Coalition.

Postwar interrogations of seven Iraqi generals and hundreds of field grade officers as well as thousands of enlisted men captured in the fighting also revealed a widespread conviction that Saddam Hussein would somehow find a eleventh-hour alternative to war.[187]

Interrogations further exposed considerable tension between the officer corps, which among other things was living high off the hog of looted Kuwaiti foodstuffs and consumer goods, and the enlisted ranks, which even before Desert Storm were poorly supplied with such essentials as food, water, and soap. A European journalist who remained in Kuwait from the beginning of the Iraqi invasion through its liberation by the Coalition has written of Iraqi soldiers that "food was near the top of their looting list,"[188] and that when Baghdad announced on February 15 that it was willing to withdraw from Kuwait, "Iraqi troops were on a high . . . , firing their guns into the air in premature celebration. . . . Their delight at the prospect of pulling out confirmed what we had always suspected: they did not want to fight and their morale was low."[189] American troops may have grumbled about their MREs (Meals Ready to Eat), but they never had to scavenge for food and water. The mass surrender of entire Iraqi units, many of them throwing down their arms at first contact with Coalition forces, testifies to their acute demoralization. True, some units, including Republican Guard divisions, did put up a stiff fight here and there, but Iraqi forces in the KTO as a whole lacked the moral cohesion to fight effectively.

The contrast in leadership was no less enervating for the Iraqis. Professionalism and trust formed the basis of officer-enlisted relations in the U.S. military, whereas fear governed those relations in the Iraqi army, whose senior officer ranks, as noted, were also highly politicized. Moreover, whereas Iraq's "victory" over Iran formed the referent experience to be emulated in the selection of Iraqi military leaders and the formulation of Iraqi military doctrine, the U.S. military leadership that planned Desert Storm was determined to avoid the myriad mistakes that its predecessors had made in Vietnam. Iraq's military experience against Iran was fatally irrelevant in the Gulf War. The Iranians had a small, crippled air force and a demoralized professional army with little capacity for armored warfare, and were never in a position to isolate the Iraqi army from its sources of supply. The rigid, static Iraqi defenses that proved so murderous to mass frontal assault by wretchedly armed Iranian teenagers provided no security against the Coalition's magnificent army, much of which was directed against Iraq's open right flank in the KTO.

In contrast, lessons learned from Vietnam and from other unpleasant post-Vietnam experiences were all critical to the Coalition's unqualified military victory over Iraqi forces in the KTO. Among those lessons were: the need for quality manpower, for clear and clean lines of command authority, for the placement of different service aviation forces under a single air component commander, for the elimination of civilian and senior military micromanagement of combat operations, and for realistic training and "free-play" exercises. U.S. forces entered the Gulf War with a leadership and operational doctrine that not only reflected a systematic appraisal of what went wrong in Indochina, Iran, Grenada, and Lebanon, but also incorporated the new strategic and operational opportunities afforded by post-Vietnam revolutionary advances in military technology.

The Coalition's qualitative superiority over Iraq in technology was as pronounced as its advantage in manpower. Iraq lacked such key technologies as space-based sensors and surveillance satellites, effective airborne warning and surveillance aircraft (including one, like the U.S. JSTARS, capable of detecting and tracking enemy ground force traffic), stealthy bombers and attack aircraft, cruise missiles, night-vision equipment, submarines, large warships, and global positioning receivers that permitted ground units to determine their precise location. The disparity in intelligence capabilities was critical. Baghdad had no satellites and no airborne reconnaissance capable of detecting key Coalition military activities. The Gulf War was a contest with a blind enemy. Even in almost all of the technologies it did field, Iraq suffered a decided qualitative disadvantage. Iraq's MiGs and Mirages were no match for the Coalition's F-16s, F-15Es, and F/A-18s; its vaunted T-72 main battle tanks served as little more than cannon fodder for the U.S. M-1 Abrams tanks, which had excellent night sights and main guns significantly outranging those of the Iraqis; and Baghdad's collection of gunboats presented helpless targets for Coalition battleships, cruisers, frigates, and naval aircraft. Worse still for Iraqi forces in the KTO was their unparalleled transparency to Coalition visual, photographic, infrared, and electronic surveillance and detection capabilities. The Iraqi military's eyes and ears were virtually paralyzed in the first few hours of the war, whereas the Coalition throughout the conflict maintained a relatively clear view of Iraqi forces—their locations, movements, and other activities. The Pentagon's own interim report on the war declares categorically: "No combat commander has ever had as full and complete a view of his adversary as did our field commander."[190]

Again, the contrasts with the Korean and Vietnam wars could not be more startling. In those two conflicts, the combination of an operationally and tactically stealthy enemy, foul weather, closed or covered terrain, and lack of surveillance technologies available to the Pentagon in the Gulf War served to deny U.S. forces all but a fragmented and often dangerously erroneous picture of the enemy's order of battle and his movements. In Korea, for example, the movement of massive Chinese forces across the Yalu in the fall of 1950 went undetected until they fell upon overextended U.N. forces with a fury that produced the longest retreat in American military history. Similarly undetected was the scope of the Communist Tet Offensive in 1968 in Vietnam.

TIME

Saddam's greatest boon to the Coalition—and it was his to give—was time. To have any chance whatsoever of forcibly overturning Iraq's aggression against Kuwait, the Coalition needed months (almost six as it turned out) to mobilize and deploy its forces to Saudi Arabia—and to train and acclimatize them in the unfamiliar theater of operations where they were expected to fight. An early Iraqi invasion of Saudi Arabia, or Iraqi air and chemical attacks on Saudi air bases and such logistically critical ports as Dammam and Jubail, could have severely disrupted Operation Desert Shield, even to the point of shattering the Coalition's political cohesion, and certainly would have significantly delayed the timing of Desert Storm. However, to the mystification of many, including the Pentagon, Saddam did nothing as the Coalition painstakingly amassed overwhelming military force on his very doorstep. His inaction converted a potentially major Iraqi advantage into a gift for the Coalition.

Saddam's unwillingness to interfere with Desert Shield, which among other things allowed the Coalition to gather specific kinds of detailed intelligence, and to erect Desert Storm's command arrangements and its associated communications systems, also permitted the Coalition, in Lawrence Freedman's words, to fight "a war by appointment."[191] The Coalition could and did pick the time and place to fight, and did so in the face of a fully mobilized enemy that seemingly could think of nothing more imaginative to do than simply to await attack. Such a situation is uncommon in the history of warfare, and unprecedented in American military experience. Before Desert Storm, U.S. military commanders had never had the time and de facto authority to pick a fight with a menacing foreign foe. That inestimable advantage had usually accrued to America's enemies—the Japanese at Pearl Harbor, the North Koreans along the 38th Parallel, the Communists in Indochina, the Hezbollah in Beirut.

The Coalition was quite vulnerable to an Iraqi spoiling attack in the early stages of Desert Shield, but by the time Desert Storm was launched there was nothing that Saddam Hussein could have done to save his army in Kuwait, except surrender it in advance. The Coalition had managed to convert all aspects of the Gulf's strategic and operational setting to its advantage. In combination, Iraq's isolation and military conventionality, Saudi Arabia's logistical abundance, the region's favorable weather and terrain, the Coalition's secure lines of communication, its numerical and qualitative superiority, and time's generosity made the Coalition invincible. One can only pity the common Iraqi soldiery, betrayed by Saddam Hussein, abused by uncaring officers, and now condemned to be fed piecemeal into the jaws of Coalition air and ground forces. And many were indeed pitiable, as recounted in this tragicomic vignette involving a British officer during the hundred-hour ground war:

> . . . a divisional staff officer . . . had taken his shovel way out into the desert, and had squatted down to attend to the calls of nature. While so occupied, he looked up to find himself surrounded by 20 Iraqi soldiers who obviously wanted to surrender. He tried to indicate that he was temporarily rather busy, but they were not to be deterred. They just

solemnly stood in a circle around him and watched interestedly as he completed the task at hand. He then took them prisoners.[192]

EXCHANGE RATES

The unparalleled degree to which the strategic and operational setting favored the Coalition was nowhere more evident than in the history-making smallness of its combat losses in people and weapons in proportion to the total committed. For example, of a total of 540,000 American military personnel committed to Desert Storm, only 148 were killed in combat, including 35 by friendly fire, or only one death for every 3,649 troops.[193] There are few American ghettos where one would have a better chance of surviving a night on the streets. Coalition air losses also were breathtakingly small. A total of 45 Coalition aircraft were lost to hostile fire in a 43-day air campaign of 111,500 sorties flown—or a loss of one plane for every 2,477 sorties flown.[194] This compares to the loss of one aircraft for every 33 sorties flown by the British Bomber Command over Germany in World War II; 23 sorties flown by British Spitfires in the 1940 Battle of Britain; 71 sorties flown by the Israelis in the 1967 Six-Day War; and 25 sorties flown by U.S. aircraft over North Vietnam during the period 1965–68.[195] A loss rate of only 1 percent would have cost Coalition aircraft over 1,000 aircraft—or over one-third the number committed to Desert Storm. Coalition losses in ground systems were equally minuscule. For example, of a total of 1,956 U.S. Abrams tanks employed in combat, fewer than two dozen were destroyed or disabled, most of them by friendly fire,[196] and only a handful of the more than 2,200 deployed U.S. infantry fighting vehicles were destroyed or damaged, most of them, again, by friendly fire.[197]

There were, of course, more than a few deficiencies in the Coalition's performance, "Scud-busting" being one of them. Desert Storm was not a perfect military operation. Other deficiencies, some serious, others inconsequential, included, for U.S. forces: inadequate battle damage assessment; inadequate friend-or-foe identification capabilities; insufficient heavy equipment transporters; poor night-vision technology for helicopter pilots in featureless terrain; low lethality of Army light forces;[198] Navy shortages of "smart" weapons and heavy penetrating bombs; often ineffective joint communications and inadequate tactical reconnaissance; and woefully insufficient countermine warfare capabilities.[199] However, none of these problems, singly or together, had any significant effects on the course of Coalition military planning or the war itself. The one possible exception was General Schwarzkopf's decision to forgo an amphibious assault against Iraqi coastal positions, a decision that was influenced by the presence of at least twelve-hundred Iraqi sea mines off Kuwait's coast.[200] In the event, an amphibious assault proved unnecessary, since the mere presence of two hovering Marine Corps Expeditionary Brigades tied down many Iraqi divisions to coastal defense. A landing would have contributed nothing to the campaign plan finally selected, and could have involved substantial U.S.

military and Kuwaiti civilian casualties. According to the Pentagon's interim report, "One reason for the maneuver plan adopted for the ground campaign was the fact that it avoided populated areas, where U.S., Coalition, and Iraqi casualties and damage to civilian objects necessarily would have been high."[201]

Of the Gulf War, Eliot Cohen has written that it "looks like the battle of Omdurman,"[202] the 1898 clash in the Sudan in which Lord Kitchener and his Maxim guns mowed down thousands of sword-wielding Dervishes and their horses at practically no loss to himself. Others have asserted of the war that after "the first few days of air combat, both air and ground operations bore more resemblance to training exercises than real combat."[203] And another, recalling the American Civil War's Union general most noted for timidity and hesitation, has concluded that it "would have taken a McClellan to avoid scoring a rout" of the Iraqis.[204] These views underscore the presence in the Persian Gulf in 1990–91 of strategic and operational conditions so averse to the survival of Iraqi forces in the KTO, to say nothing of Iraqi prospects for victory, that it would indeed have taken either a General H. Norman *Dum*kopf, or an Iraqi Napoleon or Alexander the Great, to have significantly altered Desert Storm's outcome.

Such a combination of conditions so favorable to one side rarely arises in history, and is quite foreign to U.S. military experience, except against such nuisances as the occasionally obstreperous banana-republic dictator. The Seminoles, Santa Anna's armies, the Plains Indians, and the Philippine *insurrectos* mounted more effective resistance to American arms than did the "world's fourth largest army." Baghdad failed to impose the "mother of all battles" on Coalition forces, but it did inadvertently create "the mother of all military anomalies,"[205] which, as we shall see in a later chapter's discussion, makes it difficult to extract Desert Storm's real military meaning for the future. At a minimum, it would be recklessly imprudent to assume that other aspiring Third World hegemons will remain as passive as Saddam Hussein did in the Gulf crisis.

6

Saddam as Generalissimo

ALL WARS ARE A mixture of action, reaction—and inaction. None of these ingredients is inherently good or bad, effective or ineffective. It all depends on the circumstances at hand, including the degree to which those in charge of directing military forces have an accurate picture of what is going on around them—"situational awareness," to use a term of psychology recently appropriated by U.S. military planners.

In its first postwar assessment of Saddam Hussein's behavior throughout the Persian Gulf crisis of 1990–91, the Pentagon declared: "We do not understand the reasoning underlying many of Saddam Hussein's strategic decisions."[206] Prominent among the Defense Department's sources of mystification, shared by many expert observers of the Gulf War, was what Saddam did *not* do at seemingly critical junctures of the crisis, beginning with the scope of his invasion of Kuwait. If many of Saddam's overt actions and reactions were explainable, many of his inactions were not. Examples include his failures to limit his initial aggression in Kuwait, to push on further southward into Saudi Arabia, to attack early arriving Coalition forces, to retain custody of the thousands of Western "human shields" trapped by the crisis in Iraq and Kuwait, to evacuate Kuwait before the United Nations deadline of January 15—and, once Desert Storm was launched, to employ his abundant chemical munitions and to mount a major terrorist campaign against exposed Coalition targets in the Persian Gulf and elsewhere.

These potential actions, had they been taken singly and certainly in combination, would have both impeded, and possibly aborted, the Coalition's military response to Saddam's invasion of Kuwait, and raised the price in blood to the Coalition of Desert Storm, when it came. The reasons for Saddam's inertia in the face of these opportunities to damage the Coalition before and after the beginning of Desert Storm must remain matters of speculation. Throughout the crisis and its aftermath the dictator's assumptions and thinking about events and choices remained cloaked to Western observers and probably even to his closest henchmen, men whose positions in the Baathist hierarchy and even whose very lives existed at the sufferance of a megalomaniacal thug who had time and again demonstrated a personal relish for torturing and murdering those his paranoid personality suspected of disloyalty.[207] One can only deduce tentative conclusions based on Saddam's visible behavior.

IRAQI INCOMPETENCE AND AMERICAN UNPREDICTABILITY

What is clear, however, is that the dictator's "situational awareness," especially his picture of the United States, its political will and its military prowess, was so flawed as to propel him into a series of strategically catastrophic actions and inactions from which the Coalition profited immensely. Saddam squandered his military potential, in large measure because he consistently underestimated the Coalition's will to fight and capacity to deliver the kind of swift and crushing military defeat that marked Desert Storm. To be sure, before August 2, 1990, Saddam had little reason to expect any meaningful U.S. military response to his invasion of Kuwait; as discussed in Chapter 2, preinvasion U.S. policy toward Iraq if anything encouraged Saddam to believe that he could get away with it. Once, however, U.S. and allied troops began arriving in Saudi Arabia, and certainly after the White House's announcement on November 8, 1990 that it was doubling U.S. troop deployments for a possible re-invasion of Kuwait, Saddam had good reasons to reconsider his options.

Saddam was certainly not the first aspiring Third World hegemon to be surprised by America's unpredictability. The North Koreans and the Chinese were clearly taken aback by the Truman administration's decision to commit U.S. military power and prestige to South Korea's defense in the summer of 1950; only months before, Secretary of State Dean Acheson had publicly excluded Korea from America's defense perimeter in Asia, reflecting an assessment by the Joint Chiefs of Staff (and shared by General Douglas MacArthur) that Korea was a strategic liability.[208] Fifteen years later, the North Vietnamese also had little reason to expect that their campaign to subvert South Vietnam would provoke the American response that it did; President Lyndon Johnson had, after all, campaigned in the 1964 election against "sending American boys to fight a war that should be fought by Asian boys."[209] But the very facts of American behavior in Korea and Vietnam and frequent U.S. declarations in the 1970s and 1980s of oil as a vital interest in the Persian Gulf might have had a cautionary effect on a more cognizant and wordly leadership in Baghdad.

Nor was Saddam America's first strategically incompetent adversary. Underestimation of American resolve and capacity, and an excess of imperial ambitions over the economic and military wherewithal to support them characterized Wilhelmine and Nazi Germany as well as imperial Japan.[210] All three adversaries entered war with the United States questioning America's moral fiber, capacity for national unity, and military professionalism; and all three took on coalitions of opponents, including the British Empire, Soviet Union (Russia), and the United States, whose crushing superiority in human and economic resources—and ultimately military power—in the end more than canceled out Japanese and especially German superiority at the operational level of warfare.[211]

Saddam's picture of the world was what he wanted it to be, in part because he knew so little about it, including the United States (of which his image may have been distorted by *The Godfather,* reportedly his favorite film, viewed ad nauseam), and in part because he surrounded himself with "advisers" either equally ignorant or afraid to tell him otherwise. As a CIA political psychologist testified before the House Armed Services Committee before Desert Storm:

> While he is psychologically in touch with reality, he is often politically out of touch with reality. Saddam's worldview is narrow and distorted, and he has scant experience out of the Arab world. . . . He is surrounded by sycophants, who are cowed by Saddam's well-founded reputation for brutality and are afraid to contradict him. He has ruthlessly eliminated perceived threats to his power and equates criticism with disloyalty. While Hussein is not psychotic, he has a strong paranoid orientation. He is ready for retaliation and, not without reason, sees himself as surrounded by enemies. But he ignores his role in creating those enemies, and righteously threatens his targets. The conspiracy theories he spins . . . genuinely reflect his paranoid mind-set.[212]

A poorly educated small-town thug, and later, a professional assassin, and finally, a "personality cult" dictator who fancied himself as a modern-day Saladin come to restore the Arab world to its lost glories, Saddam Hussein had practically no direct exposure to the non-Arab world other than a few ceremonial trips to Paris and Moscow; and given his paranoia and capacity for self-delusion, he probably would have rejected presentation of unpleasant facts as the product of conspiracy on the part of their messenger. It is more than coincidental that Saddam's two greatest foreign policy misjudgments—vis-à-vis Iran in 1980 and the United States in 1990—involved the reactions of non-Arab states. Even his trusted and well-traveled foreign minister, Tariq Aziz, served as little more than a Molotov-like conduit for Saddam's every wish and whim. Consider, for example, the following account of Saddam's refusal to accept positive proof of last-minute Coalition ground-force redeployments well to the west of prepared Iraqi defense positions along the Kuwait-Saudi border (i.e., General Schwarzkopf's "Hail Mary" play):

> On the eve of the ground campaign, the Iraqi foreign minister was shown clear evidence [in Moscow] of the [new Coalition] deployment in northern Saudi Arabia through updated Soviet satellite pictures taken hours before. . . . The Iraqi minister was extremely shocked as he received clear indications from Soviet military experts who did not mince words to explain the hopeless situation on the ground once the Coalition began to move. Beating a hasty path back to Baghdad, Tarek Aziz displayed the photographic evidence to his leader, urging him to act. But the latter waved off the military facts as a Soviet deception, in

concert with the Americans: he made no change in his dispositions at the front, nor did he move any other forces to bolster the defense in his rear. He simply opted to ignore the warning, playing exactly into the hands of his opponent.[213]

This episode is instructive. It forms as yet one more proof of Saddam's paranoia when confronted with unpleasant realities. The apparent unwillingness of Tariq Aziz to insist that his boss face reality is further testimony to the utter servility and fear that pervaded Iraq's decision-making process. More important, however, is the fact that firm evidence of General Schwarzkopf's decision to place the Coalition's main blow on the ground opposite the least defended approaches to Iraqi forces in Kuwait ought to have been anticipated by the Iraqi dictator, given his expressed belief in his interview with April Glaspie and elsewhere that the United States was unduly sensitive to casualties. It is clear in retrospect that Saddam expected that the Coalition offensive would be limited to two main thrusts, one along Kuwait's coastline and the other up the Wadi al-Batin that forms the border between Kuwait and Iraq, and that he deployed his forces accordingly.[214] For example, of the forty-two Iraqi divisions deployed in the KTO, as many as eleven, including four armored and mechanized infantry divisions, were effectively removed from combat because they were positioned along Kuwait's coast in anticipation of a U.S. Marine Corps amphibious assault that never came.[215]

But this vision of the Coalition's impending ground offensive, which would certainly have cost the Coalition far more blood than was actually spilled in the event, cannot be reconciled with Saddam's expressed view that it could not risk long casualty lists for domestic political reasons. If the Americans were, in fact, unable to stand much human pain on the battlefield, then why would they be so stupid as to choose the thickest Iraqi defenses for their *Schwerpunkt?* There has to be an explanation, of course, for this particular instance of disastrous misjudgment. Some have suggested that Saddam was so fixated on Kuwait proper that he could not imagine anything other than a frontal assault on the emirate.[216] Others have argued that Saddam deluded himself into believing that the Coalition ground forces were precluded from violating Iraqi territory for political reasons, perhaps because of Egyptian and Syrian concerns over participating in an operation in which Western forces entered another Arab state as hostile and potentially occupying powers.[217] Still others believe that Saddam was persuaded by his generals that the scope of a potential "left hook" of the size of Schwarzkopf's plan was logistically insupportable (as indeed it would have been for the logistically immature Iraqi army), or that in any event the desert floor in Iraq west of the Wadi al-Batin would not support movement of main battle tanks and other heavy equipment. This latter conclusion was an initial Coalition assumption until Schwarzkopf sent U.S. special operations teams to take soil samples, which showed that the ground was firm enough.[218]

Saddam's own invasion of Kuwait was certainly an unimaginative affair. Despite a crushing numerical superiority, no attempt was made to encircle the Kuwaiti army or to preempt the emirate's tiny air force on the ground. Accordingly, much of Kuwait's military managed to escape to Saudi Arabia, including up to seven thousand of its twenty thousand army troops, forty of fifty-three air force jet fighters, and most of the emirate's navy.[219] Moreover, Iraqi armored formations were directed to go straight through, rather than around, Kuwait City, where they got bogged down for a full three days; as a result, they did not reach the Saudi border until four days after the invasion began—a sorry rate of advance that revealed an incomprehension of the true potential of the armored forces.[220]

The fact nevertheless remains that Saddam Hussein, whose strategy for Kuwait's defense consisted mainly of inflicting as many Coalition casualties as possible, precisely because he understood the Coalition's sensitivity to them, apparently never asked himself the obvious question: if I were directing the Coalition's military operations and were charged with doing so with as few casualties as humanly possible, where would be the best place to attack? Ironically, the first part of the answer to that question was already staring him in the face: in the air, where the Coalition was pitting its single greatest comparative strength against Iraq in order to minimize its ground losses if and when a ground offensive became necessary.

What makes Saddam's blindness to a Coalition end-run around his right flank all the more remarkable is that most American military analysts who were openly speculating about General Schwarzkopf's likely ground campaign had reached the same conclusion: that the key to overturning Iraq's military position in Kuwait would be a *Schwerpunkt* somewhere against Iraq's open right flank—west of the Wadi al-Batin. Although few predicted how far west the "Hail Mary" would be, the imperative of casualty minimization and a quick and conclusive win ruled out restricting the Coalition offensive to frontal assaults on prepared Iraqi defenses inside Kuwait. For example, weeks before the ground offensive was launched, David C. Morrison, the *National Journal's* highly respected defense correspondent, wrote: "Among other elements, the Central Command's ground attack plan seems to entail a 'left hook' across the Saudi-Iraqi border, in an attempt to draw out the Republican Guards."[221] Dunnigan and Bay have commented that the "knowledgeable never doubted that there would be a major attack around the Allied left flank, and that was the textbook solution to the problem. . . . It was discussed openly in the Western media months before even the air war began."[222] And a postwar study of Operation Desert Storm observed that "the fact that the coalition would strike around the Iraqi right flank was a foregone conclusion to everyone except Saddam."[223] There was also ample precedent in military history, including the American Civil War: "Stonewall" Jackson's surprise appearance on the Union right flank at Chancellorsville.

Saddam's own lack of professional military experience, and the Iraqi military's lack of war-fighting experience relevant to the military challenges posed by the American-dominated Coalition, deprived both the dictator and his army of a capacity to comprehend the true military situation they faced. Moreover, the domination of the Iraqi government and military by a single, all-knowing personality, incapable of recognizing weakness or error except on the part of others, precluded the emergence of genuine professionalism within Iraqi military ranks. It suffocated the kind of initiative, flexibility, and innovation required to deal with democratic armies based on voluntary service, trust among officers and men, and an unpoliticized pursuit of military excellence for its own sake. As General Schwarzkopf noted of the Iraqi army even before Desert Storm, it was one in which "generals . . . are shot if they fail and shot if they succeed"[224]—hardly an atmosphere likely to produce Guderians, Rommels, or Pattons.

Paradoxically, Saddam's picture of the United States as a morally soft society preoccupied with material gain and pleasures, no longer tough enough to endure the kinds of sacrifices on behalf of overseas causes that it had made on behalf of preventing Indochina's Communization, was in some respects true. "No more Vietnams" has been a governing principle of post-Vietnam American foreign policy, and throughout the Persian Gulf crisis of 1990–91 President Bush repeatedly reassured the American people that another Vietnam would be avoided if military push came to shove against Iraq. What Saddam failed to grasp was that for Americans, the trauma of Vietnam was not a function of casualties alone—U.S. losses in World War II were more than seven times greater—but of the war's prolonged and indecisive character. Americans have always been willing to risk blood and treasure on behalf of clearly defined political and military objectives in combat against an unambiguous threat to their vital national interests. The threat in Vietnam was never as unambiguous and odious as that posed earlier by Hitler and imperial Japan, or later by Saddam and his invasion of Kuwait. Moreover, the Johnson administration never provided a clear and convincing definition of victory, and worse still pursued a gradualist strategy based on a then-chic (and pathetically erroneous) academic theory that held war to be first and foremost a form of discrete political communication rather than brute force aimed at demolishing the enemy's capacity or will to fight.

Saddam also seemed to credit neither America's political nor its military leadership with any capacity to learn from the mistakes of Vietnam. After the war, President Bush concluded that the Iraqi dictator "was still living back in the Vietnam days. He didn't know we had a different ball game on here, different levels of technology, a different military force, a different President."[225] The idea that U.S. political and military authorities, indolent and effete though they might be, could be capable of drawing lessons from Vietnam in order to avoid their repetition apparently escaped him. In fact, the Vietnam experience had not altogether deterred the United States from ever again using force in the Third World, but rather encouraged the country to devise political ways and military means of using force more effectively. Additionally, Saddam's invasion of Kuwait and the vulnerability of his conventional army to U.S. military power presented a situation that was everything Vietnam was not: a clear and morally despicable threat that could be overpowered at reasonable cost using a simple and attainable definition of victory.

General Schwarzkopf characterized Saddam Hussein as "neither a strategist nor is he schooled in the operational arts, nor is he a tactician, nor is he a general, nor is he a soldier. Other than that, he is a great military man"[226]—a judgment that was borne out in both the Iran-Iraq War and the Gulf War. The question, especially important for those charged with drawing lessons from the past in order to plan and fight better in the future, nevertheless remains: could a more intelligent, alert, and worldly leadership in Baghdad have done better against the Coalition? In the author's view the answer is unreservedly "yes." The fact that Saddam was a militarily (though not politically) incompetent generalissimo should not obscure the opportunities that were available to Iraq both to derail Desert Shield, and failing that, to make Desert Storm a most unpleasant affair for the Coalition. If Saddam failed to exploit those opportunities, an Iraqi Atatürk, Ben Bella, Ho Chi Minh, or Mao Zedong certainly would have.

THWARTING DESERT STORM

An Iraqi leadership more conscious of American power, purpose, and policy in the Persian Gulf—notably, its consistent and long-standing determination to prevent the region's domination by a single hostile power, be it the Soviet Union (throughout the Cold War), Iran (in the 1980s), or Iraq—could have thwarted an effective U.S. military response to Iraq's conquest of Kuwait. For example, Operation Desert Storm rested entirely on Operation Desert Shield. In turn, Desert Shield rested entirely on Saudi acquiescence to a huge Western force presence on its territory. Without abundant ground forces and land-based aviation, which only Saudi Arabia could host and support, there was no prospect of forcibly overturning Saddam's aggression.

That presence, however, was by no means a sure thing. Saudi Arabia had always resisted a visible U.S. force presence on its soil, and during those critical first few days following Iraq's occupation of Kuwait, the House of Saud was deeply divided over the issue of seeking U.S. military intervention. Crown Prince Abdul-Aziz opposed intervention,[227] and King Fahd's initial reluctance was overcome only after Secretary of Defense Cheney and General Schwarzkopf presented convincing U.S. satellite and other intelligence information suggesting that Iraqi forces were massing on the Saudi border for a possible invasion of the Kingdom itself—a prospect made all the more real by three apparently inadvertent Iraqi incursions across the Saudi border the day after the invasion (Baghdad apologized for the first, but not the rest).[228] The king's decision, made on August 6, was unprecedented, especially for an Arab country that had managed to avoid the clutches of European colonial empires. According to Prince Bandar, Saudi

Arabia's ambassador to the United States and a proponent of U.S. intervention, King Fahd declared to his American guests: "I never dreamt that we would have to ask for foreign forces to help us against an Arab brother. But Saddam did the unthinkable and therefore we had to do the unthinkable."[229]

The question remains whether Saddam could have achieved his objectives in Kuwait without frightening the Saudis into requesting U.S. intervention. As noted in Chapter 2, the Saudis were traditionally contemptuous of the Kuwaitis, and before August 2 shared Baghdad's anger at Kuwait's violation of its OPEC oil production quota. As also noted, Iraq's long-standing dispute with Kuwait centered on four other issues: unresolved borders; Kuwait's refusal to ease Iraq's access to the sea by selling or leasing the islands of Warbah and Bubiyan; Kuwait's alleged theft of oil from the Iraqi side of the shared Rumaila oil field; and Kuwait's refusal to write off loans made to Iraq during that country's long war with Iran.

Had Saddam been half as clever as Adolf Hitler in the late 1930s—another dictator he admires and to whom he has been compared—he might have considered a limited "Sudetenland" solution of the "problem" of Kuwait, rather than gobbling up the country in one fell swoop. Specifically, he could have restricted his invasion to the northern one-third of Kuwait's territory. This would have given him the islands of Warbah and Bubiyan, the entire Rumaila oil field, and all of the disputed border areas—and almost certainly would have cowed Kuwait's Sabah dynasty into forgiving past loans and obeying its OPEC quota.

It is also almost equally certain that a limited invasion, especially if accompanied by reassurances that no further aggression was contemplated, and by humane treatment of the relatively small number of Kuwaitis who inhabit the northern part of the country, would not have stampeded the Saudis into considering American military intervention. In any case, it is highly improbable that any American President could have mustered sufficient public, congressional, and international support for a military attempt to reverse a limited aggression that left most of Kuwait and its population untouched, and that posed no clear and immediate danger to Saudi Arabia.

In sum, by limiting his attack on Kuwait, Saddam Hussein not only could have achieved his main aims in that country, while at the same time preserving his burgeoning military power intact, but also could have aborted any chance of effective American intervention.

Even having taken all of Kuwait, however, Saddam could still have avoided Desert Storm, or at least raised its price in time and American blood and treasure to perhaps politically unacceptable levels. One of the mysteries of the Gulf War is why Saddam did not push right on into Saudi Arabia following his conquest of Kuwait—specifically, why he sat by passively for almost six months while the United States and its Coalition partners amassed overwhelming military power in Saudi Arabia. Whether he ever intended to do so, and was or was not deterred by the prospect of an

American response, is beside the point. The point is that an invasion of Saudi Arabia, or even Scud strikes on Saudi ports and airbases during the pre–Desert Storm U.S. buildup, would have greatly complicated an American response, and his failure to invade mystified many observers. Military analyst James Blackwell, monitoring the crisis for Washington's Center for Strategic and International Studies, later commented that "we could never figure out why Saddam stopped in Kuwait. Until the [U.S.] 24th Infantry and 1st Cavalry Divisions completed their moves into Saudi Arabia in late October, there were insufficient armored forces to prevent Saddam's massive armored forces from taking the Saudi oil fields."[230] General Schwarzkopf agreed: "Militarily, [a push into Saudi Arabia] would have been the course of action. The major miscalculation on the part of Saddam and his military is that they never thought that the Free World would care if Kuwait was taken."[231] The Pentagon's own postwar assessment concluded that a "successful Iraqi attack could have led rapidly to the occupation of Saudi Arabia's most significant oil-producing regions and the primary ports through which United States and Coalition forces would otherwise enter."[232]

Fear of an Iraqi move on Saudi Arabia formed the premise of Desert Shield, though the circumstantial evidence strongly suggests that Saddam had no such immediate or even distant intention. As noted, he did not expect his conquest of Kuwait to elicit a U.S. military response, and therefore had little reason to push across the Saudi border in force. Additionally, he may have had little confidence in his army's logistical ability to sustain a quick and long drive down the Saudi coast—a prudent assumption given the Iraqi army's ponderous "offensive" performance in combat against Iran and even against Kuwait. More important, at the end of the first week of Kuwait's invasion, Saddam began withdrawing all of his "elite" Republican Guard divisions back to positions deep inside Iraq; these divisions inevitably would have formed, as they did in Kuwait, the spearhead of any invasion of Saudi Arabia.[233] King Fahd initially did not believe his kingdom to be in danger, and as early as August 9 Pentagon spokesman Pete Williams declared that Iraqi forces in Kuwait "seem to be in a defensive posture."[234] At no time prior to August 2, 1990, did Saddam threaten Saudi Arabia, as he did Kuwait and the United Arab Emirates; on the contrary, Baghdad sought Riyadh's support and good offices in dealing with its dispute with Kuwait.

Evidently, Saddam Hussein believed that the United States could not bring itself actually to use force against him—that Desert Shield was a gigantic bluff aimed at scaring him out of Kuwait. After all, the White House had declared that initial U.S. deployments to Saudi Arabia were purely defensive, aimed at protecting the kingdom, and it was not until November 8, three months after Kuwait's fall, that President Bush announced a doubling of the deployment for possible offensive operations against Iraqi forces in Kuwait. Saddam appears not to have taken seriously the possibility that the growing Coalition ground forces in Saudi Arabia were aimed ultimately at throwing him out of Kuwait, which probably explains in part his refusal to launch early spoiling attacks against them.

It is generally conceded by military experts that during at least the first three or four weeks of August 1990, there was little standing in the way of an Iraqi thrust into Saudi Arabia's oil fields and down the coastal highway to the key Saudi ports of Jubail, Dammam, and Dhahran, through which subsequently flowed the great bulk of U.S. forces and their supplies. Saudi Arabia's small and inexperienced army was no match for its huge Iraqi counterpart, and early arriving U.S. forces, such as the 82nd Airborne Division, were simply too light in firepower and tactical mobility to have withstood an advance by the Iraqi army's thousands of tanks, armored personnel carriers, and heavy artillery pieces. Until the arrival of the U.S. 24th Mechanized Infantry and 1st Cavalry Divisions in October, even the employment of available Air Force and carrier-based air power, though capable of inflicting severe punishment, probably could not have stopped a determined Iraqi drive into Saudi Arabia.

Iraqi control of the Saudi Gulf coast from Khafji to Dhahran would have compelled U.S. forces to enter Saudi Arabia from the kingdom's operationally remote ports of Jiddah and Yanbu on the Red Sea, a confined body of water crowded with commercial traffic and geographically controlled at one end (the Bab-al-Mandeb Strait) by a country sympathetic to Iraq (Yemen). From Jiddah and Yanbu, also uncomfortably close to the religiously sensitive sites of Mecca and Medina, Coalition forces would then have been compelled to trek all the way across Saudi Arabia, a country almost the size of the Louisiana Purchase, via narrow mountain passes and hundreds of miles of open desert simply to reach Iraqi ground forces. More important, an attempted U.S. ejection of Iraqi forces entrenched in northeastern Saudi Arabia from Red Sea staging areas would have confronted the Bush administration with the one thing it had to avoid throughout the crisis: a protracted war with a possible large loss of American lives. From the very outset of the crisis, the administration recognized, as did Saddam Hussein, that critical public and congressional support for a military response to Iraqi transgressions could be fatally undermined by long casualty lists, which the "Red Sea" scenario might well have imposed. But Saddam remained inert.

In sum, if Saddam Hussein was too *incautious* to consider a limited move into *Kuwait* (but stupid enough not to have made sure that his troops stayed away from the Saudi border), he also was too *cautious* to consider a limited advance into *Saudi Arabia.* Such a move, while probably not deterring a U.S. military response, would have seriously prolonged and complicated it in a fashion that might have gravely undercut domestic American political support for the war.

Of course, by far the simplest way Saddam could have avoided the fury of Desert Storm would have been to retire his forces from Kuwait before the expiration of the United Nations deadline on January 15, 1991. As noted, the prospect of his doing so was the Bush administration's worst nightmare, since it would have left Saddam unpunished and his military power intact, including his disturbing chemical and nascent nuclear weapons capability. That Saddam chose not to withdraw voluntarily was probably attributable to the great amount of "face" he had invested in Kuwait's conquest, and a concomitant desire not to be seen to capitulate to Western demands without at least the show of a fight.

His resistance to any realistic diplomatic solutions was manifest in his rejection, both before and during Desert Storm, of repeated Soviet diplomatic initiatives designed to thwart a final military showdown with the Coalition, and later, to limit the damage to Iraq once hostilities commenced.[235] Though Moscow clearly was seeking to prevent a military humiliation of its former client—and, by extension, the reputation of Soviet arms, already badly tarnished by the Israeli-Syrian conflict of 1982—Saddam Hussein remained suspicious of a Soviet Union that was collaborating with the United States in supporting U.N. resolutions condemning Iraq and calling for its unconditional withdrawal from Kuwait—a Soviet Union increasingly dependent on American good will for a resolution of its mounting domestic crises. Like the Ayatollah Khomeini before him, Saddam regarded both Washington and Moscow as hostile centers of power conspiring against him. In so doing, however, he displayed a persistent lack of sound political judgment. Moscow was trying every means possible to extricate Saddam from certain military defeat, but Baghdad remained obdurate.

If considerations of prestige were at stake, there were also other reasons in Saddam's mind for "toughing out" the crisis. His own inflated self-esteem "as one of the great leaders of history, ranking himself with Nasser, Castro, Tito, Ho Chi Minh, and Mao Zedong,"[236] all of whom survived Western or Soviet challenges to their governance, may have encouraged him to believe that he and enough of his military power to ensure his political continuance could survive anything the Coalition might throw at him—a correct judgment, as an embarrassed Bush administration was later to learn. Saddam also clearly believed as, ironically, did much "expert" American opinion, that his forces in the KTO would put up more of a fight than they did. He, further, seemed convinced that the fragile political cohesion of the Coalition could not survive Israeli intervention in the Gulf War, which Saddam (and many others) expected to be the inevitable consequence of Iraqi Scud attacks on Israel.

Saddam also may have believed that if the war came and turned out badly, he could cut some kind of deal with the Coalition amounting to a less than unconditional surrender. As distorted as his worldview was, Saddam had repeatedly demonstrated a strong pragmatism when faced with extreme adversity. When confronted in 1975 with an Iranian-backed Kurdish rebellion that threatened to get out of hand, Saddam swallowed his pride and signed a treaty, the Algiers agreement, that acceded to the Shah's position of the disputed Shatt al-Arab waterway in exchange for Iranian withdrawal of support for the Kurds. Seven years later, when the Iran-Iraq

War was going badly for Baghdad, Saddam offered Teheran a unilateral cease-fire and a return to the status quo ante. And less than two weeks after his invasion of Kuwait, Saddam, seeking to avoid the possibility of a war on two fronts, cut his losses against Iran by capitulating to the Iranian position on every issue left unresolved by the Iran-Iraq cease-fire of 1988.

The author believes, however, that underlying all of these considerations was a bedrock conviction that the United States, in spite of its rhetorical and military posturing, did not have the political guts to use force against Iraq. Saddam's picture of the United States as an effete, Vietnam War–traumatized society, coupled with his misinterpretation of the vigorous public and congressional debate in the United States over the efficacy of sanctions and the utility of force as potentially fatal weaknesses that would carry over into hostilities with Iraq, seem to have persuaded him that no U.S. administration would dare risk the fate that befell the Johnson administration in Vietnam. If before August 2, 1990, the United States and its key Arab friends did not take seriously Saddam's thinly veiled threats vis-à-vis Kuwait, then after August 2, Baghdad seemed no more persuaded that the United States and its "artificial" Coalition allies meant military business. No other explanation can satisfactorily account for Saddam's "irrational" intractability right up to the launching of Desert Storm. A less intransigent and better informed dictator might have avoided Desert Storm by making enticing concessions before the U.N. deadline, concessions aimed at splitting Coalition ranks and playing to pro-sanctions audiences in the United States. But Saddam seemed determined to play the very role the White House wanted him to play: an idiot ogre.

Even after the Coalition air assault began, Saddam Hussein appeared convinced that the Coalition would seek to avoid offensive ground operations against Iraqi forces in the KTO. Apparently believing that his forces could ride out the Coalition's air campaign with enough fighting power left on the ground to inflict enough American loss of life to turn U.S. public and congressional opinion against the war, Saddam sought to goad the Coalition into an early ground offensive. Such was the common interpretation of the January 29, 1991, Iraqi ground attack on Khafji, an abandoned Saudi coastal town whose capture by Iraqi forces, Baghdad undoubtedly hoped, would provoke a broader Coalition counter attack that would draw it unwillingly deep into Iraqi positions inside Kuwait. General Schwarzkopf, however, was not provoked; the Iraqi attack was decimated by Coalition air and ground forces, and when Iraqi forces were driven out of Khafji, Coalition ground forces reverted to their pre-Khafji defensive posture until February 24, when General Schwarzkopf was ready to launch his hundred-hour ground offensive against Iraqi forces. By then, of course, many of those forces had been reduced by an additional three weeks of unremitting Coalition air bombardment to little more than leaderless lumps of confused and demoralized cannon-fodder.

Even with the onset of the ground war, Iraq nevertheless again surprised the Coalition by failing to do something the Coalition had expected and that unquestionably would have increased Coalition casualties: employ chemical weapons. Iraq's failure to do so continues to perplex many observers, as do other events, including the mysterious flight of over one hundred Iraqi military aircraft to Iran; Saddam's December 6, 1990, release of remaining Western hostages, whose positioning as human shields at key Coalition target sites in Iraq also would have raised the blood price of Desert Storm; his relatively humane treatment of Coalition prisoners of war (other than the first batch of captees, who were beaten and paraded on television); and the curious absence of Iraqi-inspired terrorist attacks on exposed Coalition targets in the Persian Gulf and abroad. Once war, especially the ground war, was joined, why did Saddam Hussein apparently abjure options that would have made the Coalition's task more difficult, and which he had previously shown no hesitation in employing against Iran and his own people?

With respect to Iraq's chemical weapons arsenal, opinion remains divided. Some claim that Iraq was deterred from using the weapons by public White House statements and leaflet drops on Iraqi forces in Kuwait threatening dire consequences, including war crimes trials for Iraqi commanders, and presumably the threat of nuclear retaliation (the U.S. cruiser *San Jacinto* on station in the Gulf was pointedly referred to as a "special weapons platform," traditional Pentagon jargon for nuclear weapons).[237] Others claim that the Iraqis were self-deterred by unfavorable winds, deterioration of the munitions during the months of the prewar embargo, and Iraqi forces' own lack of effective protection against chemical agents.[238] It also has been suggested that Iraqi field commanders lacked the authority to fire chemical munitions, and were victimized by disrupted lines of communication from Baghdad.[239]

The fact remains, however, that not a single Iraqi chemical shell, bomb, or other device was exploded during the entire forty-three-day Coalition campaign against Iraq, even though such munitions were available, including at least thirty chemical warheads ready to be used on Iraq's Scud missiles.[240] Nor was there a single major incident of Iraqi-directed terrorism against Coalition forces in the Persian Gulf or civilian targets outside the Gulf. To the author, this suggests that something more was at play than deterrence or practical difficulties. Specifically, the author is prepared to argue that Saddam's "restraint" with respect to chemical munitions and terrorism, and to his treatment of both Western "human shields" and POWs, was a calculated attempt to avoid provoking the Coalition into undertaking retaliatory military actions that would have jeopardized Saddam's postwar prospects for remaining in power in Baghdad. On January 3, 1991, in an almost forgotten interview with visiting French parliamentarian Michel Vanzelle, Saddam reportedly declared: "I know I am going to lose. . . . Shall I lose militarily or politically? I shall lose militarily."[241] Throughout the crisis, the dictator's personal actions seemed riveted entirely on political rather than military outcomes, and Saddam appeared utterly indifferent to the fate of his forces in the KTO, except for the politically critical Republican Guards. The view is reinforced by Saddam's proclamation of victory on February 26, even as his forces were being routed in Kuwait. The rhetoric of his proclamation, appealing to Iraqi pride in simply having survived a war with the overpowering and perfidious West, bespeaks a political image of invincibility, come what may, in very much the same way that Nasser sought to convert his own military disaster at Suez in 1956 into a domestic political triumph.

> The harvest in the mother of battles has succeeded. After we have harvested what we have harvested, the greater harvest and its yield will be in the time to come, and it will be much greater than what we have at present, in spite of what we have at present in terms of victory, dignity, and glory that was based on the sacrifices of a deep faith which is generous without any hesitation or fear. . . .
>
> Shout for victory, O brothers; shout for your victory and the victory of all honorable peoples. O Iraqis. You have fought thirty countries, and all the evil and the largest machine of war and destruction in the world that surrounds them. . . .
>
> The soldiers of faith have triumphed over the soldiers of wrong. O stalwart men. Your God is the one who granted you victory. . . .
>
> Victory is sweet with the help of God.[242]

The author believes that shortly before, during, or after the beginning of the air war on January 16, Saddam recognized the hopelessness of his position in Kuwait and decided to write off most of his forces there. Far more important to the megalomaniacal dictator was his personal and political survival—a goal for which in the past he had demonstrated a readiness to sacrifice important state interests and any number of his own people. However, once the war began, Saddam had to do two things to have any real chance of preserving his regime: he had to preserve as much of his military power as possible to defend his regime against inevitable postwar Kurdish and Shia uprisings. Second, he had to refrain from taking any actions that might provoke the U.S.-led Coalition into going beyond the U.N. mandate of liberating Kuwait. He could cut his losses in Kuwait, but he could not tolerate a U.S. advance on Baghdad, which almost certainly would have prompted his removal via a coup or direct Coalition action.

A desire to husband as much of his military power as possible could explain the transfer of Iraqi planes to Iran, in the hope that the Iranians would return them when the war was over. The strategy may also explain in part the Iraqi army's lethargy. Offensive ground action requires a great deal of movement, and almost anything Iraqi that moved on the ground in the KTO was promptly attacked by Coalition air forces. Whatever the number of Iraqi casualties in the KTO may have been, they would have been much higher if Saddam's forces had moved out of their fortified positions. Keeping the Americans from marching to Baghdad meant refraining from behavior that might incite them to abandon the U.N.-imposed political limits on Desert Storm. Clearly, blowing up American innocents abroad, gassing U.S. forces in Saudi Arabia, and torturing and murdering American POWs would have inflamed American public opinion, and could have provoked President Bush into issuing an on-to-Baghdad order.

It is testimony to Saddam's single-mindedness and his cunning pursuit of power and self-glorification, as well as to the White House's naivete and pathological fear of becoming "bogged down" in Iraq, that Saddam's Baathist regime continues to tyrannize Iraq today, having survived the most "successful" air campaign ever mounted and the swiftest and most lopsided ground offensive in modern military history. Saddam was clearly prepared to sacrifice most of his army in Kuwait as long as he retained sufficient postwar military power of his own to crush rebellious Shias and Kurds— conditions ironically promoted by an early cease-fire and administration unwillingness to stop Saddam's slaughter of the Shias and Kurds.

It goes without saying that had Saddam managed to marry his Scuds with nuclear warheads, he could have placed at extreme risk not only Coalition forces but also Saudi and Israeli cities. This raises the question of why he made his move on Kuwait before acquiring usable nuclear weapons. How close Saddam was to becoming a nuclear power in 1990 remains a matter of dispute, but as has been noted, postwar U.N. inspections have revealed that the scope of Iraq's nuclear program far exceeded prewar intelligence estimates, and many experts believe that on August 2, 1990, Iraq was perhaps only months away from having a nuclear weapon.

In retrospect, Saddam's timing of his invasion of Kuwait could not have been strategically worse, whatever the immediate considerations involved: *after* the Cold War's demise had eliminated the Soviet Union as a reliable Iraqi sponsor and freed crack U.S. forces in Europe for release to the Gulf, but *before* he had obtained nuclear capabilities that might have deterred U.S. military intervention, or more likely and specifically, a Saudi request for it, or at the very least made intervention a far more risky proposition.

In sum, a more worldly and strategically competent Iraqi leadership could in several ways have either derailed Desert Storm or significantly increased its costs. Fortunately for the United States and its allies, in Saddam Hussein they were dealing with a "military" leader with the prudence of Custer and the strategic grasp of Mussolini.

7

The Air War

THE COALITION AIR WAR against Iraq and Iraqi forces in Kuwait has been widely hailed as the most successful in history. It has also been cited as a conclusive vindication of the classic yet heretofore unfulfilled air power prophecy that an enemy state's will and capacity to wage war can be demolished by aerial bombardment alone.

For example, Colonel Dennis Drew, director of the Air Force's Airpower Research Institute, has declared that Desert Storm is "clear evidence to all doubters of air power" that "air power now dominates land warfare."[243] Lieutenant General Charles G. Boyd, commander of Air University, believes that Desert Storm has relegated the primary function of ground forces to that of "provid[ing] security for air forces," adding that the air campaign "dismantled the Iraqi armed forces and pretty much made [the Coalition ground offensive] a walkover."[244] Air Force Chief of Staff Merrill A. McPeak has claimed that the Gulf War "is the first time in history that a field army has been defeated by air power"[245] (which may come as a surprise to German survivors of the failed Ardennes offensive of 1944 and to North Vietnamese survivors of Hanoi's disastrous road-bound conventional "Easter" offensive of 1972). Secretary of Defense Cheney has called the Coalition air war "brilliantly orchestrated,"[246] and the Pentagon's own interim report on the war has also labeled it "the most discriminate in history."[247] *Air Force* magazine editor James W. Canan dubbed the campaign "unprecedented in its intensity, precision, and lethality. Never before in war had so many air forces worked together so well and with such telling effect."[248]

AN AIRMAN'S PARADISE

There is no question that air power's contribution to the outcome of the Gulf War, compared to the roles of Coalition ground and naval forces, far exceeded that in any other previous conflict. For the first thirty-nine of the war's forty-three days the Coalition relied almost exclusively on air power as a functional substitute for offensive ground operations. There was no "AirLand Battle," just a massive air assault; and the brevity and ease of the ground offensive, when it finally came, are an acknowledged product of the air campaign. Few would quarrel with General Powell's assessment, given on the eve of the hundred-hour Coalition ground assault:

Air power has been the decisive arm so far, and I expect it will be the decisive arm through the end of the campaign, even if ground and amphibious forces are added to the equation. If anything, I expect air power to be even more decisive in the days and weeks ahead.[249]

Indeed, air power, intelligently applied, could not have been anything other than decisive under the conditions in which it operated in the Persian Gulf in early 1991. During the Gulf War, Coalition air operations were little inhibited, as were air operations in World War II, Korea, and Vietnam, by inclement weather, "closed" terrain, long distances to targets, inaccurate munitions deliveries, fragmented employment of available air assets, politically delineated sanctuaries in enemy territory, civilian meddling in the planning and execution of air operations, enemy counter–air action and ground-based defenses, or enemy logistical and tactical behavior on the ground aimed at minimizing vulnerability to air attack. As Michael Armitage noted during the air campaign, it:

has been little inhibited by the kind of concerns that have limited other air campaigns during the past three decades or so. During the three Arab-Israel wars, for example, targets in or near cities were off-limits; in Korea the main Communist airfields were in sanctuary areas beyond the Yalu River; in Vietnam whole stretches of the north could not be attacked; while during the Falklands campaign, geography and the lack of resources combined to restrict the action to the island and the surrounding seas.[250]

One prominent air power proponent has even said of the Gulf War:

In reality that competent and professional use of force was not a war at all, but a brief, if intense, punishment of a third-rate power, using air power under nothing less than benign conditions. There were unique circumstances peculiar to that conflict characterized by unusually short basing distances, the absence of ground-to-air defenses, and no requirement to deal with an effective repelling air arm. Under these unwarlike circumstances, strategic bombers did attack tactical targets and tactical fighters engaged strategic targets—but this proves nothing beyond the flexibility of air power.[251]

The contrast with the air war in Vietnam certainly could not have been greater. However, those who believe that a Desert Storm–like air campaign against North Vietnam and Communist forces in the field could have quickly cowed Hanoi into submission—that civilian meddling and a gradualist approach to air power's application denied what otherwise would have been a decisive instrument of victory—fail to take into account the vastly different enemies and operational environments the United States faced in Indochina in the mid-1960s and in the Persian Gulf a quarter of a century later. Vietnam War historian George C. Herring has properly warned:

To jump to the conclusion . . . that the unrestricted use of American power could have produced victory in Vietnam at acceptable cost raises troubling questions. We can never know whether a bombing campaign of the sort advocated by the Joint Chiefs of Staff in Vietnam, and actually applied in the Gulf War, would have forced Hanoi to accept a settlement on U.S. terms, but there is ample reason to question whether it would have. The technology of 1991 was not available in 1965, and in any event North Vietnam was not vulnerable to air power in the way Iraq was vulnerable. The capacity of air power to cripple a preindustrial society was in fact quite limited. Even if the United States had destroyed the cities and industries of North Vietnam, there is considerable evidence to suggest that the Vietnamese were prepared to fight on, underground if necessary.[252]

Fifty years ago, no less an unregenerate air power prophet than Alexander de Seversky also questioned air power's utility against preindustrial societies. "Total war from the air against an undeveloped country or region," he wrote, "is well nigh futile; it is one of the curious features of the most modern weapon that it is especially effective against the most modern types of civilization."[253] In the wake of Desert Storm, claims that the Vietnam experience proved only that "air power can't do it all *if it isn't applied correctly*" should be approached with great caution.[254]

Iraq, of course, to say nothing of its forces marooned in Kuwait, presented a target array that would have made the Vietnam air war planners drool. Yet, notwithstanding the obvious facts of an air campaign that was both decisive and exquisitely planned and executed, and which inflicted remarkably few direct losses among Iraq's civilian population, the Coalition air war was not an unqualified success. Some of its features, moreover, have sparked considerable criticism.

Before discussing these matters, it is worthwhile to review the air campaign's scope. The campaign's brevity was in large measure offset by its intensity. According to Air Force and other authoritative sources,[255] a total of almost 2,800 U.S. and allied aircraft participated in the campaign, of which almost 1,680, or 60 percent, were combat aircraft (e.g., bombers, fighters, attack and electronic warfare aircraft). A total of about 111,500 sorties, or almost 2,600 per day, of all types were flown during the war, including 68,500 combat sorties. Of the latter, 8,000 were classified as offensive counterair, 9,600 as defensive counterair, 4,850 as suppression of enemy air defenses, 5,500 as close air support, 28,400 as interdiction, and 12,500 as strategic bombardment. The weight of munitions dropped totaled 88,500 tons, of which 6,250 were precision-guided. The air campaign's short duration and expenditure of munitions were among its more remarkable features. Air operations in World War II, Korea, and Vietnam lasted years, not weeks, and expended far greater amounts of ordnance. For example, compared to Desert Storm's total bomb tonnage of 88,500, Anglo-American air forces operating against European targets in World War

II dropped a total of 2.7 million tons of bombs. During the Korean War U.S. forces dropped 698,000 tons; and during the Vietnam War, a staggering 6,476,000, or seventy-four times the amount dropped on Iraq and Iraqi forces in the Kuwaiti theater of operations.[256] Even more noteworthy were Coalition air losses: only forty-five aircraft, or about one per day.[257] (The long, indecisive air war in Vietnam claimed a total of 3,700 U.S. Air Force, Navy, and Marine Corps fixed-wing aircraft of all types.)[258]

STRATEGIC VERSUS TACTICAL

Never in the history of air power has so much been accomplished so quickly and at so small a cost. Gauging the success of the Coalition air war, however, requires careful analysis of its military and political objectives. It further requires recognition that the Coalition waged two distinct air wars, each with different targets and different results. The first was a tactical campaign against Iraqi forces in the KTO and their lines of supply to Iraq proper. Targets included deployed Iraqi units, supply dumps, and bridges, roads, and rail lines connecting Iraq and the KTO.

The second was a strategic bombardment campaign aimed at Iraq's leadership itself (attacks on Saddam Hussein's known residences and command bunkers, key government ministries, and Baathist party, secret police, and Republican Guard headquarters); the leadership's ability to communicate to its people and military forces (attacks on telecommunications centers, command and control nodes, radio and television transmission facilities); and Iraq's military-industrial base, especially those components related to production of ballistic missiles and munitions of mass destruction (attacks on known Scud manufacturing facilities and chemical, biological, and nuclear weapons research and fabrication sites.) Also targeted, though under the rubric of shutting down the foundations of the Iraqi war machine, was the country's supporting economic infrastructure (attacks on electrical power generation plants, oil refineries, railroad marshaling yards, and other transportation targets). The Pentagon's postwar report on the conflict to the Congress declared the principal strategic "centers of gravity" in Iraq to be "the command and control and leadership of the Saddam Hussein regime," "Iraq's weapons of mass destruction capability," and "the various elements of the Republican Guards."[259] General Charles A. Horner, Desert Storm's overall air commander, has listed the strategic bombardment campaign's main objectives as to "isolate and incapacitate [the] Hussein regime," to "destroy Iraqi nuclear, biological, and chemical warfare capability," and to "eliminate Iraq's offensive military capability."[260]

The success of the tactical campaign was unqualified. Whatever questions may continue to surround the size of Iraqi deployments in the KTO and U.S. Central Command claims regarding them, there is no doubt that Coalition air forces decimated Iraqi forces in place and gravely compromised their lines of supply from Iraq. This is the virtually universal testimony of captured Iraqi soldiers of all ranks, who surrendered in droves at first contact with Coalition ground forces. Air power did, in fact, defeat a field army almost single-handedly, though significant Republican Guard elements did survive intact enough to fight another day.

The strategic bombardment campaign was another matter. Note already has been made of the air campaign's failure, for quite understandable reasons, to suppress fully Iraqi launches of Scud missiles—Saddam's only strategically significant weapons. Note also has been made of Saddam's continued governance of Iraq, along with the survival of his regime and much of his now-forbidden military-industrial infrastructure. Iraq's leadership, its ability to communicate, and its capacity to make enough war (e.g., against the Kurds) to stay in power and even to threaten Kuwait again remain intact, despite prewar U.S. convictions that Saddam could not politically survive the war that the Coalition was planning to wage against him. Even during the war, it is questionable whether Saddam's ability to communicate with his forces was effectively severed—or whether, had it been, what real difference it would have made, since it remains unclear whether Iraq forces in the KTO had any operational instructions other than simply to stand fast and to scourge Kuwait before withdrawing. After the first week of the air war, General Colin Powell paid tribute to the resiliency of Iraqi military communications:

> With respect to their national command authority and their command and control systems, they are very good at this. They have redundant systems, resilient systems, they have work-arounds, they have alternatives, and they are still able to command their forces. They have not lost command and control of their forces or of the country. . . ."[261]

Moreover, barring the dictator's untimely demise (always a possibility, even before the war) or the unlikely ability of the U.N. to maintain indefinitely a level of economic strangulation of Iraq's economy precluding any meaningful recovery, the world can look forward to the possibility of a Saddam militarily resurgent and lusting for revenge against his tormentors. Strategic bombardment no more dislodged the Iraqi regime than it did Hitler's, Kim Il Sung's, or Ho Chi Minh's.

The imperviousness of the Iraqi regime and much of its most disturbing military paraphernalia to strategic air assault has embarrassed Air Force spokesmen, including Chief of Staff McPeak, into suggesting that eliminating Iraq's political leadership and mass destruction weapons capability were never really U.S. war aims, which they say never went beyond Kuwait's liberation—notwithstanding repeated wartime White House, Defense Department, and U.S. Central Command statements to the contrary.[262] Indeed, the air war against Iraq proper disappoints the central claim that has been made on behalf of strategic bombardment since the 1920s, and that continues to command widespread currency within some U.S. Air Force circles today. Almost from its very inception the Air Force has been captivated by the idea that air power, specifically strategic bombardment, is capable of winning wars with little if any assistance from surface forces. As the Italian Giulio Douhet, American "Billy" Mitchell, and other early air power prophets argued, an enemy state's military forces in the field could be defeated indirectly by flying over them to strike directly at the political leadership that commanded those forces and the economic activity that sustained them.[263] Aerial bombardment–induced economic paralysis would quickly erode both the will and capacity of the enemy state to fight on; supplies would dry up for its military forces, and popular discontent and even rebellion would bring down the government or compel it to sue for peace.

This was the theory with which the U.S. Army Air Forces entered World War II, and that formed the basis for the USAAF's planning and execution of the strategic bombardment of Germany. Throughout the conflict, which ended only when Germany had been overrun on the ground by Soviet and Anglo-American ground forces, those in charge of the strategic bombardment campaign fiercely resisted diversions of bomber forces to such "peripheral" tasks as supporting the invasions of North Africa and northwestern France, and attacking German V-1 and V-2 missile launch areas in the Low Countries, arguing that dissipation of bombardment resources impeded prospects for victory through air power alone. Faith in strategic bombardment as a potential war-winner survived not only World War II but also the equally contrary experiences of Korea and Vietnam, where, it was argued, potentially decisive applications of air power were wrongly subordinated to political considerations and, in the case of Vietnam, enervated by a gradualist approach to the use of force.[264]

Proponents of "victory through air power" thus saw the Gulf War as a unique and long-overdue opportunity to prove strategic bombardment's decisiveness, as well as to try out new stealthy aircraft and precision-guided ordnance. The enemy seemed unusually vulnerable to air attack, and the Air Force–dominated air campaign planning staff of the U.S. Central Command was given a relatively free hand to plan the air war as it saw fit—no sanctuaries, no constant meddling from Washington, no separate service campaigns; and there *was* a cornucopia of new stealthy aircraft, precision-guided munitions, and other advanced technologies.

The possibility exists, of course, that the Bush administration never intended to use too much force against Iraq—that it desired a continuation of strong central political authority in Baghdad, albeit without Saddam Hussein, and therefore encouraged a restrained strategic air campaign.[265] Baathist party headquarters at the regional level in Iraq were not targeted, nor were Republican Guard units around Baghdad and elsewhere outside the KTO. In fact, few, if any, of the twenty-two Iraqi army and Republican Guard divisions Saddam Hussein deliberately withheld from combat in the KTO, many of them deployed opposite Iraq's Syrian and Turkish borders, were attacked by Coalition forces.[266] Indeed, the haste with which the White House declared a cease-fire only one hundred hours into the ground war, and its subsequent refusal to assist Kurds and Shias rebelling against

Saddam Hussein, suggest a conviction that a central government of almost any stripe in Baghdad was preferable to Iraq's disintegration into a Lebanon writ large. This may account for the seeming lack of conviction with which some strategic targets were attacked. Some targets were attacked only once and just partially damaged, as if to warn Iraqi authorities of what Coalition air forces could do rather than what they were actually doing.

Air Force planners, especially those back in Washington, where planning was dominated by a conviction that air power could win the war virtually single-handedly, clearly favored placing the main effort into the strategic bombardment campaign, and resisted pressures for according top priority to the tactical campaign.[267] "The air force," writes Norman Friedman, "decided that its most valuable contribution to war planning would be a strategic bombing campaign," and "hoped that a sufficiently intense strategic air campaign would win the war."[268] Initial air war plans coming out of Air Force Headquarters focused heavily on the strategic bombardment of Iraq at the expense of attacks on Iraqi forces in Kuwait and their supply lines—so much so that General Powell, General Schwarzkopf, and the latter's own Air Force subordinates insisted on revisions. General Schwarzkopf wanted major air operations against Iraqi forces in the KTO, especially Republican Guard divisions, from the first day of hostilities on, not as a later phase of operations to follow the strategic campaign.[269]

As it turned out, the Coalition had sufficient air power to conduct both the strategic and tactical air wars simultaneously. Air Force reluctance to be drawn into "peripheral" missions that might dilute the potency of the strategic campaign also was manifest in its initial refusal to deploy to Saudi Arabia the A-10 close air support "Warthog" and the JSTARS aircraft, designed to detect and "fix" enemy ground force movements. The A-10, foisted on an unenthusiastic Air Force by Congress in the 1970s, was built specifically to perform a mission long regarded by the Air Force as relatively unimportant. It could make no contribution to the strategic bombardment campaign, and might (and indeed did) prove so spectacular as a tank killer as to raise new congressional interest in building another close air support plane. Like the A-10, the JSTARS also threatened to direct resources and attention away from Iraq's bombardment. Fortunately for the Coalition, the A-10 and JSTARS were deployed to Saudi Arabia at General Schwarzkopf's insistence. The A-10's performance impressed General Horner, who later said, "I take back all the bad things I've ever said about the A-10. I love them. They're saving our asses."[270] Horner had reason to change his opinion. During Desert Storm, a total of 144 A-10s were credited with destroying almost 1,000 Iraqi tanks, over 900 artillery pieces, and 750 other vehicles.[271]

TARGETING THE IRAQI ECONOMY

If the strategic bombardment campaign "missed" Iraq's leadership and much of its military-industrial complex, it nevertheless inflicted great hardship on Iraq's civilian population, with whom the Coalition presumably was not at war. Air attacks paralyzed much of Iraq's economic infrastructure, which, unlike Saddam's chemical, biological, and nuclear weapons programs, was neither hidden nor hardened. Attacks on electrical power generation plants, oil refineries, commercial telephone exchanges, and those bridges, roads, and rail lines having no immediate bearing on Iraq's ability to fight in Kuwait might have occasioned less criticism had the tactical air campaign failed to isolate Iraqi forces in the KTO, or had air campaign planners, as in World War II, anticipated a long war. The potential for controversy was, of course, heightened by near-instantaneous commercial television coverage in Baghdad of the bombing's unintended effects. Desert Storm planners, however, anticipated a conflict lasting no more than one or two months—far too short a time for the indirect and delayed military consequences of attacks on economic infrastructure targets to take effect. They also could not have failed to foresee that Saddam Hussein would exploit every means available, including Cable News Network TV coverage, to portray the Coalition strategic air campaign as indiscriminate.

Why, then, was Iraq's economic infrastructure targeted? Ingrained doctrinal preferences stemming from persistent confidence in strategic bombardment's efficacy? A mirror imaging in Iraq of the attempted victory through air power against Germany in the 1940s, in which the German economy was savagely assaulted? Perhaps. But the evidence suggests at least two other reasons. The first was a desire to bring the war home to the Iraqi people, a desire certainly consistent with the objective of fomenting sufficient discontent inside and outside the Iraqi government to prompt Saddam's removal from power. The idea seems to have been not to kill Iraqi civilians outright—on the contrary, great care was taken to avoid unnecessary collateral damage in a discriminate approach (as we shall see below) that produced an historically unprecedented dearth of civilian deaths. Rather, the objective seems to have been to make Iraqi civilian life most inconvenient and frustrating; for example, the absence of electrical power forced many Iraqis to make do with candles and scarce kerosene, and eliminated tens of thousands of jobs and the income they brought home. Saddam Hussein had managed to shield his population from much of the Iran-Iraq War, in part because Iran lacked an effective air force and in part because of a policy of maintaining sufficient supplies of food, fuel, and consumer goods. This time, however, a taste of war, and perhaps even a recognition of Saddam's responsibility for it, would be forced upon all classes of Iraqi society. Yet the Iraqi people were not in a position to overthrow their government, and the history of strategic bombardment shows that deliberately irritating a people in no position to do anything other than sit at home and contemplate their hardship more often than not hardens public sentiment against the "aggressor" and for their own government, however detestable. The loss of electrical power, telephone service, and potable water may well have embarrassed Saddam Hussein before his people; clearly, the regime was incapable of protecting the population from the indirect effects of Coalition air attacks. But Saddam was simply not the kind of leader who dreaded the grass-roots public reaction that proponents of strategic bombing seem to have expected. After all, he had devoted virtually his entire political career to creating a system of government in which the opinion and fate of only one individual counted.

The second and more important reason was a desire for postwar leverage against Iraq. The Gulf War was not a total war; the Coalition did not seek to replace totalitarianism in Baghdad with democracy, and had no intention of occupying Iraq and imposing the kind of political revolution in Iraq's internal affairs that was dictated to the Japanese aboard the battleship *Missouri* in 1945. However, to ensure Iraq's compliance with the terms of the Coalition-imposed cease-fire, the Coalition needed to be in a position to exert strong economic leverage on Iraq in the form of a continued embargo whose effects were *deliberately accelerated* by wartime air attacks on Iraqi economic targets. Specifically, the Coalition wished to place the Iraqi economy in a position where recovery was impossible without the Coalition's permission and assistance. This could be accomplished without utterly demolishing those targets, which would have denied any timely economic recovery and invited great international criticism, but rather by damaging them enough to render them dysfunctional but repairable. This scheme has been both openly and privately acknowledged by key planners of the Coalition air war, with whom the author has discussed the matter. Colonel John A. Warden III, a major architect of the air war and author of an influential book extolling the virtues of strategic bombardment,[272] told the *Washington Post* after the war the reason behind Coalition attacks on Iraq's electrical power sources:

> Saddam Hussein cannot restore his own electricity. He needs help. If there are political objectives that the U.N. coalition has, it can say, "Saddam, when you agree to do these things, we will allow people to come in and fix your electricity." It gives us long-term leverage.[273]

Another Air Force planner put it this way:

> We wanted to let the [Iraqi] people know, "Get rid of this guy and we'll be more than happy to assist in rebuilding. We're not going to tolerate Saddam Hussein or his regime. Fix that, and we'll fix your electricity."[274]

Like the prewar economic embargo of Iraq, however, deprivation induced by air attacks on the country's economic infrastructure continues to fall first and most heavily on the most helpless and politically inconsequential segments of Iraqi society, and in the case of Saddam Hussein and his gang of murderous thugs, on a regime morally indifferent to popular suffering. Cynical use of that suffering to gain sorrow and sympathy from the international community was evident in Baghdad's release of videotapes of sick and malnourished children, of harvests failed because of powerless irrigation systems, and of raw sewage in waters where many Iraqis have been forced to drink and bathe. The very people with whom the United States said it had no quarrel paid the heaviest price for the behavior of a regime once believed incapable of surviving the very strategic bombardment campaign whose most lasting effects have been nonmilitary in nature. Air power expert Roy Braybrook has written:

> ... it was clearly right to give the military the freedom needed to minimize their own casualties. However, as the air offensive continued, it became increasingly clear that air power was being used, not only to attack Iraqi forces, weapons production facilities, oil refineries, and surface lines of communication, but also in an attempt to make life unbearable for the civil population. . . . The result was obviously far short of total war, since all reasonable efforts were made to avoid civilian casualties. Nonetheless, the loss of civilian facilities such as electricity, water supplies and sanitation did not fit comfortably with the declared policy of having no argument with the Iraqi people.[275]

Indeed, the wartime image of a clean, surgical application of air power, remarkable for its avoidance of significant collateral damage, excludes delayed postwar deaths and debilities stemming indirectly from attacks on Iraq's economic infrastructure, as well as Iraqis killed and injured directly by Coalition bombs during the war. The number of civilians killed directly by Coalition bombs was by most accounts remarkably small, given the air campaign's scope and intensity. The absence of high levels of collateral damage was attributable largely to stringent rules of engagement designed to minimize unwanted casualties, exclusive reliance on precision-guided munitions in the Baghdad area, the absence of civilian populations around many targets, and the superb training and discipline of Coalition pilots. The Iraqi government has declared that 2,278 Iraqi civilians were killed by the Coalition air war, a figure that Greenpeace expert William Arkin, who personally surveyed many bombed sites in Iraq shortly after the war, believes is substantially correct.[276] Middle East Watch, a human rights organization that also conducted its own survey, estimated the upper limit of Iraqi civilian dead at between 2,500 and 3,000.[277] Unofficial Air Force estimates provided privately to the author range from 1,500 to 2,000. Other observers who toured Baghdad and other Iraqi cities were also impressed by the paucity of collateral damage. "What struck me most," wrote Joost Hiltermann, a Dutch sociologist who visited Iraq right after the war on behalf of Physicians for Human Rights, "was how little damage allied air raids had actually caused to civilian areas, relative to the amount of bombs said to have been dropped. Especially in Baghdad, the bombing was eerily precise."[278]

Visual impressions were deceptive, however, because precision strikes on economic targets had delayed consequences for Iraqi agriculture, heavily dependent on electric and gasoline-powered irrigation pumps, tractors, combines, etc.; water purification facilities, all of them electrically powered;

motor transportation; and other key life-supporting functions. As Gregg Easterbrook has observed:

> ... the very conscientiousness of American pilots in avoiding indiscriminate bombing backfired in one respect on the citizens of Iraq. Because bombing accuracy has always been poor, in previous wars attempts to destroy economic targets such as bridges, power plants, and refineries have never met expectations. In Desert Storm, the bombs finally hit home. Accurate weapons have moral advantages over the older kind; far fewer civilian deaths are caused. Yet all Iraqi citizens will suffer for years to come from the precision with which coalition pilots smashed their infrastructure.[279]

CONSEQUENCES

The consequences of Coalition air attacks on Iraq's infrastructure, which critics believe clearly exceeded any conception of "military necessity" in a war which Coalition planners expected would last no more than sixty days, were detailed in a comprehensive United Nations report based on an immediate postwar survey of conditions in Iraq. The so-called Ahtisaari Report, which focused on food and agriculture; water, sanitation, and health; transportation, communications, and energy; and refugees and other vulnerable groups, prefaced its conclusions with the following declaration:

> [N]othing that we had seen or heard had quite prepared us for the particular form of destruction which has befallen the country. The recent conflict has wrought near-apocalyptic results upon the economic infrastructure of what had been, until January 1991, a rather highly urbanized and mechanized society. Now, most means of modern life support have been destroyed or rendered tenuous. Iraq has, for some time to come, been relegated to a preindustrial age, but with all the disabilities of postindustrial dependency on an intensive use of energy and technology.[280]

There are, of course, no accurate figures on the number of Iraqi noncombatants who died as a result of malnutrition, disease, and inadequate medicines and medical services induced by the Coalition's air assault on Iraqi economic targets. The Harvard Study Team Report estimated that infant and child mortality would increase by 100 percent during the first year following the cease-fire, or by some 70,000, as a result of gastroenteritis, cholera, typhoid, and malnutrition, and many thousands more aged and infirm Iraqis almost certainly succumbed to the same causes.[281] Greenpeace expert William Arkin estimated a total of 100,000 extra deaths in the first twelve months, tapering off sharply as Iraq began to recover.[282]

Whatever the actual number, however, a clear contradiction existed between, on the one hand, official U.S. declarations that "we bear no animus toward the Iraqi people who have suffered too long under a brutal regime," and on the other, the combination of a Coalition strategic bombardment campaign encompassing militarily inconsequential economic targets and postwar "sanctions [that] will continue as long as the ruthless dictator Saddam Hussein remains in power."[283] Even if it were fair to pursue a policy described by Robert Gates as one in which "Iraqis will pay the price while [Saddam] is in power,"[284] the fact that the dictator remains in power, and continues to defy the Coalition, suggests that the policy has failed and that alternatives should be examined, ranging from lifting the embargo to renewed military action to covert operations aimed directly at Saddam himself.

As was the case in World War II, Korea, and Vietnam, the Gulf War (again) calls into question the utility of strategic bombardment as a means of cowing or bringing down a determined and ruthless totalitarian regime. Strategic bombardment campaigns (and embargoes) can and have wrecked economies, but wrecking economies is not tantamount to wrecking regimes. In any event wrecked economies impose levels of human suffering and deprivation that, in conflicts short of total war, undercut moral claims of discrimination between enemy armies and noncombatant civilian populations.

Yet whatever the failures of the strategic bombardment campaign, there is no question that air power, broadly defined to include both land-based and sea-based tactical combat and support operations, came far closer to winning a war single-handedly than in any previous conflict in air power's history. The tactical air war isolated Iraqi forces in Kuwait and pummeled many units into zombie-like incoherence. By the time the Coalition ground offensive began, the four highways and one rail line linking those forces to supplies from Iraq proper had been all but obliterated, with a resulting decrease in supplies from twenty thousand to two thousand tons a day—barely enough for subsistence.[285] The limited nature of the Coalition's primary operational objective (Kuwait's liberation), an abundance of resources, and the enemy's unusual vulnerability to air attack all joined to guarantee air power's decisiveness. Coalition ground forces, so it seemed, were needed for just a few days of mopping up bomb-shocked Iraqi forces in Kuwait.

Coalition ground forces did indeed play a supporting role in the main event—the air campaign. It must, however, be recognized, especially by those now wont to declare air power the dominant form of warfare, that ground forces proved strategically indispensable to the Coalition's ability to undertake a decisive air campaign. Early in the crisis, long before U.S. and allied ground forces arrived in Saudi Arabia in sufficient strength for offensive operations, some impatient warhawks in the United States were calling for the immediate initiation of the air war. Such calls never received serious official consideration, and for a very good reason: a premature air offensive could have provoked Saddam Hussein into a ground invasion of Saudi Arabia that would have threatened the very Saudi ports and air bases upon which Desert Storm's indispensable precursor, Desert Shield, depended. Coalition ground forces of a size and caliber able to protect Saudi Arabia were required to prevent Saddam from playing his single strongest comparative advantage over the Coalition in the first months of the crisis—numerically superior Iraqi ground forces perilously close to vital Coalition facilities. Thus Coalition ground forces provided the critical shield from behind which Coalition air power could operate without fear of disruptive enemy surface attacks. They deterred Saddam from having even first thoughts about exploiting an initial and glaring Coalition vulnerability.

Moreover, Iraqi forces in the KTO, notwithstanding almost six weeks of relentless pounding from the air, did not abandon Kuwait until they saw Coalition ground forces advancing directly against them. This suggests that the Coalition's demonstrated ability and willingness to take territory, especially to place 100,000 troops on a broad front 90 by 300 miles inside Iraq,[286] and not its capacity to bomb territory, was the straw that broke the camel's back. The Gulf War was, after all, about territory, and Saddam Hussein's nineteenth-century preoccupation with territory, and concomitant preoccupation with ground warfare and events on the ground at the expense of any appreciation of modern air and naval power, were manifest throughout his behavior in both the Persian Gulf crisis of 1990–91 and the Iran-Iraq War of 1980–88. The commitment of ground forces to battle carries with it a degree of political seriousness and sense of finality that air and naval forces cannot convey, especially to Third World opponents accustomed to viewing warfare in largely one-dimensional terms. Thus the Coalition's ground offensive, brief though it was, was probably politically decisive. Not until the third day of the Coalition ground offensive did Saddam finally make the political decision that had eluded the Coalition throughout the preceding air war: unconditional withdrawal from Kuwait. For Saddam, ground forces and the taking (or losing) of territory constituted the only politically meaningful military currency. His behavior suggested a willingness to permit the aerial decimation of his forces in the KTO, most of which were "throw-away" infantry divisions composed largely of disaffected Shias and Kurds—but an unwillingness to risk the consequences of a Coalition ground advance deep into Iraqi territory, possibly to Baghdad, which threatened his own political and personal survival.

THE OTHER SERVICES

If the air war's domination of Coalition military operations suggested to many air power proponents a military revolution portending future relegation of surface forces to supporting roles (i.e., ground-helps-air displaces air-helps-ground), it also breathed new life into the long-standing Air Force–Navy debate over the relative strengths and weakness of land-based versus sea-based aviation. Desert Storm was in many respects an unpleasant experience for the Navy. Until the Gulf crisis of 1990–91, the Navy had served as America's primary instrument of force in the region because of universal Gulf state refusal to permit the presence of U.S. Army and Air Force combat forces on their territory. The Persian Gulf, even during America's undeclared war against Iran during the latter half of the 1980s, was a "Navy–Marine Corps theater of operations" by political default.

Saudi Arabia's agreement in August 1990 to host huge U.S. and other foreign combat forces on its soil, however, quickly reduced the Navy to a supporting actor on a stage increasingly dominated by the Air Force and Army. Moreover, Desert Storm underscored the inherent limitations of carrier-based aviation as well as specific weaknesses in U.S. carrier operations. Though the Navy deployed a total of six carrier battle groups for Desert Storm—the most it had ever maintained on station in a shooting war since World War II—its contribution to both the strategic and tactical air campaigns was greatly overshadowed by the Air Force, which had not only a lot more aircraft of all types in the theater (1,400 versus 445 for the Navy),[287] but also an even larger edge in offensive strike aircraft, heavy bombs, and precision-guided munitions.[288] Generally speaking, naval aircraft, because they are compelled to operate from small flight decks and to endure the shock of catapult launches and mechanically arrested landings, lack the range and payload of land-based planes, whose size is comparatively unlimited (only long runways ashore can accommodate heavy bombers, large tankers, and big transport aircraft). Moreover, because the carrier battle group relies on its own aircraft to defend itself from enemy air, missile, and submarine attack, threats which the Soviets sought to maximize down to the very eve of Desert Storm, the Navy traditionally has chosen to devote 50–60 percent of the group's complement of aircraft to perform such defensive missions as fleet air defense and antisubmarine warfare. This, of course, reduces the number of available aircraft designed for the kind of air-to-surface strike missions that dominated the Coalition air war.

Worse still for the Navy, it entered the Gulf War having failed to replace its Vietnam-era premier strike aircraft, the A-6 Intruder; it also lacked stealthy aircraft like the Air Force's F-117A, and had but a fraction of the kind of Air Force heavy and precision-guided ordnance that proved indispensable to destroying such key Iraqi targets as telecommunications centers in urban areas and hardened aircraft shelters and ammunition bunkers. The positioning of most carriers in the distant Red Sea and central and southern Persian Gulf, farther away from Iraqi targets than many Saudi air bases used by Air Force units, exacerbated the penalties of carrier aircraft's limited range. This weakness was overcome only by heavy reliance on Air Force tankers for in-flight refueling, without which naval aviation would have played a marginal role in Desert Storm.[289] In many respects, including dependency on Air Force tankers and the Air Force's domination of the air campaign's planning and assignment of targets among the various services and allied air forces, U.S. naval aviation performed at the sufferance of its larger, land-based counterpart.

Yet defenders of carrier-based air power are quite correct in pointing out the singularity of the Gulf War, in terms of the political availability of one of the finest network of air bases to be found anywhere overseas, especially outside Europe and Northeast Asia. What would the Air Force have done, they ask, had Saudi Arabia said "no" to the deployment of U.S. combat forces on its territory? Such a Saudi refusal, particularly if accompanied by similar decisions on the part of the other Gulf states and Turkey, would have left the Navy carriers as the principal arm of any air war against Iraq. Under the circumstances, the Air Force's contribution would have been restricted largely to long-range strikes by B-52 and F-111 bombers operating at great distances from outside the theater—from Diego Garcia and bases in Europe and even the United States. The result would have been an air campaign of far less intensity and much longer duration to achieve the same results—a probably indecisive air war portending a politically unattractive protracted war, and probably one also of greater collateral damage, given the absence of F-117As and primary B-52 reliance on unguided "dumb" bombs.

U.S. air power entered the Gulf War determined to prove its real capabilities, which for a variety of reasons were hobbled in Vietnam. Were those capabilities reaffirmed in the Gulf? As one looks back on air power's history, one can only conclude that it was militarily decisive in the Gulf in 1991, but that its decisiveness in Desert Storm was exceptional, perhaps never again to be repeated, unless one presumes that the United States will again be lucky enough to pick a fight with a country so naked to air power as was Iraq and that future adversaries will have learned nothing from Iraq's experience. To be sure, there is, as Harry Summers has noted, "almost complete agreement on the critical role of air forces in support of ground operations, either through close air support or through interdiction of the enemy's lines of supply and communications." But, he adds, "after all these years, we are still on square one. There is no disagreement on the importance of the air war, but considerable disagreement continues over whether in and of itself air power could have been decisive."[290]

Indeed, those now wont to see in Desert Storm an imperative for all the services to change their doctrine to reflect air power's domination of all surface operations[291] need to recognize the particular political salience of ground forces as a tool of compellence against Third World leaderships who refuse to recognize air power's "decisiveness." They also need to concede strategic bombardment's failure, notwithstanding Desert Storm's ideal conditions, to destroy or even paralyze the institutional foundations of Saddam Hussein's political domination of Iraq and Iraqi military forces. To be sure, air power's relative contribution to the outcome of conventional U.S. military operations against conventional forces is likely to grow, especially in terms of its ability to create conditions for success on the ground. But as Mark Clodfelter has wisely cautioned, "the Gulf War offers no blueprint guaranteeing a successful application of air power in the future" because the combination of a fragmented, semi-industrialized, Third World enemy waging conventional war with Soviet equipment in a desert environment and being led by an international pariah who personally made all key military decisions and relied on an intricate command and control network for their implementation is unlikely to recur.[292]

Among other things, the Air Force cannot count on facing another "Iraq," or on the kind of freedom of action it enjoyed in the Gulf. Those in charge of the air war against Iraq were accorded unprecedented operational latitude in planning and carrying out the air campaign, presumably vindicating both a "lesson learned" from Vietnam as well as the reforms mandated by the Defense Reorganization Act of 1986. The evidence suggests, however, that contrary to officially sponsored impressions, U.S. civil-military relations during the Persian Gulf crisis were less than completely harmonious.

8

Of Presidents, Generals, and Service Rivalries

THE GULF WAR HAS been hailed as a model of what U.S. civil-military relations should be in a war-threatening crisis—a vindication of a great lesson learned from the Vietnam War, and of the wisdom of the Defense Reform Act of 1986 (also known as the Goldwater-Nicholas Act). This time, unlike the 1960s, there was no attempt to run every aspect of the war directly from Washington; no White House interference in day-to-day operational minutiae; no presidential or Pentagon meddling in the proper prerogatives of the commander on the scene; no splitting up military operations to satisfy parochial service "turf" demands; no presidentially imposed sanctuaries in enemy territory, other than standard proscription of attacks on civilian targets; no political barriers to reservists' call-up. And above all, there was no attempt to shackle the employment of military force to a gradualist strategy based on the notion of war as more a form of political communication than an act of violence. In the Gulf War, the President told the military what he wanted done, and then stayed out of the way while the generals decided how to do it, and then did it.

This rhapsodical image of harmony does not altogether square with reality. To be sure, the Gulf War, certainly when compared with the Vietnam War, was characterized by U.S. military operations relatively free of both micromanagement from Washington and debilitating interservice rivalry. The commander on the spot was given the resources he wanted, the time to deploy and exercise them, and the authority to overrule individual service pressures for bigger pieces of the action, such as Marine Corps pressure for an amphibious assault and Air Force argument for extending the air war in hopes of compelling an Iraqi capitulation without a Coalition ground offensive.[293] Air Force, Navy, and Marine Corps fixed-wing aviation, rather than being permitted to run their own separate air wars, were placed under a single air component commander, and operated from the same sheet of music in the form of a daily Air Tasking Order. Division and corps commanders were given mission-type orders and then granted wide latitude in pursuing them. And so on.

There was nonetheless much civil-military tension, as well as a startling lack of communication. For example, in late July 1990 the White House and

State Department overruled the reluctant Joint Chiefs of Staff to place a U.S. aircraft carrier (the *Independence*) in the Arabian Sea as a caution to Saddam Hussein against taking military action against Kuwait. In September, Secretary of Defense Cheney relieved Air Force Chief of Staff Michael J. Dugan, the first time a Secretary of Defense has fired a sitting service chief, because Dugan publicly (and presciently, as it turned out) affronted the other services, Secretary Cheney, and General Powell by suggesting that air power alone could win a war against Iraq virtually single-handedly. In February 1991, following the Air Force's bombing of a public bomb shelter in Baghdad thought to be a military command post, Cheney and Powell revoked the U.S. Central Command's authority to select strategic targets without clearance from Washington. Cheney and Powell previously had deleted other air war targets from CENTCOM's Baghdad list, including a giant statue of Saddam Hussein and a huge arch celebrating Iraq's victory over Iran in 1988. Then, of course, there was the matter of the cease-fire and its timing. President Bush wanted a cease-fire before General Schwarzkopf believed his military business was finished. There is also evidence of continual pre–Desert Storm Washington pressure on Schwarzkopf for unrealistic campaign plans, and for military action before he felt the Coalition was ready. Paradoxically, it can also be argued that in some respects Washington exercised too little supervision—e.g., in giving the Air Force a free run against Iraq's economic infrastructure.

ADVICE UNSOLICITED AND GIVEN NOT

But perhaps the most intriguing—and unsettling—aspect of the civil-military drama of the Gulf War was not what went on between Washington and Central Command Headquarters in Riyadh, but what went on between the Pentagon and the White House. The facts appear to be that President Bush early on in the crisis made up his mind on possible U.S. military action to eject Iraqi forces from Kuwait *without* bothering to canvass the opinion of his principal military adviser, the Chairman of the Joint Chiefs of Staff; and further, that General Powell, who apparently opposed a war with Iraq, did *not* offer the President the benefit of his professional counsel. So says Bob Woodward in his book *The Commanders,* [294] which remains undisputed by any of the principal Bush administration actors during the Gulf War, including Powell, Cheney, and Brent Scowcroft. A dovish Powell and James Baker, a hawkish Cheney and Scowcroft, and a bellicose Bush have emerged in other accounts of administration decision-making during the Persian Gulf crisis.[295]

According to Woodward, President Bush's public statement on August 5, 1990, three days after the invasion, that Iraq's aggression against Kuwait "will not stand," took Powell completely by surprise, because the "President had now clearly, categorically, set a new goal, not only to deter an attack on Saudi Arabia, but to reverse the invasion of Kuwait." The

Chairman of the Joint Chiefs of Staff "was stunned. He had not been consulted."[296] Woodward goes on to declare:

> There had been no NSC meeting, no debate. The Chairman could not understand why the President had laid down this new marker, changing radically the definition of success. . . . Reversing an invasion was probably the most difficult military task imaginable, and Powell, the number one military man, had been given no opportunity to offer his assessment.[297]

Powell endorsed a defense of Saudi Arabia, but had serious reservations about Kuwait's forcible liberation—perhaps because he, like many of his colleagues in uniform, was understandably preoccupied by unfolding events in Europe and a sharply declining defense budget, and regarded the world's "fourth largest army" with more respect than it deserved. Powell almost certainly assumed that the President would consult his senior military adviser before committing the United States to a possible military invasion of Kuwait. Even after the President's August 5 statement, however, the dutiful Powell did not confront the White House with his concerns as, perhaps, some of his predecessors might have (e.g., Admiral William Crowe).

All of this suggests the presence of strong practical limitations on legislative attempts to reform civil-military relations. The Goldwater-Nichols Bill did much to curb the pernicious effects of interservice rivalry, and straightened out lines of authority from Washington to commanders in the field. By increasing the power of the JCS Chairman and field commanders at the expense of the individual service chiefs, the legislation effectively removed the service chiefs from meddling in the planning and conduct of military operations; and by elevating the Chairman to the position of the President's senior military adviser, and granting the Chairman a powerful joint staff, the 1986 bill presumably improved the quality of military advice, which before 1986 all too often represented bland compromise among contending service chiefs.

There is broad agreement that Goldwater-Nichols was a key element of Desert Storm's success. House Armed Services Committee Chairman Les Aspin has fairly summed up the legislation's impact:

> The act gave new powers to the chairman of the Joint Chiefs of Staff. It made him the chief military adviser to the president. No more was he merely the committee chairman who brought the lowest common denominator opinion from the other chiefs. It also gave new authority to field commanders like General Schwarzkopf. No longer was it necessary to assign tasks among the services for parochial reasons. An operational commander could make the best uses of his resources regardless of service. It created one clear line of command, one integrated operational plan and one focal point for decisions on the ground.[298]

Aspin also has described the pre–Goldwater-Nichols era:

> Before Goldwater-Nichols, things were quite different. In Vietnam, we had two ground armies and four air forces, each with their own chain of command. In Desert One there was no single ground commander of the mission. There was an Army commander for the ground operation, a Marine in charge of Marine helicopters flying an unfamiliar mission and an Air Force commander, also on the ground in Iran. More recently, in Grenada, we had a tiny island divided into Army and Marine sectors. In Beirut, we had a serpentine line of command that . . . went from Washington to Brussels to Frankfurt to London to Naples to the task force afloat off Lebanon to the Marine unit in Beirut.[299]

This assessment is echoed by William J. Taylor and James Blackwell of the Center for Strategic and International Studies:

> For many years, theater commanders did not have adequate control over their forces, due to complicated chains of command that involved the individual services themselves. This organizational muddle was responsible for many of the operational problems that were experienced in the abortive attempt in 1980 to rescue Americans held hostage in Iran . . . , as well as in action in 1983 in Beirut and Grenada, for example. The 1986 Goldwater-Nichols Act addressed this problem by elevating the position of the Chairman of the Joint Chiefs of Staff and by placing full command of all forces in the field squarely under the Commander-in-Chief in the theater.
>
> In *Desert Shield* and *Desert Storm,* both General Colin Powell . . . and General Norman Schwarzkopf exercised this authority with tremendous effect. Given broad political guidance, General Powell made the basic decisions on what the objectives of the war were to be, the strategy to achieve them, and the forces that would be sent to the field to accomplish them. Gen. Schwarzkopf was given leeway to develop the operational plan, to decide on its execution, and to resolve any disagreements among air, sea and ground components as to which would have priority at different phases of the campaign.[300]

Larry Korb has noted the contrast with Vietnam:

> In Vietnam, General Westmoreland ran only the ground war in South Vietnam while the air campaign against North Vietnam was run by a navy admiral in Hawaii. Westmoreland could not even order Marine aviation units stationed in South Vietnam to support Army ground troops without getting all five members of the JCS in Washington to vote on the issue.[301]

It goes without saying, of course, that Goldwater-Nichols' effectiveness in war depends very much on the caliber of those individuals serving as JCS Chairman and field commanders. The new chairmanship in the hands of a

George McClellan, Douglas MacArthur, or Curtis LeMay is not a comforting thought; and jointness for its own sake could be counterproductive in situations not requiring the participation of more than one or two services. Goldwater-Nichols also might encourage Presidents to give too much leeway to military organizations and commanders in the field.

For better or worse, neither Goldwater-Nichols nor any other legislation can compel the President to seek military advice from the Chairman, or the Chairman to offer it—even in an overseas crisis involving high risk of war. The assumption of those who crafted Goldwater-Nichols seems to have been that Presidents will invariably seek military opinion from their senior advisers on any decision to risk war, and certainly on the conduct of military operations—as had Lincoln of Halleck and Grant, Wilson of Pershing, Roosevelt of Marshall, Truman of Bradley, and Johnson of Wheeler.

That Bush initially did not consult Powell is to condemn neither. Once the decision to dispatch U.S. troops to Saudi Arabia had been made, President Bush and Secretary Cheney relied heavily on Powell's counsel and on the military appreciations coming out of Central Command headquarters in Riyadh. Moreover, the war's outcome put to rest questions that Powell and others may have initially had about Desert Storm's feasibility. There is still something unsettling about this early lack of critical communication between a President and his senior military adviser on the vital issue of whether to place U.S. military forces in harm's way. Political considerations rightly should be paramount, but they should be disciplined by a clear knowledge of what is militarily possible, of probable costs and risks, knowledge that the Chairman is paid to convey to the President. Overruling military advice is one thing; not bothering to ask for it is quite another.

The case sets a bad precedent. Future crises may involve risks of war with truly competent opponents, and U.S. security interests will not be well served by a President who impulsively commits the country to the possibility of war, and only later seeks out professional military advice, perhaps to be surprised at how unpleasant that advice might be. Presidents can and have overruled their military advisers, with mixed results. Sometimes military advice has been bad (McClellan's to Lincoln), at other times superior to presidential judgment. For example, had President Reagan followed the unanimous opinion of his own Joint Chiefs of Staff, he would have refused to place U.S. forces ashore in Lebanon in 1982–84, and thus spared his administration and the country a major humiliation. Conversely, Harry Truman wisely resisted General Douglas MacArthur's call for an expansion of the Korean War.

Presumably, one of the lessons learned from Vietnam was the danger of ignoring military opinion on military matters. Many Presidents (e.g., Madison, Lincoln, Wilson) and even some Secretaries of Defense (e.g., Louis Johnson, Charles Wilson, Clark Clifford) come to office utterly ignorant of military affairs, which places a premium on both the quality of professional counsel and its routine solicitation.

CALLING THE WAR OFF

Moreover, as noted, just before Iraq's invasion of Kuwait the White House overruled Pentagon objections to sending the *Independence* to the mouth of the Gulf as a signal to Saddam. The Joint Chiefs of Staff argued, correctly, that such a show of token force would not impress the Iraqi dictator.[302] As for General Dugan's firing, which many observers regarded as motivated by an angered Powell and by Cheney's determination to preserve interservice harmony, there was little if anything in his *Washington Post* interview that would have opened Iraqi or other eyes to the probable outlines of a U.S. air campaign against Iraq.[303] That war, if it came, would begin with a preliminary air campaign whose targets would include Iraq's leadership and military-industrial complex, was predictable by anyone with a casual knowledge of the history of U.S. air power, or who viewed the parade of military experts holding forth on CNN and the major networks, including, later, retired General Dugan. Dugan's sacking appeared almost gratuitous, especially coming in the middle of a deployment crisis, and can hardly be said to have been evidence of civil-military harmony. The poor general had the temerity to suggest not only that air power would dominate any ground clash with Iraq, but also that Iraq's military was far less of a challenge than others in the Pentagon were making it out to be.

The aftermath of the Air Force's February 13, 1991, bombing of the Ameriyya air raid shelter in Baghdad reveals yet another example of civil-military tension during the Persian Gulf crisis. Whether or not the shelter was, in fact, as the Pentagon claimed, being used for military purposes in violation of the laws of war remains unanswerable. Postwar inspection of the shelter provided no hard evidence to support the Defense Department's judgment; the edifice was one of at least ten district public air raid shelters built to common specifications during the 1980s. The fact that it was camouflaged and ringed with barbed wire means little, since camouflage and wire are common characteristics of government structures of all types throughout Iraq.[304] In any event, even had the shelter been misused by the Iraqi military, the laws of war would have required prior U.S. notification to Baghdad of an intent to destroy it.[305]

The killing of several hundred Iraqi civilians in the Ameriyya shelter caused an international outcry, including protests in Jordan and other Arab countries.[306] Another such incident would have been politically intolerable, and CNN's coverage of the grisly carnage at the Ameriyya shelter played into Iraqi charges that the Air Force was conducting an indiscriminate bombing campaign. Understandably, therefore, Cheney and Powell moved quickly to ban further attacks on shelters, suspect or not, and asserted their authority from there on out to review the target list of each daily Air Tasking Order before the targets were attacked. Washington's reassertion of some measure of control over the strategic bombardment campaign was a far cry from the suffocating micromanagement of the Vietnam War, but it was testimony nonetheless to the possibility that at least one lesson of the Vietnam War had perhaps been "overlearned."

By far and away the most controversial incident of civil-military disharmony was the timing of President Bush's unilateral cease-fire—just one hundred hours after the Coalition's ground offensive commenced. General Schwarzkopf clearly wanted at least another day or two to completely seal off Iraqi forces remaining in the KTO, and to finish off remaining Republican Guard units in the theater. As he told David Frost in a television interview shortly after the cease-fire:

> Frankly, my recommendation had been, you know, to continue the march. I mean, we had them in a rout and could have continued to wreak great destruction on them. We could have completely closed the doors and made it in fact a battle of annihilation. . . . There were obviously a lot of people who escaped who wouldn't have escaped if the decision hadn't been made to stop where we were at that time.[307]

Schwarzkopf's views on when to cease fighting had been solicited not by President Bush, but rather by Powell, who may or may not have passed them on to the White House, and who may have been victimized by "too rosy" reports of the destruction of enemy forces in the KTO.[308]

It is certainly clear in retrospect that the cease-fire's timing permitted significant Iraqi forces to escape to fight another day. An estimated total of 700 Iraqi tanks, 1,430 armored personnel carriers, and about 110,000 Iraqi troops escaped the KTO back to Iraq, where they and their crews were then immediately reemployed to put down Shia uprisings in Basra and elsewhere in southern Iraq.[309] Of critical importance was the apparent escape of at least four Republican Guard divisions relatively intact—the Adnana, Nebuchadnezzar, Al Faw, 8th Special Forces, and part of the Hammurabi. Together with the capital-based, four-brigade Baghdad Division, which was never seriously bombed by Coalition air forces, these divisions formed the basis for Saddam's political and military staying power in the tumultuous months following the cease-fire.[310] Indeed, two days after President Bush ordered the cease-fire, the U.S. Army's 24th Mechanized Infantry Division collided with the Hammurabi Division, much of which was still intact as well as ignorant of the cease-fire. In the ensuing four-hour battle, the 24th took over 3,000 Iraqi prisoners and destroyed about 250 Iraqi tanks and armored fighting vehicles and 500 trucks and other wheeled vehicles.[311]

Schwarzkopf was not the only one who regarded the cease-fire as premature. The British government and British field commanders in the KTO also wished to continue pursuit of Iraqi forces, and had serious misgivings about what they regarded as unfinished business.[312] The Soviets, too, "appeared dumbfounded" that Bush ended the war so soon and let Saddam get away with much of his army intact.[313] General Barry McCaffrey, commander of the 24th Infantry Division, stated after the war: "Going to

Basra was easily within our grasp the next day [after the cease-fire], and we had plans to do so. The Republican Guard was crumbling. . . . All of our forces together were crushing them."[314] And one of the 24th's brigadier generals, Joe N. Frazar, offered this account:

> I don't know if we were surprised by the cease-fire, but maybe we had a question in our minds as to why we were stopping. From our perspective it seemed premature, but we did not have the whole picture. We had plenty of supplies and a good plan to get to Basra. We would have taken it. The 1st Infantry Division was closing in from the south. Two divisions were therefore poised and we were ready to go. We had a detailed plan for the capture of Basra, down to brigade and battalion level. We were going to cut it off, and leave the 101st and 82nd Airborne to sweep through the town. There were a couple of bridges to the north of Basra over which the Republican Guard were escaping. They were all boxed around Basra. As we had planned, we were pushing the battle to the enemy. Then it was called off. Obviously, if we had taken Iraq's second city, Basra, it would have had a significant impact.[315]

President Bush, however, who presumably had the whole picture, was determined to order a cease-fire after only one hundred hours of ground combat, and so ordered it, even though Baghdad had not requested a cessation of hostilities. Rarely in history has a victorious army unilaterally stopped fighting—*in the absence of any request for terms by the vanquished;* and a man with Saddam Hussein's mentality almost certainly interpreted Bush's haste in unilaterally calling off the war as a sign of weakness. Indeed, in a speech "celebrating" the first anniversary of Desert Storm's beginning, Saddam pointedly remarked: "It was George Bush with his own will who decided to stop the fighting. Nobody had asked him to do so."[316]

It is not altogether clear why President Bush was in such a hurry to call the war off. A number of reasons have been offered: fear of getting sucked into bloody street fighting in Basra; fear of being drawn into Iraq's impending civil war; fear of so decimating Iraq's remaining military forces as to endanger the survival of central political authority in Baghdad; deference to Saudi and Kuwaiti fears that further fighting would pave the way for a dreaded Shia takeover of Iraq; and concern that continued decimation of the Iraqi army would place Mikhail Gorbachev in a politically untenable position vis-à-vis Kremlin hard-liners.[317] The President also seems to have been concerned that images of overkill, of mass slaughter, such as television coverage of the Iraqi wreckage on the "Highway to Hell" leading out of Kuwait City, would tarnish victory's bloom and ricochet politically in the Congress and among America's Arab Coalition partners. Perhaps, despite Saddam Hussein's demonstrated capacity to survive seemingly overpowering internal and external challenges to his authority, the President also believed that this time, surely, he could not survive the terrible hand that the Coalition had already dealt him. Given these assumptions—and an utter moral indifference to the likely fate of rebellious Kurds and Shias inside Iraq—the prudent course of action was to suspend military operations once Kuwait had been liberated.

The President clearly did not wish for Iraq's disintegration into a giant Lebanon surrounded by neighbors—Syria, Iran, and Turkey—hostile and covetous of its territory. But what he got was a weakened Iraq still ruled by a defiant Saddam Hussein.

The most detailed account of the cease-fire decision appeared in an issue of *Newsweek* a year after Desert Storm was launched.[318] General Powell reportedly was eager to terminate the war as soon as possible, because he was under the erroneous impression that Iraqi forces in the KTO had been destroyed or effectively encircled, and he believed that it would be (in his words) "un-American and un-chivalrous" to continue the killing. The apparent slaughter along the "Highway to Hell" also reportedly had "a profound effect all the way up the chain of command," even though General Schwarzkopf "knew that [Iraqi escape] roads out of Basra . . . had not been blocked and . . . he told Powell this was so." Ironically, images of mass slaughter of Iraqi soldiers proved grossly misleading. Contrary to initial and highly suspect Defense Intelligence Agency estimates of up to 100,000 Iraqi troops killed in action in the KTO, more careful postwar analysis suggests that as few as 8,000 may have been killed.[319]

Whether allowing General Schwarzkopf a few more hours or days to continue his offensive would have decisively altered events in postwar Iraq will undoubtedly remain a matter of intense speculation for years to come, especially if Saddam manages again to become a major threat to the Persian Gulf's security. From a purely military standpoint, the early cease-fire was, however, a mistake, similar in effect to Hitler's famous "stop" order in 1940 to German armored forces on the verge of obliterating Anglo-French forces corraled with their backs to the Channel at Dunkirk—forces that escaped to England to fight another day. It was also politically unwise to evacuate U.S. forces from southeastern Iraq so hastily after the cease-fire. A continued U.S. force presence on Iraqi territory, within easy reach of Basra and the Shatt al-Arab, might have provided stronger leverage against Baghdad than the combination of the embargo's continuance and of unarmed U.N. inspection teams forced to play cat and mouse with a regime that continues to defy the Coalition. The argument that staying behind in Iraq would have entangled the United States indefinitely in Iraq's tumultuous internal political affairs is not persuasive. By virtue of the Coalition's victory over Iraqi forces in Kuwait, the survival of Saddam Hussein and his regime, and U.N. Security Council Resolution 687 (which in effect asserts Security Council sovereignty over Iraq's economic and defense decisions), the United States *is* and *will* remain deeply involved in Iraq's internal affairs, at least until a change of leadership comes in Baghdad. Moreover, those areas of Iraq occupied by U.S. forces at the war's end, while strategically critical to Iraq's future, were sparsely populated and therefore politically safe.

It is sad to say, given the magnificent performance of Coalition military forces during the war, that the decisions to call off the ground war so soon, and then to high-tail it out of southeastern Iraq, may have simply postponed a final Western reckoning with Baghdad—a reckoning, should it transpire, that will likely take place in far less favorable circumstances than those surrounding Desert Shield and Desert Storm. A few weeks after the war's end, a *Newsweek* editorial summed up the feelings of many:

> There's still relief at getting Saddam's forces out of Kuwait, and pride in the achievements of American forces. And the war clearly satisfied the primary goals: to restore Kuwaiti sovereignty and cripple Iraq's offensive capability. But on more sweeping war aims, both stated and unstated, President Bush's haste to go to war—and to wrap up Desert Storm quickly—has left an incomplete victory. . . . For all of Bush's disparagement of the "Vietnam Syndrome," he was influenced by two of its central tenets: that any long-term military involvement is a potential "quagmire" and that the Third World will inevitably view U.S. forces as occupiers.[320]

It was, of course, the President's prerogative to make the decisions he did, and it was General Schwarzkopf's duty to carry them out. The euphoria over an easy Coalition military victory and the widespread conviction that Saddam could not survive it heavily influenced both the White House and Central Command headquarters in Riyadh.

The fact nonetheless remains that U.S. civil-military relations during the Gulf crisis were far from blissful, and that while U.S. military operations against Iraq were mercifully free of the kind of debilitating meddling from Washington that characterized U.S. military performance in Vietnam, the Vietnam experience and Goldwater-Nichols may have encouraged too little White House attention to military planning and its potential consequences. Also, as noted, the strength of Goldwater-Nichols also rests heavily on the caliber of the JCS Chairman and the regional commander-in-chief; the legislation elevated the former's authority to a standing well above the level of *primus inter pares.* A chairman determined to run a distant war from Washington, to micromanage a theater commander, now has far more stature and authority to do so than he would have had before 1986. Conversely, the combination of an imperious, run-amok theater commander and a politically weak White House and Pentagon could produce the kind of civil military crisis that burgeoned during the Korean War's first ten months. Moreover, as the Gulf crisis revealed, the President can commit first to war's possibility and ask the hard military questions later, and no law can compel a JCS Chairman to speak his professional mind to his only client.

STILL THE SQUABBLING SERVICES

Goldwater-Nichols's enshrinement of jointness also has its downside. While mitigating the pernicious effects of interservice rivalry on the battlefield (assuming a strong theater commander), it may encourage jointness in situations where the participation of all four services is unnecessary and even harmful. Clearly, a military undertaking on the scale of the Korean and Vietnam conflicts, and of Desert Shield and Storm, which involved major prewar and combat operations ashore, afloat, and in the air, required significant contributions from all the services. On the other hand, smaller and more specialized hostile challenges to U.S. security interests overseas may not objectively demand more than a single- or two-service response. The attempt to liberate American hostages in Iran in 1980 should not have been an all-service venture; the invasion of the tiny island of Grenada in 1983 probably could have been more smoothly accomplished had it been left entirely to the two services—the Navy and the Marine Corps—whose experience in ship-to-shore operations against tiny islands remains unparalleled; it is far from certain that the limited, one-shot punitive air strikes on Libyan targets in 1986 mandated the employment of both Navy and Air Force aviation; and the 1989 invasion of Panama from land positions inside the Canal Zone itself made the participation of Marine Corps units superfluous.

Moreover, notwithstanding passage of Goldwater-Nichols, interservice rivalry is likely to intensify, if not on the battlefield, then certainly in the planning of force structures and strategies—given the collapse of the Soviet Union, deep cuts in U.S. defense expenditure and force structure, and contending "lessons learned" from the Gulf War. Indeed, the Pentagon's *Final Report* on the war, due in mid-January 1992, was delayed for weeks because of bitter interservice bickering over the report's wording and each of the services' relative contribution to the war's outcome.[321] The Air Force's disproportionate contribution to Desert Storm's success (and the continuing crisis in U.S. naval aviation) have placed it in a position to claim that an even larger share of the country's air power should heretofore be land-based. The Army, whose performance in Desert Storm surely has put to rest any doubts about its qualitative human and technological comparability with the other services, is also in a position to take advantage of the Gulf War. Though it will have to contend with an Air Force now wont to behave as if ground forces are secondary to air power as instruments of decision in future conflict, an attitude whose public expression contributed to General Dugan's relief from command, the Army's image has gained at least temporarily at the expense of its principal service competitor, the Marine Corps.

During the Gulf War, there was no discernible difference between the Army and Marine Corps on matters in which the latter has long cultivated an image of superiority: leadership, training, esprit de corps, small unit cohesion under fire (hardly tested, to be sure, in the brief and victorious ground war), and flexibility of operational doctrine. Additionally, the Marine Corps ground forces' relative dearth of heavy armor and artillery placed them at a potential disadvantage against Iraqi forces, to the point where it was deemed prudent to assign to the 1st Marine Expeditionary

Force a brigade from the Army's 2nd Armored Division.[322] The Marine Corps also fought in a nonamphibious mode, alongside the U.S. and other Coalition armies, and took no part in the Army-dominated decisive "left hook" around the exposed Iraqi right flank in the KTO.

Indeed, the absence during the Gulf War of an amphibious assault, the Marine Corps' most distinctive mission and the post–World War II statutory basis of its independence from the Army, is significant for a number of reasons. First, despite considerable Marine Corps pressure at Central Command Headquarters for an amphibious assault, the decision was made to keep the assault force at sea as an operational reserve, and it was made by an Army officer, General Schwarzkopf. Second, General Schwarzkopf's decision proved correct. A landing anywhere through the mine-strewn coastal waters of Iraq and Iraqi-held Kuwait would have contributed nothing but potentially significant American casualties to a campaign plan, based on an inland rolling up of a virtually undefended Iraqi right flank, that promised (and delivered) a quick and decisive victory. The Marine Corps landing force in the Persian Gulf played its most valuable role by simply hovering threateningly offshore, thereby tying down Iraqi divisions that otherwise might have been deployed elsewhere. Third, the continuing absence of a significant U.S. amphibious assault since the Inchon landing of September 1950 breathes new life into old questions about the mission's utility and feasibility, especially against prepared shore and inshore defenses, which in turn strikes directly at the argument for maintaining, particularly in times of defense budget scarcity, so heavy an investment in amphibious infantry and such costly accouterments of amphibious warfare as specialized assault shipping and air and naval gunfire support. If the Marine Corps, as some asked even before Desert Storm, is going to continue to fight, as it has now for over four decades, largely as just another ground force, why not meld it into the Army?[323] The Corps' dilemma is exacerbated by the Navy's long-standing distaste for amphibious operations (or at last for the costly burden of maintaining amphibious preparedness), which during the Gulf crisis was manifest in a lack of any enthusiasm for the Marine Corps' bid to have an amphibious assault incorporated into the Desert Storm campaign plan.

The Navy certainly has other fish to fry. Its embarrassing performance in countermine warfare prompted the Senate Armed Services Committee in 1991 to authorize the transfer of much responsibility for the mission to the Marine Corps.[324] Far more threatening, however, was U.S. naval aviation's relative unproductivity during Desert Storm, which not only bears directly on the future of the centerpiece of U.S. naval power since World War II, but also lends credence to old Air Force assertions that carrier-based aviation is approaching cost-ineffectiveness relative to land-based air power— especially when called upon, as it was in Korea, Vietnam, and the Persian Gulf, to conduct operations against enemies ashore. The Navy's failure to field a stealthy aircraft or a modern dedicated attack aircraft, and cancellation of programs to upgrade the A-6 Intruder and to produce a ground attack–capable version of its F-14 Tomcat, have further reduced naval aviation's competitiveness with the Air Force.

Consider the following statistics: The Navy committed half of its carriers to Desert Storm, and 24 percent of all U.S. combat aircraft that participated in the operation, but accounted for only 17 percent of all U.S. air-to-ground attack sorties flown. In contrast, Marine Corps aircraft, which operated from bases ashore in Saudi Arabia, flew 6 percent more bomb-dropping sorties than Navy aircraft, even though the Corps had only about half the Navy's number of aircraft in the theater.[325] The Navy's relative ineffectiveness was attributable to the significantly defensive orientation of its carrier air wings, and to the comparatively short range of naval aircraft. For example, the combat radius of the Navy's two principal attack and fighter/attack planes range from 160 nautical miles for the F/A-18 to 390 for the venerable Intruder. In contrast, the combat radii for Air Force aircraft employed in attack operations in Desert Storm ranged from 500 nautical miles for the F-16, 600 for the A-10, 650 for the F-15E, and 4,342 for the B-52G.[326] As one Navy officer remarked to the author shortly after the war, "There were two losers in Desert Storm: Saddam Hussein and the U.S. Navy."

If interservice rivalries are likely to be intensified by the Soviet collapse, budget cuts, and the "lessons" of the Gulf War, the same can be said of intraservice rivalries—i.e., competition for dollars within the individual services. The greatest competitive hardship will confront those service elements that staked their primary claim for resources on the now vanished Soviet threat, *and* whose capabilities proved incidental or even superfluous in defeating Iraq, and by extension, many other potential Third World challenges to U.S. security interests. Events in the Soviet Union and the experience of the Gulf War have significantly devalued the importance of nuclear weapons, especially those of the strategic (i.e., intercontinental) variety, which will most affect the Air Force and the Navy. With respect to conventional military capabilities, the demise of the Soviet military threat, traditionally centered in Europe and the North Atlantic, together with experience in the Gulf, suggest downward readjustment of the following mission priorities: Navy antisubmarine warfare and fleet air defenses; Army and Air Force air defenses; and Marine Corps amphibious assault capabilities. Conversely, military events of the past several years argue strongly for either increased investment, or at least no reductions, in the following capabilities: airlift, and especially sealift; maritime prepositioning; antimine warfare (ground and sea); special operations; *theater* ballistic missile defense; precision-guided munitions and delivery systems; and logistical sustainability.

It is increasingly difficult, for example, to justify continued heavy Navy investment in antisubmarine warfare. The Soviet Union posed the only significant subsurface threat to U.S. naval operations, and few Third World aspiring regional hegemons, including Iraq, have submarine forces at all, or at least any worth the name. Likewise, the Army's continued retention of light infantry divisions should be reexamined. They played no role in Desert Storm, for the same reason that they lacked any convincing utility against Soviet forces in Europe: a potentially fatal dearth of organic firepower and tactical mobility. Moreover, the Cold War's demise significantly reduced prospects for major U.S. involvement in the kind of Third World low-intensity conflicts that formed the primary rationale for their creation in the first place. Desert Storm dealt a heavy blow to a widespread conviction in the U.S. Army that the Soviet Union's disintegration presaged a kind of back-to-the-future return to an era of small wars that could be handled without the kind of heavy ground forces required to take on the Soviet Army in Europe.

Additionally, the Gulf War underscored the attractiveness to Third World hegemons of several technologies well within their budgetary and technological reach that the U.S. armed services have long demonstrated an inability or unwillingness to counter effectively. Topping the list are mines, ballistic missiles, and chemical munitions—and the ability of Third World police states to conceal much of their military-industrial activities and capabilities from Western intelligence agencies.

9

Lessons, Nonlessons, and Others' Lessons

ANY ATTEMPT TO DETERMINE what the Gulf War may—or may not—have provided in the way of useful instruction for U.S. behavior in future crises and wars cannot be conducted in a vacuum. The war took place against the backdrop of events elsewhere—notably, the Soviet Union's disintegration, and the collapse of Communist political authority and military power throughout Eastern Europe and most of the Kremlin's Third World outposts—having a far more profound and lasting influence on America's foreign and defense policies than a brief war in the Persian Gulf that appears to have little altered the enduring sources of instability and violence in the region. Indeed, the war itself probably would not have been possible except for the Cold War's demise. A Soviet Union that had always exerted significant political and military discipline on Iraq might have sought to restrain Saddam Hussein's reckless behavior, and a U.S. military response to Iraq's invasion of Kuwait would have been severely impeded by a reluctance to uncover Western Europe's defense against the threat of a Soviet blitzkrieg for the purpose of dealing with aggression in the Gulf. Think also of the difficulties of cobbling together a U.N. coalition in the face of a probable Soviet Security Council veto, to say nothing of attracting key Arab allies in the presence of a Soviet Union still hostile to the United States and still influential in the Middle East. The United States returned from the Gulf War, not back to Cold War business as usual, but rather to a "new world disorder" produced by the Cold War's end.

In assessing the meaning of the war, it is also important to keep in mind the distinction between major U.S. military undertakings, on the order of World War II, Korea, Vietnam, and Desert Storm, and such minor enterprises as U.S. interventions in the Dominican Republic, Lebanon, Grenada, and Panama. The former generally require much greater amounts of time, force, and allied support, and more often engage intense and often divisive public and congressional debate, whereas the latter can usually be conducted quickly, unilaterally, and with minimum dissent.

LESSONS GALORE

In the wake of Desert Storm, drawing lessons from the Gulf War became a premier growth industry in an otherwise shrinking U.S. defense analytical community. It remains a sport open to all, and has been played hard by the Defense Department, the individual services, defense contractors, congressional committees, public and private think tanks, and lone armchair strategists. The community is positively awash in lessons, ranging from the microtechnical aspects of specific technologies employed in Desert Storm to the political and strategic context in which the conflict was waged.

Not surprisingly, many of the lessons being drawn appear suspiciously congenial to the interests and agendas of those offering them. As one group of distinguished observers has commented, ". . . just as all politics is local, so all lesson-drawing is political."[327] This is especially true at a time of sharp defense budgetary decline and mounting uncertainty over the locus and character of future threats to U.S. security interests overseas. For example, the Air Force claims that the Gulf War vindicated the utility of the B-2 bomber, even though that monstrously expensive aircraft was designed to deliver nuclear ordnance on targets in a now-defunct Soviet Union, and has little conventional bombardment capability. The Air Force has also cited the war as proof of the inherent superiority of land-based over sea-based air power, while the Navy, claiming the conflict to be an aberration, by virtue of the availability of Saudi Arabia's massive port and basing infrastructure, has reasserted arguments on behalf of carrier aviation's flexibility and independence of regional political goodwill. The Army believes the war demonstrated the need, once justified almost exclusively by the prospect of a Soviet invasion of Western Europe, for continued investment in heavy, high-technology armored and attack helicopter forces, whereas the Marine Corps sees in the conflict a revalidation of continued preparation for large-scale amphibious warfare.

Elsewhere, proponents of active strategic defenses against intercontinental ballistic missile attacks against the United States point to the Patriot antitactical missile system's performance against relatively short-range Iraqi Scuds as evidence of the Strategic Defense Initiative's desirability and feasibility. Supporters of virtually every other major U.S. system used in Desert Storm, from such old reliables as the A-6 and B-52 to such combat untested ones as the M-1A1 Abrams tank, Bradley Fighting Vehicle, JSTARS sensor aircraft, F-117A stealth fighter, and Tomahawk cruise missile, also believe they have cause for joy. On the debit side, the Gulf War presumably discredited conscription, pre–Goldwater-Nichols command arrangements, those skeptical of high-technology's cost-effectiveness, and opponents of the Reagan administration's defense buildup of the 1980s. Democrats claim that most of the new technologies that performed well in Desert Storm, including the Patriot, F-117A, Abrams tank, and JSTARS, were initiated by the Johnson or Carter administrations.[328]

Many lessons being drawn amount to little more than self-evident platitudes. Few would disagree that well-trained and well-led volunteer professionals are superior to poorly prepared, sullen conscripts; that there is no substitute for technological superiority in modern warfare; that the ability to deliver munitions precisely confers significant operational and political benefits; that one is better off fighting alongside politically significant and militarily helpful allies than going it alone; that having to deploy to a distant battlefield before hostilities commence beats having to fight your way to it; that maritime prepositioning pays big dividends in places like the Persian Gulf; that Goldwater-Nichols provided command arrangements far more satisfactory than those that prevailed in Vietnam; and that for short wars entailing small loss of American life, conscription is militarily irrelevant.

The real issue is what if any genuinely new and meaningful lessons can be drawn from the war. The performance of U.S. forces did expose a number of obvious albeit nonfatal weaknesses requiring remedy, though most of them were evident to impartial scrutiny long before Desert Storm. It did not take a war in the Persian Gulf to reveal chronic inadequacies in America's shrinking defense industrial base; U.S. merchant shipping and military sealift; the Navy's mine warfare capabilities, strike aviation, and ability to communicate with the other services; Army and Air Force ability to distinguish between friend and foe; the Army's heavy lift vehicle capability; the Air Force's ability to gather timely battle-damage assessment and to detect and destroy mobile missile launchers; and so on. Every military establishment has weaknesses, and the Pentagon was fortunate that Saddam Hussein was in no position to exploit America's in the Persian Gulf.

In fact, it can be argued that the Gulf War provided no genuine test of U.S. fighting power, that because it was "the mother of all military anomalies,"[329] it cannot—and should not be permitted to—serve as a model for the future. To put it another way, leaving aside the heartening performance of some new technologies that had heretofore been untested in combat, the Gulf War taught us very little that we did not already know or suspect about our own military strengths and weaknesses, though we did learn, to the apparent surprise of many "experts," that Iraq's vaunted "war machine" was more a comic-opera force. Caution is to be advised even in assessing the performance of new weapons. As a Soviet analysis of the war noted, "After all, to be objective, they were employed essentially under ideal conditions, in the absence of any serious return fire and electronic countermeasures. In essence, [the Coalition] conducted wide-scale testing of new and promising models of weapons and military equipment of the twenty-first century under conditions close to those of the proving ground."[330]

Nor is it self-evident that the war had much to offer in the way of new perspectives on modern warfare in general. Euphoric claims that Desert

Storm heralded a revolution in warfare tantamount to the invention of gunpowder and the airplane's appearance, that it was "a defining moment in military history . . . as momentous as Cannae, Agincourt, Waterloo, the Somme, or Normandy,"[331] certainly must be approached with great caution. After all, in Iraq we were dealing with an enemy having a gross national product about equal to Portugal's and only about 60 percent of Portugal's per-capita income. We were also dealing with an adversary who could not put up much of a fight precisely because his appreciation of warfare was one-dimensional, and mired in the paradigm of the Somme and Passchendaele as revisited in the Iran-Iraq War seventy years later. The war's exquisite strategic and operational setting, together with an enemy leadership that seemed to go out of its way to accommodate both our strengths and weaknesses, not only reduced what Carl von Clausewitz called war's "friction" to minor nuisance levels, but also made it extremely difficult to extract meaningful guidance for the future. We know that U.S. forces performed superbly against Iraq, but it is far from clear that Iraq represented much more than a large punching bag that could have been almost as easily defeated by a much smaller and less technologically elegant Coalition force. Bobby Inman, Joseph Nye, William Perry, and Roger Smith quite correctly caution that the "first lesson of the Gulf War is to be very wary about drawing any so-called lessons of the Gulf War."[332]

WHAT WE DID NOT LEARN

Indeed, what we did *not*—because we *could* not—learn from the Gulf War is likely to be far more pertinent to future force planning than the plethora of "lessons learned" now deluging the Pentagon. The same can be said for lessons other potential adversaries can draw to our future disadvantage in combat. The Gulf War's success is not likely to be repeated precisely because the war demonstrated to future Iraqs some of the "dos and don'ts" in attempting to challenge Western military power.

With respect to the war's myriad nonlessons, for example, Desert Storm's very brevity and paucity of U.S. casualties left unchallenged two acknowledged potential U.S. vulnerabilities that could well surface in a future war of longer duration and larger American losses: the patience of the American people and their elected representatives for protracted conflicts, and the all-volunteer force's military stamina. Much has been written on the subject of American impatience with long wars, though the historical evidence is rather mixed. World War II engaged the United States for almost four years without any significant demoralization on the home front or among U.S. fighting forces overseas. On the contrary, the war was probably as popular as any in American history until Desert Storm came along. Even during the three years of the Korean War, which became unpopular following the Chinese rout of MacArthur's forces along the Yalu and subsequent seesaw stalemate in central Korea, there remained a grudging determination to see the war through. To the extent there was political dissent at home, it centered on partisan Republican criticism of the Truman administration policy of limiting the conflict to the Korean peninsula.

It was the Vietnam War that provided the basis for doubts about Americans' willingness to stay the course in protracted conflicts. Public and congressional support for the war began eroding significantly in the wake of the Tet Offensive of early 1968, which fueled an already large—and largely draft-induced—virulent and politically radical antiwar movement. By the turn of the decade, the war had not only destroyed the post–World War II bipartisan foreign policy consensus, but also become the dominant issue in domestic American politics. It was also the Vietnam War that provided the preferred referent experience in the pre–Desert Storm public and congressional debate over the prospect of war with Iraq. Opponents of war saw another Vietnam lurking in the Persian Gulf, whereas supporters of administration policy disparaged any analogy. Throughout the months leading up to Desert Storm, administration spokesmen repeatedly asserted that, if war came, the mistakes of Vietnam would not be repeated.

It is instructive to note that U.S. military personnel killed in the Vietnam War (58,000) only slightly surpassed those of the Korean War (54,000), and were dwarfed by those of World War II (407,000). This suggests that casualties per se are not a reliable predictor of American tolerance for wars, protracted or not. What distinguished Vietnam from World War II, and to a lesser extent the Korean conflict, was that in Vietnam casualties were being sustained with no apparent progress toward victory, or, to put perhaps a finer point on it, in the absence of an understandable or acceptable definition of victory. Moreover, World War II and Korea, like the Gulf War, were initiated by unambiguous acts of conventional aggression across internationally observed boundaries.

Americans are, in fact, willing to sacrifice much blood and treasure on behalf of what they regard, rightly or wrongly, as legitimate causes, and as long as there remains a connection between that sacrifice and visible advancement toward an end of hostilities on desirable terms—i.e., "light at the end of the tunnel." The American people will support even a costly war for a just cause, but they will withdraw their support when they no longer see a reasonable chance for realizing a preferred or acceptable outcome. The connection between sacrifice and progress was seemingly severed in Indochina by the Tet Offensive, which to many Americans viewing it through the prism of their own media appeared to portend an endless and indecisive war. American impatience, and for the same reasons, was no less apparent in the Reagan administration's intervention in Lebanon in 1982–84. What prompted public and congressional outcry, and that intervention's ultimate termination, over the deaths of 241 Americans in the October 23, 1983, truck-bombing of the Marine Corps barracks in Beirut was not just the loss of life, but that the dead seemed to have died in vain. The Reagan administration never offered a coherent or convincing statement of U.S. interests in Lebanon, or a picture of how its casual intervention in that anarchic country might foster those interests, whatever they were. By

October 1983 it appeared to many Americans that the Marines in Beirut were serving no function other than providing targets for Hezbollah snipers.

In contrast, U.S. interests in the Persian Gulf were long established and relatively clear-cut and compelling. Moreover, the easily demonized Saddam Hussein, his "rape" of tiny Kuwait, and imminent threat to Saudi Arabia greatly facilitated the political orchestration of an American-led international military response. Overwhelming wartime public and congressional support was assured once Desert Storm began. Suppose, however, that the war had lasted 430 instead of 43 days, and had claimed the lives of 14,800 instead of 148 Americans? Suppose U.S. forces had gotten bogged down in their attempt to retake Kuwait, prompting the departure of Egypt, France, and other allies from the Coalition—and maybe even a bid by Saudi Arabia for a "separate" peace with Saddam? Such a turn of events might well have fatally undermined domestic U.S. political support for the war, although we will never know, because Desert Storm was too short and sweet to try American patience.

Nor did the war constitute a real test of the military stamina of the all-volunteer force (AVF). The AVF's professionalism, skill, courage, and discipline during the Gulf crisis has rightfully been praised almost everywhere, including in these pages.[333] The Gulf War validated both the AVF's quality as well as the efficacy of the Pentagon's Total Force Policy of relying heavily on reserve components for combat support, combat service support, and even some combat functions. A notable exception was the combat unreadiness during the crisis of so-called round-out brigades attached to active-duty American divisions.[334] But the conflict was, again, too short and mild in terms of U.S. casualties to test the AVF's ability to sustain a conflict on the order of a Korea or Vietnam, to say nothing of a global war.

The AVF was created in the wake of the Vietnam War primarily for domestic political reasons. The unpopularity of that war and of conscription were indissolubly linked, and the latter could not survive the former's termination. Notwithstanding the continued massive Soviet threat to Western Europe, which during the 1960s and 1970s grew even more formidable by virtue of the dissipation of U.S. military energy and resources in Vietnam, no presidential candidate, including Richard Nixon in 1968, could hope to be elected on a platform that failed to promise at least to study the possibility of replacing conscription with a volunteer military. Nixon also correctly calculated that the prospect of the draft's abandonment would more or less demolish what remained of the student-led antiwar movement.

Thus came the famous Gates Commission of 1969, which in 1970 issued a report recommending the establishment of today's AVF.[335] Though many of the commission's suppositions about how the AVF would fare in terms of recruitment and retention, and social, racial, and sexual representativeness proved erroneous, the commission clearly understood that a smaller AVF would require augmentation via conscription in the event of a major war on the order of Korea, Vietnam, or a U.S.-Soviet conflict in Europe lasting more than a few months and involving significant casualties. In the Persian Gulf in 1991, the size of the AVF's deployments exceeded those of peak U.S. strength in Korea and more or less equaled the peak in Vietnam, but the Gulf deployments could not have been sustained, absent conscription, in a multiyear war entailing American casualty rates on the order of those sustained in Korea and Vietnam. Accordingly, the Commission recommended creation of a robust standby draft system as a backup for the AVF and hedge against a large war[336]—a recommendation that proved too politically sensitive to be implemented.

The twin issues of American popular tolerance for, and the AVF's ability to sustain, protracted and bloody combat may, of course, be moot. The Soviet Union's disintegration has dramatically reduced prospects of U.S. involvement in such a conflict, particularly if one assumes, as does the author, that the Vietnam experience itself has had an enduring cautionary effect on any latent American impulse to risk even another Korea or Vietnam for anything but the highest of stakes. It is highly improbable that the Bush or any other post-Vietnam political administration would have thrown down the military gauntlet to Saddam Hussein *except* in reasonable confidence that the Iraqi challenge could be overcome at an easily tolerable cost in time and blood. Since Vietnam, the United States has not, as some hoped or predicted, eschewed military intervention in the Third World altogether; but it has on balance been much more discriminating in picking enemies and places to fight. Moreover, the collapse of the Soviet Union and its influence in the Third World has removed a major incentive for American intervention there. There may, in short, simply be no more Koreas or Vietnams in the Pentagon's future, at least in terms of those wars' duration and cost. This in turn makes discussions of America's political and military capacity to endure such conflicts largely academic. The point is that the Gulf War taught nothing about how to sustain that capacity.

Neither did the war teach much of anything about how to sustain military operations ashore in logistically "immature" or bare regions, which are the general rule in the Third World. As Under Secretary of Defense Frank Kendall commented shortly after Desert Storm's conclusion, "We did not learn how to engage in a combat scenario without any significant preparation time or how to engage in an operation where you did not have a large indigenous infrastructure to depend on for support."[337] Saudi Arabia was a logistician's paradise, having no overseas parallel outside Europe and Northeast Asia. The availability of Saudi bases and ports to U.S. and Coalition forces in 1990 was, moreover, clinched only by the stupidly careless behavior of Saddam, which convinced an alarmed House of Saud that Iraq's invasion of Kuwait was a precursor to an assault on the kingdom itself. As discussed in an earlier chapter, a more prudent Saddam could have avoided frightening the Saudis into an American military embrace, and therefore thwarted any prospect of Desert Storm.

It is worth speculating how well Desert Shield and Desert Storm would have fared if Saudi Arabia in 1990 had been as logistically immature as

Korea was in 1950 and Vietnam was in 1965. Years of basic military construction would have been required to create an infrastructure to host and make combat-ready the Coalition forces that actually launched Desert Storm within less than six months after the Saudis requested foreign intervention. A timetable of years rather than months probably would have been politically unacceptable to the Saudis, who wished to limit as much as possible the duration of a Western force presence on their territory. It would also have afforded Saddam Hussein more or less unlimited time to consolidate Iraqi defenses in Kuwait and to play games with the Coalition's political cohesion. It would certainly have given the Iraqi dictator additional time to produce usable nuclear weapons.

In Korea, the United States entered hostilities with a ready-made albeit inadequate infrastructure in neighboring Japan; and in Vietnam, enemy military pressure in the mid-1960s was never sufficient to block the erection of such massive logistical and operational facilities as those constructed at Cam Ranh Bay, Ton Son Nhut, and Bien Hoa. In both wars the United States had time to build, and also benefited logistically from a network of regional rear-area transit bases in Okinawa, Guam, and the Philippines.

Neither a ready-made infrastructure not the time to build new ones is likely to be available for U.S. forces in the future. Potential enemies must now recognize that the United States cannot be granted a five- or six-month buildup of the kind of enormous combat power that doomed Iraqi forces in Kuwait. In this respect, the Gulf War was an experience almost unique in this century for the Pentagon, the one exception being France's reception of the American Expeditionary force in 1917–18. Politically secure U.S. military access ashore in the Third World has been eroding for decades. Budgetary pressures, and more important, host-country political sensitivity to the presence of Western (especially U.S.) forces on their territory, has slowly but steadily reduced, to a shadow of its former self, the once vast network of overseas U.S. bases—witness the Philippines' recent termination of American basing rights. To be sure, much of that network was aimed at containing the spread of Soviet power and influence, but it also had significant residual utility against non-Soviet regional threats to U.S. security. Even the Saudis, once the Gulf War was concluded, made it plain in no uncertain terms that they were not prepared to host even a token permanent U.S. force presence on their soil—even the prepositioning at remote sites of a single U.S. Army division's worth of equipment and supplies.

There is thus, at first glance at least, much credence to the U.S. Navy and Marine Corps argument that the Gulf War, specifically the availability of Saudi Arabia's abundant logistical facilities, was the exception in the Third World that proves the rule. The collapse of the Soviet conventional threat, which was centered primarily in the logistically robust theaters of Europe and Northeast Asia, places a premium on logistically self-sustaining expeditionary forces having healthy forcible-entry capabilities (i.e., amphibious assault) and being able to operate independently of local political goodwill (i.e., at sea). On the other hand, in many logistically immature or primitive areas of the Third World, places like South America, South Asia, and most of Africa, it is difficult to detect an intersection of vital U.S. security interests and formidable threats to those interests that would prompt a major U.S. military intervention. There are many plausible potential future conflicts lurking in those areas—more Indo-Pakistani, Sino-Indian, or Sino-Vietnamese wars, racial and tribal conflict in sub-Saharan Africa, etc. But it is hard to imagine direct U.S. military intervention in any of them, save of the humanitarian variety. Thus, prospects for having to fight a large conventional war in a logistically inadequate theater of operations may be all but academic. This judgment, of course, does not apply to small-scale interventions of the Panama and Grenada variety, punitive onetime raids like the air strikes on Libya in 1986, and protective actions such as the Marine Corps' extraction of endangered American and other Western nationals from Liberia in 1990.

The Gulf War also taught us nothing about how to fight a militarily self-sufficient adversary, or one having uninterrupted access to external sources of supply from powerful sponsors. Again, the Gulf War was a unique one for the Pentagon in this century. Leaving aside minor interventions against helpless enemies, the United States had, until the Gulf crisis, always confronted either major military empires (Wilhelmine and Nazi Germany, imperial Japan) or client states of an opposing superpower (North Korea and North Vietnam). And in the case of the latter two conflicts, U.S. policies regarding the interdiction of external arms and supply transfers—specifically, the basic efficacy of aerial interdiction and allegations of political constraints on its putative effectiveness—formed major sources of domestic political and civil-military division. In Korea, General MacArthur's demand for an expansion of the war across the Yalu River into Manchuria prompted President Truman to cashier the self-made legend, causing great public and congressional uproar at home. During the Vietnam War, extensive Johnson administration restrictions on air attacks on North Vietnamese sources of external supply, notably Haiphong harbor and road and rail links along the Sino-Vietnamese border, provided a constant source of bitter partisan and thinly veiled military criticism. Indeed, the controversy over the air war in Vietnam continues, with partisans of air power claiming that restrictions on its application thwarted a potentially decisive victory over both North Vietnam and Hanoi-sponsored attempts to defeat the non-Communist regime in the South.

Iraq's utter political and military isolation, especially when coupled with its military conventionality and great inferiority vis-à-vis the Coalition in war-making and war-sustaining resources, precluded either a protracted conflict or a stalemated one. The Soviet Union's abandonment of Iraq early on in the Persian Gulf crisis removed any prospect of the kind of superpower support that Pyongyang had enjoyed in the 1950s and that Hanoi counted on in the 1960s. Even before the Coalition initiated hostilities against Iraq, the U.N. embargo had imposed a degree of isolation on Baghdad that years of bombing never did on North Vietnam.

Can the United States expect to fight such "lonely" adversaries in the future? Again, the significance of recent developments in the former Soviet Union cannot be ignored. The Soviet Union's disintegration, and attendant collapse of actual and potential military support for its once robust array of Third World client states, suggests, at least with respect to those states, that they would be most imprudent to challenge U.S. or Western military power on the assumption that meaningful Russian (Ukrainian, Belarussian) military assistance would be forthcoming. The very example of Iraq's experience in 1990–91 alone serves as a stark warning of both the inability of the former Soviet Union to provide such assistance, and of the dangers of confronting the United States without allies of some kind. To be sure, such remaining Communist states as China and North Korea continue to provide peacetime military assistance, including nuclear and ballistic missile technologies, to such potential or aspiring hegemons in the Third World as Algeria, Syria, and Iran. But both China and North Korea are geographically remote from their Islamic clients, lack significant force projection capability, and are preoccupied with their own domestic and regional affairs. Both could, moreover, undergo abrupt changes in leadership as radical as those that have recently swept through most of the rest of the Communist world. In short, Iraq, at least in this one respect, could well provide a model for future Third World adversaries: a state that, while perhaps enjoying some regional political and military support, risks confronting the United States without potentially decisive "great power" patronage.

If the Gulf War did not teach the United States how to deal with Third World adversaries aided by powerful outside allies, it also underscored the continuing dependence of the United States on allies for any major military undertaking. Indeed, the war reaffirmed America's long-standing inability to go it alone in significant overseas conflicts. Occasional and often acute frustration with allied political and military behavior in World War II, Korea, Vietnam, and the Persian Gulf should not be permitted to obscure the reality of critical U.S. dependence on allies to prevail on the battlefield in conflicts other than "banana-republic" types of interventions and punitive raids. The United States could not have hoped to triumph over imperial or Nazi Germany without the assistance of such powerful continental partners as Britain, France, and the Soviet Union—allies that in both world wars collectively contributed the lion's share of ground combat forces. In Korea and Vietnam, countries hosting U.S. forces contributed significant forces of their own to combat, as did (in Korea) outside powers. In the Persian Gulf, U.S. dependence on allies both within and outside the region was critical, demolishing the dreams of some neoisolationists that the Cold War's demise would somehow free the United States from burdensome and obstreperous allies, thereby permitting unilateral exercise of American power at times and places of our own choosing.

As a postwar assessment of the Gulf War conducted by the Center for Strategic and International Studies pointed out, U.S. dependence on allies in the Persian Gulf was pervasive, encompassing "political, logistical, and industrial" dependence.[338] The report did not mention the significant contributions of high-quality albeit small ground and air contingents supplied by Britain and France, or the naval contingents provided by a host of NATO countries, which among other things largely offset the U.S. Navy's embarrassing inadequacy of mine-warfare vessels. Nor did the report mention such small but critical details as the following: General Schwarzkopf's swift redeployment of U.S. heavy Army forces to fall upon the Iraqis' largely undefended right flank—the so-called Hail Mary play— would not have been possible without sufficient heavy equipment transport- ers (HETs) to move the tanks and armored fighting vehicles along the single available tapline road. The movement required a total of over 1,200 HETs, but the Defense Department had only 480. Saudi Arabia and NATO allies supplied 715, with another 182 coming from American commercial truck- ing companies.[339]

The United States also required Arab political allies such as Egypt and Syria to legitimize a largely Western assault on a brother Arab state; logistical allies such as Saudi Arabia, Turkey, Germany to assemble the necessary forces in the region to conduct Desert Storm; and foreign industrial support to make good such critical shortfalls in U.S. capabilities as microchips and other electronic equipment now manufactured only in Japan.[340] Even in "small-war" situations susceptible to unilateral U.S. military action, U.S. administrations feel compelled for both domestic political and international political reasons to seek out allies, even token ones, to provide a veneer of legitimacy and respectability. Recall the great and often comic-opera efforts of the Reagan administration to legitimize its 1983 invasion of Grenada by enlisting the participation of such island micro-states as Dominica, Antigua, Barbuda, St. Lucia, and St. Kitts.

Even more so than in the past, conducting sizable operations in the Third World will require the logistical and political support, and even military assistance, of at least one and preferably more states indigenous to the region of conflict. The Gulf War did not teach us how to fight alone, and in all probability the United States will not be able to do so effectively—or wish to—in the future.

Nor did the war provide any instruction in dealing with an enemy capable of dictating the time and place to initiate hostilities. This is perhaps the Gulf War's single most unusual—and nonreplicable—feature. From World War II to Korea and Vietnam, and throughout the Cold War in Europe, U.S. military planning was predicated on the assumption that the enemy would strike first—that he would enjoy the powerful advantages of the operational initiative during at least the opening weeks and even months of hostilities. Waiting for others to start wars with the United States has become a long-standing American tradition, deeply rooted in conceptions of American moral superiority, abhorrence of war as a human institution, and, until Pearl Harbor, a sense of geographic impregnability.

To be sure, the Gulf War was initiated by Iraq's invasion of the emirate, which involved no assault on U.S. forces or on the territory of a country to which the United States was in any way committed to defend. But the Bush administration, after some initial hesitation, did choose to respond militarily and eventually to use force to expel Iraqi forces from Kuwait. Moreover, Saddam's passivity in the face of a U.S. military buildup whose character increasingly signaled aggressive intent afforded the U.S. military something it had rarely enjoyed before: license to pick the time and place to start hostilities, and plenty of time (almost six months) to work out the details. It was customarily the Pentagon's adversaries that enjoyed these advantages, which were often reinforced by better trained, more combat experienced, and numerically superior forces. Indeed, the starting premise of U.S. and NATO force planning for the four decades preceding the Gulf crisis was that the Soviet Union and its Warsaw Pact allies would have the advantages of operational, tactical, and perhaps even strategic surprise. This assumption was bolstered by the Korean and Vietnam experiences. In Korea, the enemy struck first, coming close to pushing U.S. forces into the sea at Pusan. And throughout the Vietnam conflict, North Vietnamese regular forces and their Viet Cong auxiliaries initiated most ground engagements and broke them off at times and places of their own choosing; only in the air war did the United States retain the initiative, though to little avail in the end. NATO continually eschewed any offensive intentions vis-à-vis the Warsaw Pact, including preemptive military action and even potential wartime ground counterattacks inside Warsaw Pact territory. Thus a U.S. military so long preoccupied with having to grapple with a Soviet offensive against numerically inferior NATO forces along a Central Front (West Germany and the Low Countries) lacking strategic depth must have been overjoyed at being handed in the Persian Gulf the kind of geographical and operational advantages denied it in Europe. It is most unlikely that the Pentagon will again have the ability to "start" a major war under such favorable circumstances in the future, if for no other reason than the unlikelihood of again encountering an opponent as accommodating and clumsy as Saddam Hussein.

But perhaps the most important nonlesson of the Gulf War was its failure to teach how to fight a wily or even competent adversary. We learned nothing about how to fight an alert, intelligent, resourceful, and innovative enemy, and it would be irresponsible to assume that other Third World national military leaderships are no more able than Iraq's, and therefore that what worked against Saddam will work against other aspiring regional hegemons. U.S. military experiences in Northeast and Southeast Asia in the 1950s and 1960s, in Lebanon in the early 1980s, and in the Persian Gulf in the late 1980s were hardly unqualified successes, and the Pentagon is certainly not the only military establishment in the world drawing conclusions from the Gulf War's uniqueness. Even within the Arab world, which has had great difficulty in challenging Western conventional military strengths, the Iraqi army, though large and relatively well-equipped, has long been regarded as mediocre. Its "victory" in the last months of an eight-year war over an isolated and exhausted Iran compelled to rely on wretchedly trained and equipped teenagers as cannon fodder against Iraq's abundant foreign-supplied tanks and artillery, was largely a Pyrrhic one. It not only bankrupted Iraq's economy, but also engendered a pervasive demoralization within the Iraqi army that carried over into the Gulf War to the Coalition's great advantage. The Egyptian army fought far better in 1973 against the Israelis, as did the Syrian army in Lebanon in 1982— products in no small part of far more sensible and politically prudent leadership in Cairo and Damascus than in Baghdad in 1990–91.

In terms of sheer strategic incompetence—i.e., an inability to calibrate political ends to military means—and capacity for self-delusion—i.e., inflation of self and country to levels of power and grandeur vis-à-vis the rest of the world, having no basis in objective reality—Saddam bears apt comparison to Benito Mussolini, a brutal buffoon who believed himself to be a modern-day incarnation of Caesar come to transform Italy into a twentieth-century Roman Empire. Like Mussolini, who presided over one of Europe's poorest and most militarily vulnerable and ineffectual states (witness the Italian army's disastrous performances against all of its adversaries in World War II, including tiny Greece, performances redeemed only by the arrival of German forces), Saddam had no objective understanding of the limits of his nation's power. There may, of course, be more Mussolinis out there in the Third World—Muammar al-Qaddafi comes to mind—but they will be the exception and not the rule.

Other lessons not forthcoming from the Gulf War include: how to conduct ground operations amidst civilian populations; how to fight in situations involving enemy employment of chemical weapons and effective theater ballistic missiles; and, how to fight in the absence of assured air superiority. This last nonlesson, like so many others, may be moot. Not since the closing months of World War II have U.S. ground and naval forces had to worry about serious enemy air attack, although achieving and maintaining air superiority over enemy territory often proved costly and difficult. However, as Air Force Chief of Staff McPeak remarked in late 1991 at a small gathering at which the author was present,[341] since 1945 the only American troops that have been killed by air attack have died at the hands of their own air forces. While mistaken air and artillery bombardment of friendly forces has long been an unavoidable curse of modern warfare, American ground forces have come to take friendly skies above their positions for granted—as indeed almost a right natural to U.S. military operations. Neither in Korea nor Indochina, nor during the Gulf War, did enemy air forces venture behind American lines, with the exception in Korea of a few "washing machine Charlie" nuisance raids. This good fortune undoubtedly would not have survived a NATO–Warsaw Pact conflict in Central Europe, but the Soviet Union's disintegration has removed the only military establishment capable of challenging U.S. superiority over its own air space. Like Iraq, most Third World countries lack air forces able or willing to challenge U.S. air power effectively, even over their own territory. This judgment, of course, assumes U.S. ability to position sufficient sea- and land-based aviation in the theater of operations to conduct major air operations. In situations not involving the commitment of U.S. ground troops, such as the punitive U.S. air attacks against Libya in 1986, the issue of achieving and maintaining a permissive air umbrella over surface forces does not, of course, arise.

Confidence in U.S. air power to protect Army and Marine Corps forces on the ground from enemy air attacks does not, unfortunately, extend to ballistic missile strikes, whose effects could be horrendous if such strikes employed chemical munitions. U.S. forces have had no experience in chemical warfare since World War I, and were ill-prepared to deal with possible Iraqi chemical attacks during the Gulf War. Though such attacks were anticipated, many U.S. armored fighting vehicles lacked collective overpressure systems designed to prevent penetration of toxic agents; individual protective gear and U.S. chemical agent detection devices were not state-of-the-art; and serious shortfalls in atropine and other antidotes persisted throughout the crisis. Saddam Hussein was either unable to use, or more likely was deterred from employing, [342] his vast chemical weapons arsenal. This is no guarantee that future Third World adversaries will be as supine, although U.S. air power's capacity to wreak vast destruction even without employing nuclear weapons should give any thinking adversary pause in contemplating "chemical" escalation. The Coalition failed to deter Saddam from launching his Scud missiles against targets in Saudi Arabia and Israel, and both ballistic missiles and chemical munitions are fast gaining favor in the Third World, precisely because they are seen as an at least partial offset to superior Western conventional air power, and because of demonstrated gaps in Western defenses against them. For example, some postwar analysis suggests that the U.S. Patriot antimissile defense system performed far less effectively than originally advertised, and probably would have exacerbated the lethal effects of chemical missile attacks had Iraqi Scuds been so armed[343]—and this against a missile that technologically represented little more than a modest improvement over its almost fifty-year-old German V-2 counterpart of World War II. To be sure, improvements over the Patriot are under development,[344] but the range, accuracy, and payload of ballistic missiles now proliferating within the Third World, including those that might be illicitly transferred from the former Soviet Union, are also improving.[345]

The "cleanliness" of the Gulf War—i.e., the locus of almost all ground combat operations away from urban and other populated areas—also stands in stark contrast to most previous U.S. conflicts, and probably many future ones. Ground combat operations in Europe, Korea, the Dominican Republic, Vietnam, Grenada, and Panama were often conducted amidst dense civilian populations, and occasionally involved bitter and bloody urban warfare (e.g., U.S. operations to retake Hue and other Vietnamese cities in the wake of the 1968 Communist Tet Offensive), which in Korea and especially Vietnam did little to endear the support of friendly populations and undermined American political support for the war. In Desert Storm the disposition of most Iraqi forces in the KTO and stringent Coalition rules of engagement spared most of what relatively few noncombatants inhabited the battle area, which consisted of some small villages and a few roving bands of Bedouins. There *were* Iraqi refugees who sought protection in U.S.-controlled territory, but they sought safety not from Coalition firepower but rather from Iraqi government reprisals for having had the misfortune of being tainted by contact with the Coalition's goodwill. Moreover, the Iraqi army's failure to put up a fight for Kuwait City, which might have claimed significant Coalition casualties had a determined house-to-house defense been mounted, further reduced potential civilian losses. Most Iraqi civilians who died in the Gulf War perished as a result of the Coalition's strategic bombardment campaign conducted against targets in Baghdad and other Iraqi cities.

Like naval campaigns on the high seas, military operations in desert environments, from the Anglo-American North African campaign against German-Italian forces in the early 1940s to Desert Storm a half a century later, have been remarkably free of civilian loss of life. But such operations are historically exceptional, and certainly have been for the American military in this century. In this regard, it would be most unwise to view Desert Storm as a model for future wars.

LESSONS OTHERS CAN LEARN

No less important than a healthy recognition of what the Gulf War did not—indeed could not—teach us is an appreciation of what lessons others can draw, especially aspiring regional hegemons having ambitions at odds with U.S. security interests. Such lessons understandably focus on U.S. political and especially military strengths and weaknesses, and on Saddam Hussein's unwillingness or inability to avoid the former or exploit the latter. The author here has chosen to identify some of the more general lessons potential Third World adversaries can draw to our future detriment, and, for the sake of clarity, to present them in instructional form.

LESSON NUMBER 1: *Beware of America's unpredictability and unsurpassed ability to move and supply major military forces to almost any shore.*

Do not be fooled, as was Saddam Hussein with respect to Kuwait, by the absence of formal American security commitments to this country or that; no such commitments existed with respect to Korea in 1950, South Vietnam in 1965, or Kuwait in 1990. When Americans, rightly or wrongly, believe their vital interests are at stake, which is often hard for outsiders—and on occasion, even Americans—to judge, they can and will move quickly, especially in circumstances involving overt aggression across accepted international boundaries, and in regions, such as the Persian Gulf, where they have manifestly paramount interests. To take American passivity for granted in such situations is to risk being as surprised as the North

Koreans, North Vietnamese, and Saddam Hussein. In challenging U.S. regional security interests, avoid direct, major, and outrageous actions, such as wanton killing of helpless American civilians, General Manuel Noriega's mindless 1989 "declaration of war" against the United States, and Saddam's gobbling up of Kuwait in one fell swoop. Be more subtle and circumspect. Take a bit here, a piece there.

Also recognize America's enormous capacity to project and maintain forces over vast distances. Time and again, her adversaries have been surprised at her ability to create a powerful military presence in areas remote from North America, and to project that power ashore, forcibly if necessary. Such endeavors require time, of course—almost six months in the case of the Persian Gulf crisis of 1990-91—and perhaps Saddam Hussein's greatest mistake was to permit the United States to amass overwhelming military power on his very doorstep. By his passivity, he converted time, an advantage initially his own, into a Coalition asset. Moreover, the Coalition's task was immensely facilitated by the presence of a robust logistical infrastructure already in place in neighboring Saudi Arabia. Note, however, that his great boon is not available to the United States in most areas of the Third World, and in the absence of regional friends and allies willing to accept a U.S. presence on their own territory, U.S. military responses will be limited to seaborne capabilities that, formidable though they are, lack the reach, punch, and staying power of shore-based air and ground forces. This, in turn, places a premium on refraining from actions that promise to scare into America's military embrace regional neighbors that might otherwise remain neutral or even hostile to U.S. intervention. Saddam Hussein should have restricted his move against Kuwait to the recovery of Warbah and Bubiyan islands and the long-standing disputed inland border areas, which in all likelihood would have compelled the Bush Administration to accept an Arab-orchestrated negotiated settlement of the matter. Alternatively, Saddam should have kept going deep into Saudi Arabia, which would have greatly complicated any U.S. military response.

LESSON NUMBER 2: *Recognize that the primary restraints on future U.S. military power's application increasingly will be internal, rather than external.*

The Cold War's demise has spurred significant and ongoing contractions in U.S. military power, and America's increasing preoccupation with its domestic social and economic problems, and with rising difficulties with her traditional allies, will exert a growing restraint on her readiness to embark on large-scale military enterprises overseas. On the other hand, the dissolution of the Soviet Union into a loose and tenuous "commonwealth" pregnant with prospects for violent self-destruction has removed the single greatest external counterweight to U.S. military power abroad. Though having smaller military forces, the United States is now much freer from external restraints than it was during the forty years of the Cold War to concentrate those forces at places and times of its own choosing. Witness the transfer to the Persian Gulf of the U.S. Army's Seventh Corps from Europe, a redeployment that would not have been risked as long as a massive and hostile Soviet army continued to menace NATO in the heart of Europe. Saddam Hussein clearly underestimated the degree of military flexibility conferred upon the United States by the vanishing Soviet threat. He also failed to grasp the bandwagon effect of a United States emerging from the Cold War as the world's only remaining superpower, with no challengers anywhere even on the most distant horizon. The United States attracted a spectrum of allies in the Persian Gulf that would have been simply impossible had circumstances included a still united and powerful Soviet Union opposed to America's response. For example, Syria certainly would not have signed up with the Coalition, and France would have had every incentive to play her favorite role of uncommitted grand intermediary.

Public, congressional, and White House moves to slash U.S. defense expenditure, which has already declined significantly in real terms since the mid-1980s, and is almost certainly to bottom out at no more than 3.0–3.5 percent of GNP—down from almost 7 percent during the Reagan administration's peak—will eliminate far more U.S. force structure than Saddam Hussein or any other Third World hegemon could hope to accomplish on the battlefield. Consider the magnitude of the following U.S. unilateral reductions in active-duty forces now planned for the period 1990–97 alone: a U.S. Army to 535,000 people and 12 divisions, from 751,000 and 18; a U.S. Navy to 12 carrier battle groups and 448 ships, from 15 and 526 respectively; and a U.S. Air Force to 215 long-range bombers and 26 tactical fighter wings, from 269 bombers and 36 wings.[346] These reductions, which may be followed or attended by additional cuts, will serve both to lengthen the time needed, and to limit the amount of force the United States can bring to bear at any given place in the future. Indeed, the United States may not be able to repeat Desert Storm. George F. Will has commented that "Desert Storm was an unrepeatable use of vanishing Cold War capabilities."[347]

LESSON NUMBER 3: *Whatever the temptation, refrain from attempting directly to challenge U.S. (and Western) military power on its own terms.*
Take heed of Lawrence Freedman's observation:

> The sweeping victory in the Gulf undermined any notion that the Third World can now compete with the West in the military sphere. Whatever high-technology systems have been acquired by Third World states, the ability to defeat formidable military capabilities with sophisticated intelligence, command and control, and training is still lacking.[348]

This caution applies first and foremost to American air and naval power, whose incomparable quality and experience eliminate any effective competition. This is not to argue that U.S. air and naval forces cannot be damaged at the hands of Third World opponents; they can and have—witness U.S. air losses over North Vietnam, and the Navy's repeated embarrassment in the Persian Gulf by Iranian and Iraqi mines. But in any situation where the United States can establish major air and naval forces in a region of contention, expect to operate in the face of hostile superiority at sea and in the air.

Circumventing or neutralizing this superiority is difficult, but not impossible. Iraq was unable to do so because its forces were compelled to operate in terrain and weather that maximized the strengths of U.S. air and naval power, and because it had chosen to mimic industrial models of military organization. "Guerrilla" and other unconventional styles of warfare were in any event unavailable to Iraq. Baghdad was not waging a "revolutionary" conflict, but rather a traditional war of territorial conquest. The precursors of the kind of "people's" or "revolutionary" war that worked so well against the West in East Asia in the 1940s, 1950s, and 1960s—i.e., a politically aroused indigenous population, and topography permitting operational strategies and tactical doctrines capable of dissipating the potentially decisive effects of superior Western conventional firepower—were simply not present or creatable in the barren desert wastes of the KTO. Iraq is hardly the only Third World paradigm with which the Pentagon may have to contend in the future. As air power historian Caroline F. Ziemke has noted:

> Iraq was unique less in the extent to which it adopted the trappings of European military power and infrastructure than in its doing so in a way that maximized its vulnerability to strategic bombing (centralized industry, communications, and military command and control) and minimized the relative advantages (operational and tactical flexibility, resilience, and military effectiveness). Iraq certainly represents one type of Third World opponent (perhaps even the most common one), but it would be dangerous to forget the other paradigm—the opponent who (like the North Koreans, Communist Chinese, Viet Cong, and North Vietnamese) played their unique cultural and political strengths to their advantage and significantly blunted the effect of Western technological superiority.[349]

Moreover, it should be noted that Saddam Hussein achieved some modest successes against the Coalition worthy of future emulation. He managed to shield much of his "forbidden" military-industrial base from destruction. Through secrecy, deception, concealment, dispersal, and simply burying valued assets deep underground, he blocked a potentially decisive strategic application of Coalition air power, and indeed managed to preserve himself and his regime against manifest Coalition expectations. Moreover, though the Iraqi air force predictably proved no match for the Coalition, Saddam, like many other aspiring regional hegemons in the Third World, saw in the combination of even primitive ballistic missiles and hyperlethal munitions a possible means of offsetting, if not countering directly, Western superiority in conventional military power. Such technologies can exert a powerful deterrent effect in the right circumstances. They can provide a relatively easy path to regional military preeminence, and require far less in the way of money and skilled manpower to acquire and maintain than attempts to duplicate U.S. and Western prowess in naval and air warfare. Note also other "poor man's" technologies that the Americans had trouble dealing with, and others that they never had to face in the Gulf. Sea mines seem to be a perennial problem for the U.S. Navy, and mobile launchers for theater ballistic missiles also proved their relative worth against the Coalition's best efforts to suppress them.

Note, further, that the Americans profited immensely from the peculiar character of Saddam Hussein's regime. While some totalitarian states, such as Hitler's Germany and Ho Chi Minh's North Vietnam, have performed brilliantly on the battlefield because they have been intelligent enough to recognize that success in modern warfare demands both a high level of politically untainted military professionalism and a willingness to grant field commanders the authority to make critical decisions on the spot, the Iraqi army suffered from a paralysis common to many personality-cult dictatorships. Modern warfare demands not only a level of training and technological expertise beyond the reach of short-service conscript armies common to Third World police states, but also a level of ingenuity, innovation, and initiative incompatible with the very concept of blind obedience. Whatever the advantages authoritarian states may once have had over democratic ones in combat, the Gulf War should be a warning to those who still believe that democratic political institutions are incompatible with military excellence. Intellectual freedom may now be a prerequisite for such excellence. Sullen soldiers motivated primarily by fear and rigidly controlled from headquarters are liabilities, not assets.

LESSON NUMBER 4: *The Americans remain extremely sensitive to casualties, notwithstanding the Iraqi Army's failure to inflict many.*

This sensitivity also applies to a lesser extent to enemy noncombatant casualties. Since the mass slaughters of World War I, Western democracies have registered an increasing sensitivity to casualties in war. In this respect, the so-called Vietnam Syndrome is very much alive and well in the United States. Indeed, the evidence suggests that the desire to minimize both U.S. military and Iraqi civilian casualties was the single most important determinant of the shape and course of Desert Storm. It accounted for, among other things, reliance on a lengthy preliminary air campaign against Iraqi forces in the KTO before launching the coalition's ground offensive; abjuration of an amphibious assault along Iraq's and Kuwait's heavily defended coasts, in favor of a move around Iraq's undefended and unpopulated right flank; stringent rules of engagement regarding air attacks on targets in populated areas; and the Bush administration's sigh of relief, before Desert Storm, upon learning that Western hostages in Iraq were to be released rather than placed as "human shields" in and about key Iraqi

military and other targets. This American sensitivity to both their own and
Iraqi civilian casualties also permitted Saddam Hussein, before and during
the Gulf War, to place key war-supporting facilities and other military
assets amidst residential areas, and even inside religious and cultural
edifices, in reasonable confidence that the Americans would not risk hitting
them for fear of the kind of outcry that did erupt with the bombing of the
civilian-packed Ameriyya air-raid shelter in Baghdad.

Saddam Hussein also astutely employed the presence in Baghdad of
CNN and other foreign television services to inflate the negative political
impact on the Coalition of such events as the bombing of the Ameriyya
shelter and Coalition air attacks along the so-called Highway to Hell.
Graphic images of Iraqi civilian dead at the shelter compelled the Pentagon
to suspend all attacks on targets in the Baghdad area for several days, and
footage erroneously suggesting a deliberate mass slaughter of helpless Iraqi
troops fleeing Kuwait helped propel the White House into an early
unilateral cease-fire. U.S. political opinion is highly sensitive to television
images of events, and the advent of continuous and instantaneous television
coverage of war's inherent horrors, as opposed to its episodic and delayed
transmission of images during the Vietnam War, provides new opportunities to adversely influence U.S. military operations. Such coverage, beyond
the Pentagon's control, can and should be treated as a military asset and
used accordingly.

The combination of U.S. restraint and Iraqi military impotence held
wartime American military and Iraqi civilian casualties to levels well below
those that might have produced domestic American political trouble or
division within the Coalition. This does not, however, mean that strategies
aimed at maximizing U.S. casualties should be eschewed by America's
future adversaries, especially ones like Saddam Hussein, and Mao Zedong
and Ho Chi Minh before him, who were politically able and morally
prepared to expend the lives of ten or even one hundred of their own
countrymen to kill or, perhaps better yet, to capture a single American.

Yet such strategies cannot hope to succeed if Americans are permitted to wage their end of the war largely with air and naval power,
which for them, especially against Third World opponents, are comparatively casualty-free. U.S. ground forces must be drawn into the fight, as the
Iraqis feebly attempted to do at Khafji, and hopefully in circumstances,
such as combat in closed terrain and urban areas, that inhibit exploitation
of their superior tactical mobility and firepower. This may or may not, of
course, be possible, depending on the locus of conflict and the operational
and tactical environment. An alternative is to strike directly at American
noncombatants themselves. Official and private Americans residing or
visiting abroad remain vulnerable to terrorist attack and hostage-taking,
and such actions, while not militarily consequential, have demonstrated a
capacity to influence both official Washington and American public opinion
alike.

LESSON NUMBER 5: *Above all, hope that Americans will conclude that the Gulf War is a model for the future.*

Nothing would better serve the interests of future Third World challengers to U.S. security interests overseas than an American conclusion that, in the Gulf War, it had discovered a way of waging war without incurring war's traditional risks, pain, and suffering. The virtually free military ride Saddam gave the Coalition; talk of "hyperwar" and the "new military revolution" apparent in Desert Storm now pervading the Pentagon; and the excessive confidence Americans have always placed in technology as a substitute for hard and dangerous work on and off the battlefield—all may combine to prompt a disastrous misinterpretation of the Gulf War's military meaning. Former Air Force Chief of Staff Michael Dugan has wisely cautioned that though "Desert Storm was a triumph, it is now the last war. The circumstances will never be repeated."[350] Future enemies are not likely to be as militarily vulnerable as Saddam Hussein's Iraq. Eliot Cohen has charged that "the greatest test of our strategic maturity will be our willingnesss to view critically our performance in this rout. Victory has a way of excusing a multitude of sins.[351]

All of these caveats are certainly in order. Victorious armies generally tend to learn less from their successes than their adversaries learn from their failures. The stunning brevity and lopsidedness of the Coalition's victory over Iraq encourages both a blindness to the degree to which remarkably good fortune played a determining role in that victory, and an assumption that what worked in the Gulf War will work again against others at different times and places. A self-satisfied French army made this mistake in the wake of World War I, as did a victorious Pentagon in the wake of World War II. To the extent that we learned so very much from our defeat in Vietnam, we may now be wont not to learn enough, or at least not the right nonlessons, from our seemingly effortless triumph in the Persian Gulf. And the burden of those lessons is to understand that Desert Storm's victory was not only guaranteed before the first U.S. aircraft entered Iraqi-controlled air space on its way to Baghdad, but also that that victory can never be repeated.

10

Pyrrhic Triumph

THE DEGREE TO WHICH the Coalition dealt Iraqi forces in the KTO a crushing military defeat was evident in the utter disorientation of those Iraqi commanders who were summoned to Safwan by General Schwarzkopf to receive the terms of the cease-fire. According to the Pentagon's own account:

> Following the Iraqi accounting of Coalition prisoners of war in Iraqi hands, Lieutenant General Al-Jabburi asked that the Coalition reciprocate and provide an accounting of Iraqi prisoners of war being held by the Coalition. When told that the counting was still going on, but at that time the number was in excess of 58,000, Lieutenant General Al-Jabburi appeared stunned. In apparent disbelief he asked the Iraqi III Corps commander if that was the correct number. Major General Al-Dughastani replied that it was possible, but that he did not know.
>
> General Schwarzkopf proposed that a line be drawn on a map from which all forces would be withdrawn at least one kilometer to prevent inadvertent contact between Iraqi and Coalition forces. Lieutenant General Al-Jabburi agreed. When shown the CENTCOM proposed line, the Iraqi asked why the line was drawn behind his troops. General Schwarzkopf said that the line was the forward line of the U.S. advance. Lieutenant General Al-Jabburi again appeared stunned. Once again he queried his III Corps commander, who said it was possible, but that he did not know. Following this, the Iraqi attitude was considerably more subdued.[352]

The Coalition's remarkable military performance is beyond dispute, and will be studied in military schools around the world for decades to come. Few military campaigns in history have been conducted as swiftly and with so little loss of friendly lives as Desert Storm. The euphoria and parades that followed Desert Storm were well deserved by a U.S. military that clearly had overcome the onerous legacies of the Vietnam War, and that performed in the Persian Gulf with a seeming flawlessness that more resembled a gigantic peacetime training exercise than war as experienced before Desert Storm.

The question nevertheless arises of what this spectacular display of force actually accomplished beyond the military realm. Wars are waged, after all, to achieve political objectives, and while the Gulf War clearly achieved

Kuwait's liberation, that objective was hardly the sole or most important reason the United States made war on Iraq in 1991. The Bush administration clearly saw in the Gulf War an opportunity to fulfill other, more significant goals than simply the liberation of a small country to which the United States had no prewar defense commitments or even particular affinity.

American war aims manifestly encompassed Saddam Hussein's removal from power and the permanent elimination of Iraq's ability to threaten its neighbors, especially with ballistic missiles and hyperlethal munitions. These objectives were subsumed under the declared aim of ensuring, in President Bush's words, "the security and stability of the Persian Gulf."[353] Saddam Hussein, by his invasion of Kuwait, and by his ill-concealed efforts to establish Iraq as the region's dominant military hegemon—and a nuclear-armed one, to boot—constituted a clear and present danger to security and stability in the Gulf.

However, while Desert Storm removed a symptom of the Iraqi "problem" (i.e., Baghdad's conquest of Kuwait), it failed to eliminate the problem's source. Saddam's continued governance of Iraq, and the survival of much of Iraq's latent capacity to threaten its neighbors, and to acquire usable ballistic missile and hyperlethal munitions capabilities, has voided Desert Storm's victory of much of its potential and intended political content. No satisfactory or enduring resolution of the Gulf crisis was possible without Saddam Hussein's removal from power, and his very survival is seen by some Arabs as an inspirational victory over a long-detested West.

The White House grossly overestimated the Iraqi dictator's vulnerability and underestimated his capacity for survival, just as it had before August 2, 1990, completely misread Saddam and his ambitions, and his susceptibility to American blandishments.

In fact, despite maintenance of the U.N. embargo and continued Coalition hostility, Saddam has made remarkable strides in restoring basic economic services, and in reconstituting the Iraqi army, which in terms of size and major equipment holdings *remains among the largest in the world.* A year after Desert Storm's conclusion, the Iraqi army retained an estimated 2,400 tanks, 4,400 armored personnel carriers and infantry fighting vehicles, 1,000–2,000 pieces of artillery (including mortars), and 250 multiple rocket launchers.[354] Iraq may also have retained as many as 200 usable Scud missiles.[355] The army has, moreover, been restructured from a ponderous and indifferent one-million-man force into a smaller, more professional force of approximately 350,000–400,000 troops, with a much higher relative Republican Guard content.[356] Saddam seems to have learned at least one very important lesson from Desert Storm.

Columnist William Safire's conclusion that "Bush snatched defeat from the jaws of victory" by failing to pursue the war until Saddam was toppled may be unfair, but there is no doubt that Iraq remains a serious menace in the Persian Gulf region.[357] Assistant Secretary Edward P. Djerejian, the

State Department's top Middle East expert, testified before a House subcommittee in November 1991 that "Even after Desert Storm, Iraq retains a considerable military capability which could pose a threat" to Saudi Arabia, and observed that "the present force structure of the Iraqi military is much larger than that of the Saudi, even after Desert Storm."[358] In January 1992, CIA director Robert Gates told the Senate Governmental Affairs Committee that "Iraq will remain a primary [nuclear, chemical, and biological weapons] proliferation threat at least as long as Saddam Hussein remains in power," and added that "the cadre of scientists and engineers trained for these programs will be able to reconstitute any dormant program rapidly."[359] Additionally, Iraq has openly defied the provisions of U.N. Security Council Resolution 687. It has repeatedly deceived U.N. inspection teams regarding the existence and location of forbidden weapons and manufacturing sites; it has violated the demilitarized zone along the Kuwaiti border; it has failed to pay compensation to Kuwait; it has violated Resolution 687's ban on military aircraft flights; and it is using Jordan, Turkey, and Iran to smuggle in food, embargoed equipment, and luxury items, and to export used construction equipment and small amounts of oil.[360] These are hardly the activities of a Desert Storm–cowed and compliant Iraqi leadership.

Indeed, Saddam has managed to convert the military disaster of Desert Storm into something of a political victory, especially among Iraq's ruling Sunni minority, and among much of the Arab world's Shia minority. It is doubtful that other Arab leaderships expected an Iraqi military victory over the Coalition, but the fact that Saddam refused to cut and run before the Coalition's gathering military forces, and that he and much of his army managed to survive the Coalition's victory, must have come as much of a surprise to other Arab governments as it did to the Bush administration. That any Arab state could emerge intact from the best that the United States and its Western allies could throw at it cannot but have increased respect and even admiration for a leader whose persona and appeal resonated quite well during the crisis among poor and powerless "street" Arabs from Rabat to Amman.

Saddam's aura of invincibility is also reinforced by the Bush administration's seeming helplessness in changing the political landscape in Baghdad. Ironically, in Desert Storm's wake the administration has been compelled to pursue the very same policies—a combination of sanctions and of publicly cajoling the Iraqi people into removing Saddam Hussein—that it rejected as ineffectual before Desert Storm. Having repeatedly compared Saddam to Hitler also damaged the Bush administration's position, since Hitler would hardly have been permitted to remain Germany's Führer after World War II. Hitlers deserve nothing less than death or capture. As for sanctions, it is difficult to see how the infliction of suffering on Iraq's politically impotent general population can be expected to dislodge a regime that has protected itself from their consequences; on the contrary, Saddam Hussein can and has used the continuation of sanctions to transfer blame for Iraq's plight from his own actions to those of a "persecuting" United States.

Desert Storm also may have damaged the legitimacy of Saudi Arabia and the other Gulf oil kingdoms and sheikdoms on whose behalf it was largely conducted. The war advertised their military helplessness against such relatively large and powerful would-be hegemons as Iraq and Iran—a condition that is certain to persist irrespective of the quantities of advanced weapons they purchase from the West. Saudi Arabia and the city-states on the Arab side of the Gulf lack the population bases and social structures necessary to field armies capable of holding their own against those on the northern side of the Gulf. In the future, as in August 1990, Western military intervention will be required to protect Saudi Arabia and the other peninsular states against the kind of threat posed by a militarily resurgent Iraq or Iran. Shahram Chubin has noted that after

> some twenty years of major defense expenditures ($150–$200 billion), Saudi Arabia still needs to call upon Western allies for most security problems. This is in part a comment on the regional imbalances in the population and, in effect, on the nature of society in the Kingdom. A credible defense of the country will not be possible until recruitment in the armed forces is broadened, which will necessitate reform in the way power is managed in the country.[361]

An abiding dependency on the United States for its ultimate security has particular political dangers for Saudi Arabia. Leon Hadar observed of the Arab Gulf states that the

> Gulf War pointed to the long-term problem facing traditional Middle Eastern monarchies: to survive politically, they must continue to rely on direct and indirect American aid and military support. This dependency exposes their populations to competing Western political and economic models and creates politically explosive expectations. . . . Opposition from both modernizing and fundamentalist forces is quite likely at some point.[362]

Saudi qualms over a residual U.S. military presence underscore the House of Saud's extreme sensitivity to delegitimizing appearances, though the very fact that it felt compelled to call upon over half a million American troops to save it from a brother Arab state may have hardened the image in the minds of many of Saudi Arabia as a surrogate for American interests in the Gulf. It is important to remember the Shah of Iran's fate; that monarch, by permitting his own country to become the Gulf's regional policeman on behalf of American definitions of "security and stability" in the Gulf, invited his own destruction by highly nationalistic and Islamic fundamentalist forces bent on expelling "infidel" power and influence in the Gulf.

Indeed, many Middle East experts believe that the Gulf War has excited even further the prewar resurgence of Islamic fundamentalism ignited by the Ayatollah Khomeini's revolution in Iran. Especially among the common peoples of the poorer Arab states, such as Morocco, Algeria, Tunisia, Sudan, and Jordan, as well as among the large, nonindigenous, and disenfranchised labor forces of the oil-rich Gulf states themselves, the war may have breathed new life into the old and bitter issue of the vast inequality of wealth separating the Arab oil-rich and oil-poor states, and within the former, between the privileged ruling clans and their economically indispensable Palestinian, Egyptian, and other foreign work forces. Kuwait's disgusting postwar abuse of Palestinian and Egyptian guest workers, along with the exiled government's refusal to embrace politically those of its citizens who stayed behind during the Iraqi occupation and were significantly democratized by the experience of resistance,[363] smacks of the same kind of arrogant and shortsighted behavior that characterized the emirate's prewar diplomacy toward Iraq. To be sure, neither Kuwait's nor Saudi Arabia's political reconstruction was ever part of the U.S. or Coalition agenda during the Persian Gulf crisis of 1990–91. But it is nevertheless legitimate to question the durability of a monarchy and a sheikdom for whom the war seems to have been little more than a temporary interruption in political and social business as usual.

Christopher Layne has concluded:

> Other than the dubious satisfaction of liberating Kuwait and restoring its government—a corrupt, repressive, and undemocratic regime that, to paraphrase Bismarck's comment about the Balkans, was not worth the bones of a single American soldier—it is hard to see what lasting gains the United States has secured from the Gulf War.[364]

The Gulf War was a magnificent military victory barren of any significant diplomatic gains. It was fought to repel Saddam Hussein's challenge to the *old* order in the Persian Gulf, not to create a new one. Accordingly, future historians may regard the war as a complete failure.

These judgments may seem unduly harsh. But the very fact that one day in the coming few years U.S. military forces might again have to return to the Persian Gulf to defend a helpless Kuwait and Saudi Arabia against a militarily resurgent Iraq, commanded by a Saddam Hussein now lusting for revenge, suggests that if Desert Storm was a crowning military achievement, it was also no less a politically bankrupt victory. While it temporarily wrecked much of the Iraqi army, it failed to eliminate an Iraqi leadership, which could well include Saddam's successors, that continues to pose, as it did before the Gulf War, the major threat to the Persian Gulf region's "security and stability." That job remains unfinished.

Veteran Middle East observer Jim Hoagland has pointed to "the falsity of the administration's argument that the only choices available on February 28 [the war's last day] were to march to Baghdad, engage in indiscriminate slaughter, or cease fire unilaterally." In his view,

> There were a range of other options, including cutting off the key escape routes of Saddam's Republican Guards to the north and "closing the

pocket" at Basra, which had in fact been planned. But it didn't happen. Guided by faulty battlefield intelligence, Bush made the unempirical decision to terminate the war unilaterally. Saddam's survival in Baghdad a year later suggests that there was something to his bet that whatever happened in Kuwait the United States still remembers Vietnam too vividly to have the patience and will to pursue him militarily to the bitter end.[365]

In retrospect, however, the political impotence of Desert Storm appears wonderfully compatible with the course of U.S. policy toward Iraq before, during, and after the Gulf War, which always lacked consistency, foresight, a willingness to follow through, and an acceptance of the risks inherent in trying to influence events inside Iraq. It took the Iraqi invasion of Kuwait to alert the White House suddenly to the fact that Saddam Hussein was an Arab Hitler rather than a "force for moderation" in the Persian Gulf. Years of coddling a ruthless and ambitious megalomaniacal dictator abruptly vanished when those manifest ambitions became reality. Then, once Desert Storm really got rolling, the White House intervened to impose a unilateral cease-fire that foreclosed continued military operations that might have prompted Saddam's departure from power. Next, the White House ordered U.S. forces to abandon positions deep inside Iraq whose retention also might have provided the political leverage to topple Saddam Hussein. Nor did the White House lift a single finger to assist those among the Iraqi population, notably the Kurds and Shias, who did rise—with U.S. encouragement—against Saddam. U.S. forces stood idly by while Iraqi tanks and helicopter gunships, many of which had been permitted to escape destruction by Coalition forces in the KTO, gunned down those who might have accomplished the one objective that eluded the Coalition's 750,000 troops.

The war was a great success while it lasted, but it lasted not long enough to bear worthwhile political fruit.

NOTES

1. A number of serious histories and studies of the war have already appeared in print. See Norman Friedman's *Desert Victory: The War for Kuwait;* James Blackwell's *Thunder in the Desert: The Strategy and Tactics of the Persian Gulf War;* James Dunnigan and Austin Bay's *From Shield to Storm: High-Tech Weapons, Military Strategy, and Coalition Warfare in the Persian Gulf;* and *Triumph Without Victory: The Unreported History of the Gulf War,* produced by the staff of *U.S. News and World Report.*

Bob Woodward's *The Commanders;* Pierre Salinger and Eric Laurent's *Secret Dossier: The Hidden Agenda Behind the Gulf War;* Elaine Sciolino's *The Outlaw State: Saddam Hussein's Quest for Power and the Gulf Crisis;* and Judith Miller and Laurie Mylroie's *Saddam Hussein and the Crisis in the Gulf* also provide well-informed accounts of the diplomatic fore-play and the Bush administration's decision-making during the crisis. Highly critical works accusing the Bush administration of turning the Gulf crisis unnecessarily into a war include Stephen Graubard's *Mr. Bush's War: Adventures in the Politics of Illusion* and Jean Edward Smith's *George Bush's War.* Other histories are undoubtedly on the way, as are anthologies to complement those already published, such as Micah Sifry and Christopher Cerf's *The Gulf War Reader: History, Documents, Opinions* and James Ridgeway's *The March to War.*

As for lessons learned, it is almost impossible to keep up with the flood of studies that has emanated from the Pentagon (for example, *Conduct of the Persian Gulf Conflict),* the individual armed services (e.g., *United States Air Force Performance in Desert Storm),* think tanks (e.g., Jim Blackwell of the Center for Strategic and International Studies' *The Gulf War: Military Lessons Learned),* professional associations (e.g., the Association of the U.S. Army's *The U.S. Army in Operation Desert Storm),* and private defense specialists (e.g., Bruce Watson's *Military Lessons of the Gulf War).*

1a. Ezio Bonsignore, "The War that Wasn't," *Military Technology,* March 1991, p. 60.

2. For an understanding of Saddam Hussein the man and political leader and the nature of his Baathist regime, see Samir al-Khalil, *Republic of Fear: The Inside Story of Saddam's Iraq* (New York: Pantheon Books, 1989); Efraim Karsh, and Inari Rautsi, *Saddam Hussein, A Political Biography* (New York: The Free Press, 1991); and Judith Miller and Laurie Mylroie, *Saddam Hussein and the Crisis in the Gulf* (New York: Times Books, 1991).

3. Bruce Watson, et al., *Military Lessons of the Gulf War* (Novato, California: Presidio Press, 1991), p. 146.

4. James F. Dunnigan and Austin Bay, *From Shield to Storm: High-Tech Weapons, Military Strategy, and Coalition Warfare in the Persian Gulf* (New York: William Morrow and Company, 1991), p. 25.

5. Martin Yant, *Desert Mirage: The True Story of the Gulf War* (New York: Prometheus Books, 1991), pp. 57–61.

6. Both Kelly and Dole quoted in Pierre Salinger and Eric Laurent, *Secret Dossier: The Hidden Agenda Behind the Gulf War* (New York: Penguin Books, 1991), pp. 4 and 25, respectively.

7. Karsh and Rautsi, op. cit., pp. 201–202.

8. John K. Cooley, *Payback: America's Long War in the Middle East* (New York: Brassey's Inc., 1991), p. 186.

9. Elaine Sciolino, *The Outlaw State: Saddam Hussein's Quest for Power and the Gulf Crisis* (New York: John Wiley and Sons, Inc., 1991), p. 140.

10. Ibid., p. 188.

11. Karsh and Rautsi, op. cit., p. 207.

12. Ibid., p. 204.

13. Adel Darwish and Gregory Alexander, *Unholy Babylon: The Secret History of Saddam's War* (New York: St. Martin's Press, 1991), pp. 33–34.

14. Sciolino, op. cit., p. 199.

15. Ibid., pp. 127–28.

16. Yant, op. cit., p. 19.

17. Darwish and Alexander, op. cit., p. 239.

18. Salinger and Laurent, op. cit., p. 75.

19. Quoted in Don Oberdorfer, "Was War Inevitable?," *Washington Post Magazine,* March 17, 1991, p. 19.

20. Shahram Chubin, "Post-War Gulf Security," *Survival,* March-April 1991, p. 144.

21. Sciolino, op. cit., pp. 207–208.

22. Kenneth R. Timmerman, *The Death Lobby: How the West Armed Iraq* (New York: Houghton-Mifflin Company, 1991), p. 214.

23. Karsh and Rautsi, *Saddam Hussein,* op. cit., p. 212.

24. "The Persian Gulf Crisis," *The Middle East,* 7th edition (Washington, D.C.: Congressional Quarterly, Inc., 1991), pp. 316–17.

25. Salinger and Laurent, op. cit., p. 32.

26. Ibid., p. 191.

27. Ibid., p. 184. Also see Yant, op. cit., pp. 77–79, and Salinger and Laurent, op. cit., p. 43.

28. Timmerman, op. cit.

29. Ibid., ix.

30. Ibid., xix.

31. Ibid., p. 389.

32. See Anthony Cordesman and Abraham R. Wagner, *The Lessons of Modern War,* Vol. I, *The Iran-Iraq War* (Boulder, Colorado: Westview Press, 1990), p. 171.

33. Dilip Hiro, *The Longest War: The Iran-Iraq Military Conflict* (New York: Routledge, 1991), p. 63.

34. Ibid., p. 119.

35. Responding to the Iraqi attack on the *Stark,* President Reagan declared: "We've never considered the Iraqis hostile at all. They've never been in any way hostile. . . . And the villain of the piece is Iran." Quoted in Darwish and Alexander, op. cit., pp. 67–68.

36. Miller and Mylroie, op. cit., p. 147.

37. Stephen C. Pelletiere, Douglas V. Johnson II, and Leif R. Rosenberger, *Iraqi Power and U.S. Security in the Middle East* (Carlisle Barracks, Pennsylvania: Strategic Studies Institute, U.S. Army War College, 1990), x.

38. Quoted in James Ridgeway, ed., *The March to War* (New York: Four Walls Eight Windows, 1991), p. 43.

39. Ibid., p. 213, and Cooley, op. cit., p. 187.

40. Stephen J. Solarz, "The Stakes in the Gulf," *New Republic,* January 7 and 14, 1991. Reprinted in Micah L. Sifry and Christopher Cerf, eds., *The Gulf War Reader: History, Documents, Opinions* (New York: Random House, 1991), p. 282.

41. Quoted in Yant, op. cit., p. 4.

42. Quoted in Ridgeway, op. cit., p. 43.

43. July 27, 1990, speech before the Senate. Quoted in Mark A. Siegel, "Saddam Hussein's Other Republican Guards," *Wall Street Journal,* March 21, 1991.

44. From transcript of meeting released by Iraq, excerpts reprinted in Sifry and Cerf, op. cit., pp. 120–21.

45. Ibid., pp. 122–23.

46. During his interview with Glaspie, Saddam threatened: "If you use pressure, we will deploy pressure and force. We know that you can harm us, although we do not harm you. But we too can harm you. Everyone can cause harm according to their ability and their size. We

cannot come all the way to you in the United States, but individual Arabs may reach you."
Ibid., p. 125.

47. See Sciolino, op. cit., p. 177.

48. Christopher Hitchens, "Why We Are Stuck in the Sand," *Harper's,* January 1991, reprinted in Sifry and Cerf, op. cit., p. 116.

49. Cooley, op. cit., p. 57.

50. Quoted in Ridgeway, op. cit., p. 57.

51. Bob Woodward, *The Commanders* (New York: Simon and Schuster, 1991), p. 223.

52. Salinger and Laurent, op. cit., p. 111.

53. Watson, op. cit., p. 153.

54. Roland Dannreuther, *The Persian Gulf Conflict: A Political and Strategic Analysis,* Adelphi Paper No. 264 (London: International Institute for Strategic Studies, 1992).

55. Quoted in John K. Cooley, "Pre-War Gulf Diplomacy," *Survival,* March-April 1991, pp. 125–39.

56. "The Persian Gulf Crisis," op. cit., p. 135.

57. The Kuwaiti Theater of Operations was the U.S. Central Command's official nomenclature for Iraqi-occupied Kuwait and adjacent areas of southeastern Iraq containing Iraqi forces deployed for operations pursuant to Kuwait's defense.

58. Quoted in Woodward, op. cit., p. 225.

59. Quoted in Sifry and Cerf, op. cit., p. 198.

60. Ibid., p. 199.

61. Ibid., p. 199.

62. Quoted in James Bennet, "How They Missed That Story," *Washington Monthly,* December 1990, reprinted in Sifry and Cerf, op. cit., p. 360.

63. Quoted in Sifry and Cerf, op. cit., p. 125.

64. Quoted in Ridgeway, op. cit., p. 62.

65. Rami Khouri, "America Will Reap a Festering Bitterness," *Los Angeles Times,* January 28, 1991.

66. Quoted in Sifry and Cerf, op. cit., p. 179.

67. Elizabeth Drew, "Letter from Washington," *New Yorker,* February 4, 1991, reprinted in Sifry and Cerf, op. cit., p. 181.

68. Ibid., p. 189.

69. Baker quoted in "The Gulf Crisis: The Road to War," Part 2, television documentary produced by the American Enterprise Institute, Washington, D.C., for the Discovery Channel, 1991.

70. Quoted in "The Persian Gulf Crisis," op. cit., p. 385.

71. See R. Jeffrey Smith and Glen Frankel, "Saddam's Nuclear Weapons: A Lingering Nightmare," *Washington Post,* October 13, 1991; Michael Wines, "U.S. Is Building Up Picture of Vast Iraqi Atom Program," *New York Times,* September 27, 1991; and "Damned Elusive," *Economist,* October 19–25, 1991, p. 46.

72. Les Aspin, address before the Center for Strategic and International Studies, Washington, D.C., December 21, 1990. Reprinted in Les Aspin, *The Aspin Papers: Sanctions, Diplomacy, and War in the Persian Gulf* (Washington, D.C.: Center for Strategic and International Studies, 1991), p. 6.

73. Les Aspin, "Securing U.S. Interests in the Persian Gulf Through Diplomacy," Report to the House Armed Services Committee, reprinted in *The Aspin Papers,* op. cit., pp. 42–43.

74. Hugh Sidey, "'Twas a Famous Victory," *Time,* January 2, 1992, p. 54.

75. "Figures That Add Up to Success," *Jane's Defense Weekly,* April 6, 1991, p. 529.

76. Helen Chapin Metz, ed., *Iraq: A Country Study* (Washington, D.C.: Federal Research Division, Library of Congress, 1990), p. 79. Hereafter cited as *Country Study.*

77. Samir al-Khalil, "Iraq and Its Future," *New York Review of Books,* April 11, 1991, p. 12.

78. Ibid., p. 12.

79. Ibid., p. 12.

80. Earl H. Tilford, Jr., *Setup: What the Air Force Did in Vietnam and Why* (Maxwell

AFB, Alabama: Air University Press, 1991), p. 93; and Barton Gellman, "Air War Struck Broadly in Iraq," *Washington Post,* June 23, 1991.

81. *The World Fact Book 1990* (Washington, D.C.: Central Intelligence Agency, 1990), p. 150.

82. Clyde Haberman, "Trade Sanctions Against Baghdad Imposed by the European Community," *New York Times,* August 5, 1990.

83. Quoted in Ridgeway, op. cit., p. 202.

84. Quoted in Woodward, op. cit., p. 313.

85. Statement of James R. Schlesinger before the Senate Armed Services Committee, November 27, 1990, pp. 4–5.

86. Ibid., p. 8.

87. Statement of William J. Crowe before the Senate Armed Services Committee, November 28, 1990, p. 4.

88. Ibid., pp. 4–5.

89. Ibid., p, 10.

90. Statement of William E. Odom before the Senate Armed Services Committee, November 30, 1990, p. 3.

91. Statement of William H. Webster before the House Armed Services Committee, December 5, 1990. Excerpts reprinted in "Documents on the Gulf Crisis," *The Middle East,* op. cit., pp. 380–81.

92. Statement of Richard Perle before the Senate Armed Services Committee, November 29, 1990, p. 4.

93. Woodward, op. cit., pp. 269–71.

94. Sciolino, op. cit., p. 33.

95. Statement of Henry A. Kissinger before the Senate Armed Services Committee, November 28, 1990, p. 9.

96. "Kuwait, Deteriorating Human Rights Conditions since the Early Occupation" (New York: Middle East Watch, November 16, 1990).

97. "Chronology of the Gulf Crisis," *The Middle East,* op. cit., p. 359.

98. "Documents on the Gulf Crisis," ibid., p. 385.

99. Statement of James H. Webb, Jr., before the Senate Armed Services Committee, November 29, 1990, pp. 2–3.

100. According to Woodward, op. cit., whose account of events remains uncontested by any of the principals involved.

101. Edward N. Luttwak, "Saddam and the Agencies of Disorder," *Times Supplement* (London), January 18, 1991. Reprinted in Sifry and Cerf, op. cit., p. 293.

102. Patrick Buchanan, "How the Gulf Crisis Is Rupturing the Right," *Washington Times,* August 25, 1990.

103. Odom, op. cit., pp. 11, 12.

104. Kissinger, op. cit., pp. 1–2.

105. Perle, op. cit., p. 2.

106. Ibid., p. 4.

107. Ibid., p. 4.

108. A. M. Rosenthal, "Reclaiming Victory," *New York Times,* September 20, 1991.

109. Opening Statement of Senator Sam Nunn before the Senate Armed Services Committee, November 27, 1990, p. 2.

110. Ibid., p. 2.

111. Ibid., p. 2.

112. Ibid., p. 3.

113. Schlesinger, op. cit., p. 15.

114. Statement of David C. Jones before the Senate Armed Services Committee, November 28, 1990, p. 2.

115. See the author's "The Air War Missed Its Biggest Target," *Baltimore Sun,* November 21, 1991.

116. Martin van Creveld, *Fighting Power: German and U.S. Army Performance, 1939–1945* (Westport, Connecticut: Greenwood Press, 1982), p. 3.

117. Stephen C. Pelletiere and Douglas V. Johnson II, *Lessons Learned: The Iran-Iraq War* (Carlisle Barracks, Pennsylvania: Strategic Studies Institute, 1990), hereafter referred to as *Lessons Learned;* and Stephen C. Pelletiere, Douglas V. Johnson II, and Lief R. Rosenberger, *Iraqi Power and U.S. Security in the Middle East* (Carlisle Barracks, Pennsylvania: Strategic Studies Institute, 1991), hereafter referred to as *Iraqi Power.*

118. *Lessons Learned,* op. cit., ix.

119. Ibid., p. 67.

120. *Iraqi Power,* op. cit., ix.

121. Ibid., p. 6.

122. Ibid., p. 58.

123. Transcript of Department of Defense New Briefing by General Merrill A. "Tony" McPeak, United States Air Force, Washington, D.C., March 15, 1991, p. 2. Hereafter referred to as McPeak Briefing.

124. "Friendly Fire in Gulf Claimed 35 Americans," *Washington Post,* October 20, 1991.

125. See Gregg Easterbrook, "Operation Desert Shill," *New Republic,* September 30, 1991, p. 37.

126. Quoted in David C. Morrison, "Weighing the Ground War in the Gulf," *National Journal,* February 2, 1991, p. 278.

127. "Defense Analysts: Limited War to Free Kuwait Could Cut Casualties by Over Half," *Inside the Army,* December 10, 1991, p. 11.

128. Ibid., p. 11.

129. James Blackwell, *Thunder in the Desert: The Strategy and Tactics of the Persian Gulf War* (New York: Bantam Books, 1991), xxxiii.

130. "CSIS: Allied Casualties Could Reach 30,000 Under All-Out Attack Scenario," *Inside the Army,* January 7, 1991, p. 11.

131. Testimony before the Senate Armed Services Committee, June 12, 1991. Reprinted in "Schwarzkopf Reports to Congress on U.S. Military in Persian Gulf War," *Inside the Pentagon* (June 20, 1991), p. 9.

132. "Schwarzkopf: 'I Got a Lot of Guff,'" *Newsweek,* March 11, 1991, p. 34.

133. U.S. Central Command Briefing, Riyadh, January 27, 1991. Reprinted in Richard Pyle, *Schwarzkopf in His Own Words: The Man, the Mission, the Triumph* (New York: Signet Books, 1991), p. 195.

134. Interview with C. D. B. Bryan, cited in Sciolino, op. cit., p. 28.

135. Pyle, op. cit., pp. 253–54.

136. Two Iraqi army divisions did participate briefly in the 1973 war, covering the withdrawal of other Arab forces toward Damascus. Both were heavily damaged by Israeli air attacks. See Blackwell, op. cit., p. 13.

137. Quoted in Sciolino, op. cit., p. 34.

138. According to the highly respected London International Institute for Strategic Studies, Iraq's army in 1990 was the world's sixth largest, following those of the Soviet Union, China, India, Vietnam, and North Korea. See *The Military Balance 1989–1990* (London: International Institute for Strategic Studies, 1990).

139. Ibid., pp. 101–102.

140. Cordesman and Wagner, op. cit., pp. 420, 412.

141. Quoted in Roger Cohen and Claudio Gatti, *In the Eye of the Storm: The Life of General H. Norman Schwarzkopf* (New York: Farrar, Straus, and Giroux, 1991), p. 242.

142. McPeak Briefing, op. cit., p. 2.

143. Ibid., p. 35.

144. See discussion, pp. 69–83, in Ronald Bergquist, *The Role of Airpower in the Iran-Iraq War* (Maxwell AFB, Alabama: Air University Press, 1988).

145. See William Scott Malone, "Did the U.S. Teach Iraq to Hide Its Terror Arms?," *Washington Post,* November 3, 1991; Paul Lewis, "U.N. to Impose New Arms Curbs on Iraq,"

New York Times, October 9, 1991; and Michael Littlejohns, "Iraq Arms Destruction 'Will Take 2 Years,'" *London Financial Times,* October 25, 1991.

146. The Manhattan Project employed 25,000 people and cost $5 billion in 1991 dollars. The Iraqi nuclear weapons program, it is estimated, employed at least 20,000 people and cost $4–$8 billion. See Smith and Frankel, op. cit.

147. See Eric Schmitt, "U.S. Says It Missed 2 A-Plants in Iraq," *New York Times,* October 10, 1991.

148. Smith and Frankel, op. cit.

149. Prewar estimates of Iraq's mobile Scud launchers ranged from forty to sixty. Iraq apparently had hundreds, though the exact number remains unknown.

150. See "Damned Elusive," op. cit., p. 46.

151. Quoted in Timmerman, op. cit., p. 104.

152. Ibid., p. 105.

153. Ibid., pp. 105–20.

154. See Malone, op. cit.

155. Benjamin F. Schemmer, "Special Ops Teams Found 29 Scuds Ready to Barrage Israel 24 Hours before Cease-fire," *Armed Forces Journal,* July 1991, p. 38.

156. Ibid., p. 38.

157. *Needless Deaths in the Gulf War, Civilian Casualties During the Air Campaign and Violations of the Laws of War* (New York: Middle East Watch, 1991), p. 348. Hereafter referred to as *Needless Deaths.*

158. Data provided to the author in oral Pentagon briefing, November 25, 1991.

159. McPeak Briefing, op. cit., p. 71.

160. Anthony Cordesman, *Weapons of Mass Destruction in the Middle East* (London: Brassey's [U.K.], 1991), p. 42.

161. Michael Armitage, "After the Gulf War," *NATO's Sixteen Nations,* February 1991, p. 19.

162. William B. Quandt, "After the Gulf Crisis: Challenges for American Policy," *Washington Quarterly,* Summer 1991, p. 14.

163. *Conduct of the Persian Gulf Conflict: An Interim Report to Congress* (Washington, D.C.: Department of Defense, July 1991), p. 1-3, hereafter cited as *Interim Report;* and Steven R. Bowman, *Persian Gulf War: Summary of U.S. and Non-U.S. Forces* (Washington, D.C.: Congressional Research Service, February 1991).

164. Watson, op. cit., p. 51.

165. Bowman, op. cit., pp. 11–12.

166. *Interim Report,* op. cit., p. 7-3.

167. William J. Perry, "Desert Storm and Deterrence," *Foreign Affairs,* Summer 1991, p. 67.

168. Vincent Thomas, "The Sea Services' Role in Desert Shield/Storm," *Sea Power,* September 1991, p. 27.

169. *The U.S. Army in Operation Desert Storm* (Arlington, Virginia: Association of the United States Army, 1991), p. 9.

170. See Charles E. Heller and William A. Stofft, *America's First Battles, 1775–1965* (Lawrence, Kansas: University of Kansas Press, 1986).

171. See Anthony Preston, "Allied MCM in the Gulf," *Naval Forces,* No. IV, 1991, p. 51.

172. J. M. Martin, "We Still Haven't Learned," *Proceedings,* July 1991, p. 64.

173. Bonsignore, op. cit., p. 61.

174. *Interim Report,* op. cit., p. 4-6.

175. Michael Dugan, "The Air War," *U.S. News and World Report,* February 11, 1991, p. 26.

176. R. A. Mason, "The Air War in the Gulf," *Survival,* May-June 1991, p. 213.

177. Quoted in Richard Mackenzie, "A Conversation with Chuck Horner," *Air Force,* June 1991, p. 60.

178. McPeak Briefing, op. cit., p. 40; and "Figures That Add Up to Success," op. cit., p. 529.

179. "The Course of the War," *Strategic Survey 1990–1991* (London: International Institute for Strategic Studies, 1991), p. 68. Hereafter cited as "The Course of the War."

180. Watson, op. cit., p. 154.

181. Anthony Cordesman, "Rushing to Judgment on the Gulf War," *Armed Forces Journal*, June 1991, pp. 67–68.

182. Dunnigan and Bay, op. cit., p. 402.

183. Easterbrook, op. cit., p. 40.

184. Perry, op. cit., p. 68.

185. "The Course of the War," op. cit., p. 60.

186. Quoted in "War in the Middle East," *Strategic Survey 1990–1991*, op. cit., p. 59.

187. "The Coalition Air Campaign and Collateral Damage," briefing presented to the author and others by William M. Arkin, Greenpeace International, at the Institute for Defense Analyses, Alexandria, Virginia, November 8, 1991. Hereafter cited as Arkin Briefing.

188. Jadranka Porter, *Under Siege in Kuwait: A Survivor's Story* (Boston: Houghton-Mifflin Company, 1991), p. 81.

189. Ibid., p. 233.

190. *Interim Report*, op. cit., p. 14-1.

191. Quoted in *Strategic Survey 1990–1991*, op. cit., p. 93.

192. Edward Fursdon, "Full Story of the 100-Hour Rout," *Asia-Pacific Defense Reporter*, April 1991, p. 8.

193. "Figures That Add Up to Success," op. cit., p. 529; and Ian Kemp, "DoD Lists 'Friendly Fire' Casualties," *Jane's Defense Weekly*, August 24, 1991, p. 302.

194. John A. Adam, "Warfare in the Information Age," *Spectrum*, September 1991, p. 26.

195. Roy Braybrook, "War in the Air: Was There Overkill?," *Asia-Pacific Defense Reporter*, April 1991, p. 9.

196. *Army Equipment Performance in Operation Desert Storm*, Background Brief (Arlington, Virginia: Association of the United States Army, April 1991), p. 1; and *Interim Report*, op. cit., p. 1-2.

197. *Army Equipment Performance*, op. cit., p. 2; and Kemp, op. cit., p. 302.

198. *Army Equipment Performance*, op. cit., p. 6.

199. Thomas, op. cit., p. 33.

200. Preston, op. cit., p. 51.

201. *Interim Report*, op. cit., p. 12-13.

202. Eliot Cohen, "After the Battle," *New Republic*, April 1, 1991, p. 22.

203. Gene I. Rochlin and Chris Demchak, "The Gulf War: Technological and Organizational Implications," *Survival*, May-June 1991, p. 260.

204. Easterbrook, op. cit., p. 40.

205. Phrase of David H. Hackworth, "The Lessons of the Gulf War," *Newsweek*, June 24, 1991, p. 22.

206. *Interim Report*, op. cit., p. 2-9.

207. al-Khalil, *Republic of Fear*, op. cit.

208. John Spanier, *The Truman-MacArthur Controversy and the Korean War* (Cambridge, Massachusetts: Harvard University Press, 1959), pp. 16–23.

209. Loren Baritz, *Backfire: A History of How American Culture Led Us into Vietnam and Made Us Fight the Way We Did* (New York: William Morrow and Company, 1985), p. 145.

210. See the author's "Operational Brilliance, Strategic Incompetence: The Military Reformers and the German Military Model," *Parameters*, Autumn 1986.

211. Ibid., p. 24.

212. Testimony of Dr. Jerrold Post, quoted in *The Aspin Papers*, op. cit., pp. 20–21.

213. David Eshel, "Desert Storm: A Textbook Victory," *Military Technology*, April 30, 1991, p. 30.

214. Blackwell, op. cit., p. 157.

215. Ibid., p. 157.

216. James W. Pardew, Jr., "The Iraqi Army's Defeat in Kuwait," *Parameters*, Winter 1991, p. 20.

217. "The Persian Gulf Crisis," *The Middle East,* op. cit., p. 337.

218. *Interim Report,* op. cit., p. 5-2; and Douglas Waller, "Secret Warriors," *Newsweek,* June 17, 1991, p. 25.

219. Blackwell, op. cit., pp. 71–72.

220. See *U.S. News and World Report* Staff, *Triumph Without Victory: The Unreported History of the Gulf War* (New York: Random House, 1992), pp. 40–41. Hereafter cited as *Triumph Without Victory.*

221. David C. Morrison, "Weighing the Ground War in the Gulf," *National Journal,* February 2, 1991, p. 278.

222. Dunnigan and Bay, op. cit., p. 351.

223. James Blackwell, et al., eds., *The Gulf War: Military Lessons Learned* (Washington, D.C.: Center for Strategic and International Studies, 1991), p. 27.

224. Quoted in Pyle, op. cit., p. 166.

225. Quoted in Sidey, op. cit., p. 54.

226. Quoted in Pyle, op. cit., p. 254.

227. *Triumph Without Victory,* op. cit., pp. 85–86; and Norman Friedman, *Desert Victory: The War for Kuwait* (Annapolis, Maryland: Naval Institute Press, 1991), p. 66.

228. Sciolino, op. cit., pp. 219–20.

229. Ibid., p. 220.

230. Blackwell, *Thunder in the Desert,* op. cit., p. 103.

231. Quoted in Pyle, op. cit., p. 114.

232. *Interim Report,* op. cit., p. 69.

233. See *Triumph Without Victory,* op. cit., pp. 97–98.

234. Jean Edward Smith, *George Bush's War* (New York: Henry Holt and Company, 1992), p. 97.

235. See Graham E. Fuller, "Moscow and the Gulf War," *Foreign Affairs,* Summer 1991, pp. 55–75.

236. Bishara A. Bahbah, "The Crisis in the Gulf—Why Iraq Invaded Kuwait," in Phyllis Bennis and Michel Moushabeck, eds., *Beyond the Storm: A Gulf Crisis Reader* (New York: Olive Branch Press, 1991), p. 53.

237. Friedman, op. cit., p. 205; also see McGeorge Bundy, "Nuclear Weapons in the Gulf," *Foreign Affairs,* Summer 1991, pp. 84–94; and Dunnigan and Bay, op. cit., p. 269.

238. Friedman, op. cit., pp. 351–52; and T. W. Danielson, "Chemical Warfare and Desert Storm," *Command,* November-December 1991, pp. 52–53.

239. Danielson, op. cit.

240. Ezio Bonsignore, "The Best Weapons Are Not Used," *Military Technology,* May 1991, p. 7.

241. Quoted in Sciolino, op. cit., p. 81.

242. "Documents on the Gulf Crisis," *The Middle East,* op. cit., p. 389.

243. Quoted in Bill Sweetman, "Catching Up with Doctrine," *Jane's Defense Weekly,* June 29, 1991, p. 1174.

244. Quoted in Joe West, "Air Power Backers Feel Vindicated by Gulf Win," *Air Force Times,* April 1, 1991, p. 27.

245. McPeak Briefing, op. cit., p. 13.

246. *Interim Report,* op. cit., p. 1-3.

247. Ibid., p. 12-3.

248. James W. Canan, "Air Power Opens the Fight," *Air Force,* March 1991, p. 15.

249. Quoted in Mason, op. cit., p. 225.

250. Armitage, op. cit., p. 10.

251. A. G. B. Metcalf, "A Backward Step?," *Strategic Review,* Fall 1991, p. 6.

252. George C. Herring, "America and Vietnam: The Unending War," *Foreign Affairs,* Winter 1991/1992, p. 110.

253. Alexander P. De Seversky, *Victory Through Air Power* (Garden City, New York: Garden City Publishing Company, 1943), p. 28.

254. Jimmie V. Adams, quoted in John D. Morrocco, "From Vietnam to Desert Storm," *Air Force,* January 1991, p. 71.

255. See McPeak Briefing, op. cit.; Charles A. Horner, "Reflections on Desert Storm: The Air Campaign," briefing presented to the Congress, Spring 1991, hereafter cited as Horner Briefing; Tamir Eshel, "The Most Successful Air Campaign Ever?," *Military Technology,* April 1991, pp. 36–44; and informal U.S. Air Force briefing provided the author on November 22, 1991. Hereafter cited as Informal USAF Briefing.

256. Tonnage figures for World War II, Korea, and Vietnam are compiled from data appearing in Patrick M. Cronin, *The Quest for Targets That Count: Lessons Learned from Allied Strategic Bombing in the Second World War* (Washington, D.C.: Center for Naval Analysis, 1989), pp. 41–48; Robert Frank Futrell, *The United States Air Force in Korea, 1950–1953* (New York: Duell, Sloan, and Pearce, 1961), p. 645; Rapheal Littauer and Norman Uphoff, eds., *The Air War in Indochina,* Air War Study Group (Boston: Beacon Press, 1972), pp. 167–73, 197–217; and Mark Clodfelter, *The Limits of Air Power: The American Bombing of North Vietnam* (New York: Free Press, 1989), pp. 166–67, 194.

257. Horner Briefing, op. cit.

258. Earl H. Tilford, Jr., "Selected Statistics, U.S. Air War in Southeast Asia," memorandum provided to the author, 1991.

259. *Interim Report,* op. cit., p. 2-5.

260. Horner Briefing, op. cit.

261. Pentagon Press Briefing by Richard Cheney and Colin Powell, Department of Defense, Washington, D.C., January 23, 1991. Reprinted in *Inside the Pentagon,* January 25, 1991, p. 6.

262. See, for example, "USAF Tries to Block PA&E Desert Storm Analysis from Reaching Congress," *Inside the Pentagon,* January 3, 1992, pp. 1–2; and "Greenpeace Analyst: Gulf War Strategic Bombing 'Irrelevant' to Winning War," *Inside the Air Force,* January 10, 1991, pp. 1, 12.

263. See, for example, Seversky, op. cit.; Giulio Douhet, *The Command of the Air* (Washington, D.C.: Office of Air Force History, 1983); William Mitchell, *Winged Defense, The Development and Possibilities of Modern Air Power—Economic and Military* (New York: Dover Publications, Inc., 1925, 1988); and E. S. Gorrell, "The Future Role of American Bombardment Aviation [1918]," U.S. Air Force Historical Research Agency, Maxwell AFB, Alabama, 248.222–78.

264. See Clodfelter, op. cit.; Barry D. Watts, *The Foundations of U.S. Air Doctrine* (Maxwell AFB, Alabama; Air University Press, 1984); Donald J. Mrozek, *Air Power and the Ground War in Vietnam* (Washington, D.C.: Pergamon-Brassey's, 1989); Earl H. Tilford, Jr., *Setup: What the Air Force Did in Vietnam and Why* (Maxwell AFB, Alabama: Air University Press, 1991); Caroline F. Ziemke, *In the Shadow of the Giant: USAF Tactical Air Command in the Era of Strategic Bombing* (Columbus, Ohio: Ohio State University, Ph.D. Thesis, 1989), and "Promises Fulfilled? The Prophets of Air Power and Desert Storm," background paper, Washington Strategy Symposium on the Future of U.S. Air Power, January 1992.

265. The discussion that follows is based on the author's numerous conversations with several key Coalition air campaign planners, who asked not to be identified or quoted directly; the Arkin Briefing, excerpts of which were reprinted in "Analyst Charges USAF's Generic Gulf War Targeting Had No Positive Effect," *Inside the Air Force,* January 17, 1992, pp. 16–20; and another briefing provided the author on November 22, 1991, by a Defense Department official conducting after-action assessments of the air war, hereafter cited as After-Action Briefing.

266. Dannreuther, op. cit., pp. 62–63.

267. *Triumph Without Victory,* op. cit., pp. 269–74.

268. Friedman, op. cit., pp. 160, 171.

269. *Triumph Without Victory,* op. cit., p. 273.

270. Quoted in Benjamin L Harrison, "The A-10: A Gift the Army Can't Afford," *Army,* July 1991, p. 23.

271. Adam, op. cit., p. 23.

272. John A. Warden III, *The Air Campaign: Planning for Combat* (New York: Pergamon-Brassey's, 1989).

273. Gellman, op. cit.

274. Ibid.

275. Braybrook, op. cit., p. 10.

276. Arkin Briefing, op. cit.

277. *Needless Deaths,* op. cit., p. 19.

278. Joost R. Hiltermann, "Bomb Now, Die Later," *Mother Jones,* July-August, 1991, p. 45.

279. Easterbrook, op. cit., p. 40.

280. So named for Armti Ahtisaari, Under Secretary General for Administration and Management, leader of the United Nations team and principal author of the *Report of the United Nations Mission to Assess Humanitarian Needs in Iraq,* 1991. Excerpts reprinted in Bennis and Moushabeck, op. cit., p. 397.

281. Harvard Study Team Report, p. 12–13; see also, "70,000 Iraqis Said to Have Died Post-War," *Washington Post,* January 9, 1992.

282. Arkin Briefing, op. cit.

283. Edward P. Djerejian, Assistant Secretary of State for Near Eastern and South Asian Affairs, "The Middle East After the Gulf War," testimony before the House Foreign Affairs Committee, November 20, 1991, reprinted in *U.S. Department of State Dispatch,* November 25, 1991, p. 862.

284. Quoted in Patrick E. Tyler, "Bush Links End of Trading Ban to Hussein Exit," *New York Times,* May 21, 1991.

285. Watson, op. cit., pp. 73, 168.

286. Ibid., p. 107.

287. McPeak Briefing, op. cit., p. 18.

288. See Thomas, op. cit., p. 33; and Riley D. Mixon, "Where We Must Do Better," *Proceedings,* August 1991, pp. 38–39.

289. Mixon, op. cit., p. 38.

290. Harry Summers, "Clash of Bombing Visions," *Washington Times,* June 27, 1991.

291. See, for example, Price T. Bingham, "Air Power in Desert Storm and the Need for Doctrinal Change," *Airpower Journal,* Winter 1991, pp. 33–46.

292. Mark Clodfelter, "Of Demons, Storms, and Thunder: A Preliminary Look at Vietnam's Impact on the Persian Gulf Air Campaign," *Airpower Journal,* Winter 1991, p. 29.

293. Gellman, op. cit.; and "The Secret History of the War," *Newsweek,* March 18, 1991, p. 28, hereafter cited as "Secret History."

294. Woodward, op. cit.

295. "Secret History," op. cit.; and Michael Massing, "The Way to War," *New York Review of Books,* March 28, 1991, p. 38.

296. Woodward, op. cit., p. 260.

297. Ibid., p. 261.

298. Les Aspin, "Desert One to Desert Storm: Making Ready for Victory," address before the Center for Strategic and International Studies, Washington, D.C., June 20, 1991, p. 3.

299. Ibid., p. 6.

300. William J. Taylor and James Blackwell, "The Ground War in the Gulf," *Survival,* May-June 1991, p. 241.

301. Lawrence J. Korb, "This Time the Military Got It Right," *Brookings Review,* Summer 1991, p. 6.

302. See Ted Gup, "A Man You Could Do Business With," *Time,* March 11, 1991, p. 59.

303. See Woodward, op. cit., pp. 290–96.

304. Arkin Briefing, op. cit.; and *Needless Deaths,* op. cit., pp. 128–47.

305. Ibid., pp. 137–47.

306. "Chronology of the Gulf Crisis," *The Middle East,* op. cit., p. 366.

307. Cohen and Gatti, op. cit., pp. 298–99.

308. Friedman, op. cit., p. 77.

309. Cohen and Gatti, op. cit., pp. 296–97. See also Douglas Waller and John Barry, "The Day We Stopped the War," *Newsweek*, January 20, 1992, pp. 16–25.

310. *Triumph Without Victory*, op. cit., pp. 404–405, 412.

311. See Patrick J. Sloyan, "A Major Battle in War Came after Cease-fire," *Boston Globe*, May 8, 1991; and David S. Harvey, "In Battle with the 24th Aviation Brigade," *Rotor and Wing International*, June 1991, p. 65.

312. See Waller and Barry, op. cit.; and William E. Schmidt, "British Misgivings at Gulf War's End Are Recalled," *New York Times*, August 20, 1991.

313. Douglas Waller, "What the Soviet Union Knew," *Newsweek*, January 20, 1992, p. 24.

314. Quoted in Cohen and Gatti, op. cit., p. 295.

315. Quoted in ibid., pp. 295–96.

316. Quoted in Bernd Debusman, "Saddam Jeers at Bush, Claims Iraq Won War," *Washington Times*, January 17, 1992.

317. *Triumph Without Victory*, op. cit., p. 401.

318. See Waller and Barry, op. cit.

319. See "Hollow Victory," *U.S. News and World Report*, January 20, 1992, p. 44.

320. "What Did Bush Win?," *Newsweek*, May 13, 1991, p. 27.

321. See Barton Gellman, "Disputes Delay Gulf War History," *Washington Post*, January 28, 1992.

322. Dunnigan and Bay, op. cit., pp. 273–76.

323. See, for example, Richard Halloran, *To Arm a Nation: Rebuilding America's Endangered Defenses* (New York: Macmillan Publishing Company, 1986), pp. 343–44.

324. "Navy Stripped on Mine Countermeasures, Maritime Prepositioning Programs," *Inside the Pentagon*, July 25, 1991, pp. 3–4.

325. See Benjamin F. Schemmer, "Six Navy Carriers Launch only 17 percent of Attack Missions in Desert Storm," *Armed Forces Journal*, January 1992, pp. 12–13.

326. See ibid; and Gordon Swanborough and Peter M. Bowers, *United States Military Aircraft Since 1909* (Washington, D.C.: Smithsonian Institution Press, 1989).

327. Bobby Inman, Joseph S. Nye, William J. Perry, and Roger K. Smith, "Lessons from the Gulf War," *Washington Quarterly*, Winter 1992, p. 58.

328. See Bruce Schoenfeld, "Parties Rush to Take Credit for Weapons," *Defense Week*, March 4, 1991, p. 3.

329. David H. Hackworth, "Lessons of a Lucky War," *Newsweek*, March 11, 1991, p. 49.

330. *Soviet Analysis of Operation Desert Shield and Operation Desert Storm* (Washington, D.C.: U.S. Defense Intelligence Agency, 1991), p. 76.

331. William J. Taylor and James Blackwell, "The Ground War in the Gulf," *Survival*, May-June 1991, p. 245.

332. Inman, et al., op. cit., p. 57.

333. See, for example, Martin Binkin, "The New Face of the American Military: The All Volunteer Force and the Persian Gulf War," *Brookings Review*, Summer 1991, pp. 7–13; and Les Aspin, "The All Volunteer Force: Assessing Fairness and Facing the Future," address before the Association of the United States Army, Crystal City, Virginia, April 26, 1991.

334. See Lewis Sorely, "National Guard and Reserve Forces," in Joseph Kruzel, ed., *American Defense Annual, 1991–1992* (New York: Lexington Books, 1991), pp. 184–201.

335. So named after Thomas F. Gates, former Secretary of the Air Force. The commission on an all-volunteer armed force consisted of fifteen prominent individuals; its report, *Report of the President's Commission on an All-Volunteer Armed Force*, was issued in February 1970, and published by the U.S. Government Printing Office.

336. See ibid., pp. 119–24.

337. Quoted in John D. Morrocco, "War Will Reshape Doctrine, but Lessons Are Limited," *Aviation Week and Space Technology*, April 22, 1991, p. 40.

338. James Blackwell, Michael J. Mazarr, and Don M. Snider, *The Gulf War: Military Lessons Learned* (Washington, D.C.: Center for Strategic and International Studies, 1991), p. 6.

339. Dunnigan and Bay, op. cit., p. 241.

340. See Blackwell, et al. op. cit., p. 8.

341. Informal remarks presented before the Center for Technology and Public Policy Research, BDM Corporation, McLean, Virginia, November 20, 1991.

342. Bundy, op. cit.

343. See "Defense Against Tactical Missiles: An Historical Perspective," briefing prepared by the BDM International Corporation, McLean, Virginia, December 10, 1991.

344. See Michael W. Ellis and Jeffrey Record, "Theater Ballistic Missile Defense and U.S. Contingency Operations," *Parameters,* Spring 1992.

345. Cordesman, *Weapons of Mass Destruction,* op. cit.

346. See the following trio of studies published in December 1991 by the Congressional Budget Office, Washington, D.C.: *The Costs of the Administration's Plan for the Army Through the Year 2010,* pp. 5, 7; *The Costs of the Administration's Plan for the Navy Through the Year 2010,* p. 2; and *The Costs of the Administration's Plan for the Air Force Through the Year 2010,* pp. 4–5.

347. George F. Will, "The Emptiness of Desert Storm," *Washington Post,* January 12, 1992.

348. Lawrence Freedman, "The Gulf War and the New World Order," *Survival,* May-June 1991, p. 203.

349. Ziemke, "Promises Fulfilled?," op. cit.

350. Michael Dugan, "First Lessons of Victory," *U.S. News and World Report,* March 18, 1991, p. 36.

351. Eliot A. Cohen, op. cit., p. 19.

352. *Interim Report,* op. cit., p. 4–10.

353. President's address of August 8, 1990, reprinted in Sifry and Cerf, op. cit., p. 179.

354. Ahmed Hashim, "Iraq, the Pariah State," *Current History,* January 1991, p. 14.

355. Charles Lane, "The Stalking of Saddam," *Newsweek,* January 20, 1992, p. 27.

356. Hashim, op. cit., pp. 14, 15.

357. William Safire, "The April Surprise," *New York Times,* January 12, 1992.

358. Quoted in Jim Hoagland, "A Year After Desert Storm: What the War Didn't Resolve," *Washington Post,* January 12, 1992.

359. Quoted in Elaine Sciolino, "Iraqis Could Pose a Threat Soon, CIA Chief Says," *New York Times,* January 16, 1992.

360. Lane, op. cit., p. 27.

361. Chubin, op. cit., p. 146.

362. Leon T. Hadar, *Extricating America from its Middle Eastern Entanglement* (Washington, D.C.: Cato Institute, 1991), p. 5.

363. See Mary Ann Tetreault, "Kuwait: The Morning After," *Current History,* January 1992, p. 7.

364. Christopher Layne, "Why the Gulf War Was Not in the National Interest," *Atlantic Monthly,* July 1991, p. 68.

365. Jim Hoagland, "Desert Storm Ticktock," *Washington Post,* January 26, 1992.

SELECTED BIBLIOGRAPHY

Books, Reports, Studies

Aspin, Les. *The Aspin Papers, Sanctions, Diplomacy, and War in the Persian Gulf.* Washington, D.C.: Center for Strategic and International Studies, 1991.

Bennis, Phyllis, and Michael Moushabeck, eds. *Beyond the Storm: A Gulf Crisis Reader.* New York: Olive Branch Press, 1991.

Blackwell, James, et al., eds. *The Gulf War: Military Lessons Learned.* Interim Report of the Study Group on Lessons Learned from the Gulf War. Washington, D.C.: Center for Strategic and International Studies, 1991.

Blackwell, James. *Thunder in the Desert: The Strategy and Tactics of the Persian Gulf War.* New York: Bantam Books, 1991.

Bullock, John, and Harvey Morris. *Saddam's War: The Origins of the Kuwait Conflict and the International Response.* London: Faber and Faber, 1991.

Carpenter, Ted Galen, editor. *America Entangled: The Persian Gulf Crisis and Its Consequences.* Washington, D.C.: Cato Institute, 1991.

Cohen, Roger, and Claudio Gatti. *In the Eye of the Storm: The Life of General H. Norman Schwarzkopf.* New York: Farrar, Straus, and Giroux, 1991.

Conduct of the Persian Gulf Conflict: An Interim Report to Congress. Washington, D.C.: Department of Defense, July 1991.

Cooley, John K. *Payback: America's Long War in the Middle East.* New York: Brassey's, 1991.

Dannreuther, Roland. *The Persian Gulf Conflict: A Political and Strategic Analysis.* Adelphi Paper Number 264. London: International Institute for Strategic Studies, 1992.

Darwish, Adel, and Gregory Alexander. *Unholy Babylon: The Secret History of Saddam's War.* New York: St. Martin's Press, 1991.

Dunnigan, James F., and Austin Bay. *From Shield to Storm: High-Tech Weapons, Military Strategy, and Coalition Warfare in the Persian Gulf.* New York: William Morrow and Company, 1991.

Friedman, Norman. *Desert Victory: The War for Kuwait.* Annapolis, Maryland: Naval Institute Press, 1991.

Graubard, Stephen R. *Mr. Bush's War: Adventures in the Politics of Illusion.* New York: Hill and Wang, 1992.

Hadar, Leon T. *Extricating America from Its Middle East Entanglement.* Washington, D.C.: Cato Institute, 1991.

Karsh, Efraim, and Inari Rautsi. *Saddam Hussein: A Political Biography.* New York: Free Press, 1991.

Khalidi, Walid. *The Gulf Crisis: Origins and Consequences.* Washington, D.C.: Institute for Palestine Studies, 1991.

al-Khalil, Samir. *Republic of Fear: The Inside Story of Saddam's Iraq.* New York: Pantheon Books, 1989.

Miller, Judith, and Laurie Mylroie. *Saddam Hussein and the Crisis in the Gulf.* New York: Times Books, 1990.

Needless Deaths in the Gulf War: Civilian Casualties During the Air Campaign and Violations of the Laws of War. New York: Middle East Watch, 1991.

Pelletiere, Stephen C., et al. *Iraqi Power and U.S. Security in the Middle East.* Carlisle Barracks, Pennsylvania: Strategic Studies Institute, U.S. Army War College, 1990.

Pelletiere, Stephen C., and Douglas V. Johnson. *Lessons Learned: The Iran-Iraq War.* Carlisle

Barracks, Pennsylvania: Strategic Studies Institute, U.S. Army War College, 1990.

Porter, Jadranka. *Under Siege in Kuwait: A Survivor's Story.* Boston: Houghton-Mifflin Company, 1991.

Report of the United Nations Commission to Assess Humanitarian Needs in Iraq. New York: United Nations, 1991.

Ridgeway, James, ed. *The March to War.* New York: Four Walls Eight Windows, 1991.

Salinger, Pierre, and Eric Laurent. *Secret Dossier: The Hidden Agenda Behind the Gulf War.* London: Penguin Books, 1991.

Sciolino, Elaine. *The Outlaw State: Saddam Hussein's Quest for Power and the Gulf Crisis.* New York: John Wiley and Sons, 1991.

Sifry, Micah L., and Christopher Cerf, eds. *The Gulf War Reader: History, Documents, Opinions.* New York: Random House, 1991.

Smith, Jean Edward. *George Bush's War.* New York: Henry Holt and Company, 1992.

Soviet Analysis of Operation Desert Shield and Desert Storm. Defense Intelligence Agency Translation. Washington, D.C.: Defense Intelligence Agency, October 1991.

Summers, Harry G. *On Strategy II: A Critical Analysis of the Gulf War.* New York: Dell Publishing, 1992.

Timmerman, Kenneth R. *The Death Lobby: How the West Armed Iraq.* New York: Houghton-Mifflin Company, 1991.

Triumph Without Victory: The Unreported History of the Gulf War. Staff of *U.S. News and World Report.* New York: Random House, 1992.

United States Air Force Performance in Desert Storm. USAF White Paper. Washington, D.C.: The United States Air Force, 1991.

The U.S. Army in Operation Desert Storm. Arlington, Virginia: Association of the United States Army, 1991.

Warden, John. *The Air Campaign: Planning for Combat.* New York: Brassey's, 1989.

Watson, Bruce W., et al. *Military Lessons of the Gulf War.* Novato, California: Presidio Press, 1991.

Woodward, Bob. *The Commanders.* New York: Simon and Schuster, 1991.

Briefings, Memoranda, Television Documentaries

"The Air Campaign: Part of the Combined Arms Operation." Briefing presented by General Merrill A. McPeak, United States Air Force, Washington, D.C., Department of Defense, March 15, 1991.

"The Coalition Air Campaign and Collateral Damage." Briefing presented to the author and others by William M. Arkin, Greenpeace, at the Institute for Defense Analyses, Alexandria, Virginia, November 8, 1991.

"Defense Against Tactical Missiles: An Historical Inquiry." Briefing prepared by the BDM International Corporation, McLean, Virginia, December 10, 1991.

"The Gulf Crisis: The Road to War." Three-part television documentary produced by the American Enterprise Institute, Washington, D.C., for the Discovery Channel, 1991.

Pentagon Press briefing presented by Secretary of Defense Dick Cheney and General Colin Powell, Department of Defense, Washington, D.C., January 23, 1991.

"Reflections on Desert Storm: The Air Campaign." Briefing presented by General Charles A. Horner, United States Air Force, Washington, D.C., 1991.

"Selected Statistics, U.S. Air War in Southeast Asia." Memorandum provided to the author by Earl H. Tilford, Jr., 1991.

U.S. Air Force briefing provided to the author, November 22, 1991.

U.S. Air Force briefing provided to the author, November 25, 1991.

U.S. Central Command briefing presented by General H. Norman Schwarzkopf, Riyadh, Saudi Arabia, February 27, 1991.

Articles and Speeches

Apple, R. W., Jr. "Bush Rattles Saber: Will Iraq Flinch?" *New York Times,* September 19, 1991.

Armitage, Michael. "After the Gulf War." *NATO's Sixteen Nations,* February 1991.

Aspin, Les. "Desert One to Desert Storm: Making Ready for Victory." Speech before the Center for Strategic and International Studies, Washington, D.C., June 20, 1991.

Atkeson, Edward B. "Iraq's Arsenal: Tool of Ambition." *Army,* March 1991.

Atkinson, Rick. "Outflanking Iraq: Go West, Go Deep." *Washington Post,* March 18, 1991.

Augustine, Norman R. "How We Almost Lost the Technological War." *Wall Street Journal,* June 14, 1991.

Barry, John, and Evan Thomas. "A Textbook Victory." *Newsweek,* March 11, 1991.

"The Battle Joined." *Newsweek,* Commemorative Edition, Spring/Summer 1991.

Bingham, Price T. "Air Power in Desert Storm and the Need for Doctrinal Change." *Airpower Journal,* Winter 1991.

Binkin, Martin. "The New Face of the American Military." *Brookings Review,* Summer 1991.

"Blitzkrieg." *Newsweek,* Commemorative Edition, Spring/Summer 1991.

Bonsignore, Ezio. "The War That Wasn't." *Military Technology,* March 1991.

Braybrook, Roy. "War in the Air: Was There Overkill?" *Asia-Pacific Defense Reporter,* April 1991.

Broad, William J. "U.N. Says Iraqi Children Dying at Accelerated Rate." *Washington Times,* October 15, 1991.

Bundy, McGeorge. "Nuclear Weapons and the Gulf." *Foreign Affairs,* Fall 1991.

"Catching Up with Doctrine." *Jane's Defense Weekly,* June 29, 1991.

"Chronology of the Gulf Crisis." *The Middle East,* 7th edition. Washington, D.C.: Congressional Quarterly, 1991.

Chubin, Shahram. "Post-War Gulf Security." *Survival,* March-April 1991.

Clodfelter, Mark. "Of Demons, Storms, and Thunder: A Preliminary Look at Vietnam's Impact on the Persian Gulf Air Campaign." *Airpower Journal,* Winter 1991.

Cohen, Eliot A. "After the Battle." *New Republic,* April 1, 1991.

Cooley, John K. "Pre-War Gulf Diplomacy." *Survival,* March-April 1991.

Cordesman, Anthony H. "Rushing to Judgment on the Gulf War." *Armed Forces Journal,* June 1991.

Dawisha, Adeed. "The United States in the Middle East: The Gulf War and Its Aftermath." *Current History,* January 1992.

Djerejian, Edward P. "The Middle East After the Gulf War." *U.S. Department of State Dispatches,* November 25, 1992.

"Documents on the Gulf Crisis." *The Middle East,* 7th edition. Washington, D.C.: Congressional Quarterly, 1991.

Draper, Theodore. "American Hubris." *New York Review of Books,* July 16, 1991.

———. "The Gulf War Reconsidered." *New York Review of Books,* July 16, 1991.

Drew, Elizabeth. "Letter from Washington." *New Yorker,* February 4, 1991.

DuBois, Thomas R. "The Weinberger Doctrine and the Liberation of Kuwait." *Parameters,* Winter 1991–1992.

Duffy, Brian. "The 100-Hour War." *U.S. News and World Report,* March 11, 1991.

Dugan, Michael. "The Air War." *U.S. News and World Report,* February 11, 1991.

Easterbrook, Gregg. "Operation Desert Shill." *New Republic,* September 10, 1991.

Eldridge, Bo. "Desert Storm, Mother of All Battles." *Command,* November-December 1991.

Eshel, David. "Desert Storm: A Textbook Victory." *Military Technology,* April 1991.

Eshel, Tamir. "The Most Successful Air Campaign Ever?" *Military Technology,* April 1991.

"Facing up to Failure." *Jane's Defense Weekly,* April 6, 1991.

"Figures That Add Up to Success." *Jane's Defense Weekly,* April 6, 1991.

"The Final Push." *Newsweek,* Commemorative Edition, Spring/Summer 1991.

Flanagan, Edward M., Jr. "The 100-Hour War." *Army,* April 1991.

Foray, G. "The Eight Lessons of Success." *Military Technology,* August 1991.

Freedman, Lawrence. "The Gulf War and the New World Order." *Survival,* May-June 1991.

Fuller, Graham E. "Moscow and the Gulf War." *Foreign Affairs,* Summer 1991.

Fursdon, Edward. "Full Story of the 100-Hour Rout." *Asia-Pacific Defense Reporter,* April 1991.

"The Fury of Desert Storm." *U.S. News and World Report,* March 11, 1991.

Gellman, Barton. "Allied Air War Struck Broadly in Iraq." *Washington Post,* June 23, 1991.

———. "Disputes Delay Gulf War History." *Washington Post,* January 28, 1991.

Gordon, Michael R., and Eric Schmidt. "Much More Armor Than U.S. Believed Fell Back to Iraq." *New York Times,* March 25, 1991.

"Gulf Crisis: Coalition Order of Battle." *The Military Balance 1991–1992.* London: International Institute for Strategic Studies, 1991.

Gup, Ted. "A Man You Could Do Business With." *Time,* March 11, 1991.

Hackworth, David H. "The Lessons of the Gulf War." *Newsweek,* June 24, 1991.

———. "We Didn't Finish the Job." *Newsweek,* January 20, 1992.

Hashim, Ahmed. "Iraq. The Pariah State." *Current History,* January 1992.

Herring, George C. "America and Vietnam: The Unending War." *Foreign Affairs,* Winter 1991–1992.

Hickman, William F. "Confrontation in the Gulf: Unintended Consequences." *Naval War College Review,* Winter 1991.

Hiro, Dilip. "A Few of Our Favorite Kings." *New Statesman and Society,* August 24, 1990.

Hoagland, Jim. "Desert Storm Ticktock." *Washington Post,* January 26, 1992.

———. "A Year After the Storm: What the War Didn't Resolve." *Washington Post,* January 12, 1992.

Indyk, Martin. "America's Choice in the Middle East." *National Interest,* Winter 1991.

Inman, Bobby R., et al. "Lesson from the Gulf War." *Washington Quarterly,* Winter 1992.

Karsh, Efraim, and Inari Rautsi. "Why Saddam Invaded Kuwait." *Survival,* January/February 1991.

Kemp, Ian. "The 100-Hour War to Free Kuwait." *Jane's Defense Weekly,* February 23, 1991.

al-Khalil, Samir. "Iraq and Its Future." *New York Review of Books,* April 11, 1991.

Khouri, Rami G. "America Will Reap a Festering Bitterness." *Los Angeles Times,* January 28, 1991.

Kissinger, Henry A. "The Game Has Just Begun." *Washington Post,* August 19, 1990.

Klare, Michael T. "Behind Desert Storm: The New Military Paradigm." *Technology Review,* May-June 1991.

Korb, Lawrence J. "This Time the Military Got It Right." *Brookings Review,* Summer 1991.

Krauthammer, Charles. "The Lonely Superpower." *New Republic,* July 29, 1991.

"Kuwait: How the West Blundered." *Economist,* September 29, 1990.

Lane, Charles. "The Stalking of Saddam." *Newsweek,* January 20, 1992.

Layne, Christopher. "Why the Gulf War Was Not in the National Interest." *Atlantic Monthly,* July 1991.

Leo, John. "Lessons from a Sanitized War." *U.S. News and World Report,* March 18, 1991.

Mackenzie, Richard. "A General's Cunning Quashed Saddam." *Insight,* March 18, 1991.

MacLeod, Scott. "In the Wake of Desert Storm." *New York Review of Books,* March 7, 1991.

Madison, Christopher. "The Blame for Losing Iraq." *National Journal,* April 13, 1991.

Margelleti, Andrea. "Special Operations in the Desert." *Military Technology,* April 1991.

Mason, R. A. "The Air War in the Gulf." *Survival,* May-June 1991.

Massing, Michael. "Can Saddam Survive?" *New York Review of Books,* August 15, 1991.

———. "The War to War." *New York Review of Books,* March 28, 1991.

Moore, Molly. "War Exposed Rivalries, Weakness in Military." *Washington Post,* June 10, 1991.

Morris, Roger. "One Year After the Iraqi Invasion of Kuwait: What Did Winning Mean and What's Next?" *New York Times,* August 2, 1991.

Morrison, David C. "Weighing the Ground War in the Gulf." *National Review,* February 2, 1991.

Morrocco, John D. "From Vietnam to Desert Storm." *Air Force,* January 1992.

———. "War Will Reshape Doctrine, but Lessons Are Limited." *Aviation Week and Space Technology,* April 22, 1991.

Nativi, Andrea. "An Early Lesson?" *Military Technology,* April 1991.

Nisan, Mordechai. "The Old Order Reborn: America and the Middle East." *Global Affairs,* Winter 1992.

Nixon, Richard. "Why U.S. Policy Is Right in the Gulf." *New York Times,* January 6, 1991.

Oberdorfer, Don. "Was War Inevitable?" *Washington Post Magazine,* March 17, 1991.

O'Donnell, Laurie. "Lessons Learned, Re-learned, and Reinforced." *Asia-Pacific Defense Reporter,* April 11, 1991.

"The 100 Hours." *Time,* March 11, 1991.

"The 100-Hour War." *Army Times,* March 11, 1991.

"Operation Desert Storm." *Army Focus,* June 1991.

Pardew, James W., Jr. "The Iraqi Army's Defeat in Kuwait." *Parameters,* Winter 1991–1992.

Perry, William J. "Desert Storm and Deterrence." *Foreign Affairs,* Fall 1991.

"The Persian Gulf Crisis." *The Middle East,* 7th edition. Washington, D.C.: Congressional Quarterly, 1991.

Primakov, Yevgeni. "My Final Visit with Saddam Hussein." *Time,* March 11, 1991.

Quandt, William B. "After the Gulf Crisis: Challenges for American Policy." *Arab-American Affairs* [n.d.].

Record, Jeffrey. "The Gulf War Is Looking Less and Less Like a Victory." *Baltimore Sun,* August 28, 1991.

———. "Why the Air War Worked." *Armed Forces Journal,* April 1991.

Rochlin, Gene I., and Chris Demchak. "The Gulf War: Technological and Organizational Implications." *Survival,* May/June 1991.

Rosenthal, A. M. "Reclaiming the Victory." *New York Times,* September 20, 1991.

Rubenstein, Alvin Z. "New World Order or Hollow Victory?" *Foreign Affairs,* Fall 1991.

Safire, William. "Bush's Bay of Pigs." *New York Times,* April 4, 1991.

Schmitt, Eric, and Michael R. Gordon. "Unforeseen Problems in Air War Forced Allies to Improvise Tactics." *New York Times,* March 10, 1991.

"The Secret History of the War." *Newsweek,* March 18, 1991.

Sidey, Hugh. "'Twas a Famous Victory." *Time,* January 6, 1992.

Siegel, Mark A. "Saddam Hussein's Other Republican Guards." *Wall Street Journal,* March 21, 1991.

Solarz, Stephen J. "The Stakes in the Gulf." *New Republic,* January 7 and 14, 1991.

Summers, Harry. "Clash of Bombing Visions." *Washington Times,* June 27, 1991.

Sweetman, Bill. "Learning the Lessons of Desert Storm." *Jane's Defense Weekly,* March 9, 1991.

Talbott, Strobe. "High Noon Minus the Shoot-out." *Time,* February 10, 1992.

Taylor, William J., and James Blackwell. "The Ground War in the Gulf." *Survival,* May-June 1991.

Tetreault, Mary Ann. "Kuwait: The Morning After." *Current History,* January 1992.

Thomas, Vincent C., Jr. "The Sea Services' Role in Desert Shield/Desert Storm." *Sea Power,* September 1991.

Tyler, Patrick E. "Who's Talking Tough? Why, Saddam Hussein." *New York Times,* October 24, 1991.

Viorst, Milton. "War and Consequences." *Washington Post,* November 13, 1990.

Waller, Douglas, and John Barry. "The Day We Stopped the War." *Newsweek,* January 20, 1991.

"War in the Middle East." *Strategic Survey 1990–1991.* London: International Institute for Strategic Studies, 1991.

Warner, Denis. "Saddam's Strategy Rested on U.S. Casualties." *Asia-Pacific Defense Reporter,* March 1991.

Weaver, Greg. "Gulf War Lessons Not to Learn." *Defense News,* August 26, 1991.

Webb, James. ". . . And the Horrors of a Desert War." *New York Times,* September 23, 1991.

Wettern, Desmond. "Sea Lines Cause Concern." *Asia-Pacific Defense Reporter,* March 1991.
"What Did Bush Win?" *Newsweek,* May 13, 1991.
Will, George F. "The Emptiness of Desert Storm." *Washington Post,* January 12, 1992.
Wills, Gary. "Who Commands the Commanders?" *Baltimore Sun,* May 10, 1991.
Zakheim, Dov. "Top Guns." *Policy Review,* Summer 1991.
Ziemke, Caroline F. "Promises Fulfilled? The Prophets of Air Power and Desert Storm."
    Washington, D.C.: Washington Strategy Seminar, January 1992.

INDEX